Reconstructing Teaching

One of the greatest resources a school has is its staff, so the education of teachers themselves and the way their work is defined are therefore of the utmost importance. Major trends of increased control and 'new managerialism' are radically altering both the content and the form of teacher education.

Reconstructing Teaching questions whether the outlined changes that have occurred in recent times have been the right ones, initiated by the right people for the right reasons and in the right ways, and explains where current practices in relation to policy-making need to be addressed and how lessons can be learned for the future. The authors

- explore how the development, role and impact of national teaching standards serve both to deliver and to legitimate the culture of performance, now widespread within the public sector;
- outline the principles of performance management, according to which teaching is currently being reorganised, in terms of their underpinning values and assumptions and the likely impacts on the nature of teaching as an activity and the structure of teaching as an occupation;
- set changes in the nature of teaching within the wider international context of changes in the structures of work;
- explain how such changes are not trivial and have broad implications for the ways in which teachers relate to one another, to the learners with whom they work and to the wider communities within which their activities are conducted.

These discussions lead to a consideration of governance and accountability and the nature of the democratic basis on which decisions of enormous social significance are currently being made. This is an important book which should be read by all those involved in education.

Pat Mahony is Professor of Education and **Ian Hextall** is Senior Research Fellow, both at Froebel College, University of Surrey Roehampton.

Reconstructing Teaching

Standards, performance and accountability

Pat Mahony and Ian Hextall

London and New York

First published 2000
by RoutledgeFalmer
11 New Fetter Lane, London EC4P 4EE

Simultaneously published in the USA and Canada
by RoutledgeFalmer
29 West 35th Street, New York, NY 10001

RoutledgeFalmer is an imprint of the Taylor & Francis Group
© 2000 Pat Mahony and Ian Hextall

Typeset in Garamond by Bookcraft Ltd, Stroud
Printed and bound in Great Britain by Clays Ltd, St Ives PLC

British Library Cataloguing in Publication Data
A catalogue record for this book is available from the British Library

Library of Congress Cataloging in Publication Data
A catalogue record has been requested

ISBN 0-415-23096-9 (hbk)
ISBN 0-415-23097-7 (pbk)

Contents

Illustrations

Figures

Tables

Abbreviations

APE	Accreditation of Prior Experience
APL	Accreditation of Prior Learning
ARTEN	Anti-Racist Teacher Education Network
AST	Advanced Skills Teacher
ATL	Association of Teachers and Lecturers
CATE	Council for the Accreditation of Teacher Education
CBI	Confederation of British Industry
CPD	Continuing Professional Development
DETR	Department of Environment, Transport and the Regions
CRE	Commission for Racial Equality
DfEE	Department for Education and Employment
EOC	Equal Opportunities Commission
FENTO	Further Education National Training Organisation
GRTP	Graduate and Registered Teacher Programme
GTC	General Teaching Council
HEFCE	Higher Education Funding Council for England
HEI	Higher Education Institution
HRM	Human Resource Management
HMI	Her Majesty's Inspectorate
ICT	Information and Communications Technology
ILO	International Labour Organisation
ITE	Initial Teacher Education
ITT	Initial Teacher Training
LEA	Local Education Authority
LGA	Local Government Association
LGMB	Local Government Management Board
LPSH	Leadership Programme for Serving Headteachers
MP	Member of Parliament
NACCCE	National Advisory Committee on Culture, Creativity and Education
NAHT	National Association of Headteachers
NAME	National Anti-Racist Movement in Education
NAPTEC	National Primary Teacher Education Conference
NASUWT	National Association of Schoolmasters and Union of Women Teachers
NC	National Curriculum
NCITT	National Curriculum for Initial Teacher Training

NDPB	Non-Departmental Public Body
NEOST	National Employers' Organisation for School Teachers
NPM	New Public Management
NPQH	National Professional Qualification for Headship
NPS	National Professional Standards
NQT	Newly Qualified Teacher
NUT	National Union of Teachers
OECD	Organisation for Economic Co-operation and Development
OFSTED	Office for Standards in Education
OPSS	Office of Public Service and Science
PAT	Professional Association of Teachers
QCA	Qualifications and Curriculum Authority
QTS	Qualified Teacher Status
QUANGO	Quasi-Autonomous Non-Governmental Organisation
SCETT	Standing Committee for the Education and Training of Teachers
SCITT	School-Centred Initial Teacher Training
SCOP	Standing Committee of Principals
SENCO	Special Education Needs Coordinator
SEO	Society of Education Officers
SHA	Secondary Heads Association
STRB	School Teachers Pay and Review Body
TTA	Teacher Training Agency
TUC	Trades Union Congress
UCET	University Council for the Education of Teachers

Preface

This has not been an easy book to write, lying as it does on the cusp of so many unknowns. We have found it challenging to write about the transformations occurring in England where 'fast' policy seems to have taken on a new meaning and what is true today will have changed by tomorrow. In recognising our own difficulties as nothing compared to the strains on those charged with implementation, we have found it difficult not to get entangled in the detail which, for practitioners, is precisely where policy bites. The general political landscape is also misty in its configurations. For example we, like many other people, are uncertain about the meaning of the terms 'UK' or even 'Britain', where current devolutionary shifts are located within a wider context of 'Europeanisation' and 'globalisation'. Moreover, the meaning and import of Third Way politics are not at all clear and their implications for teaching, if anything, are even less so.

There has been an important emotional dimension to our experiences in doing the research. At times we have felt angry or sad as interviewees have detailed their struggles to integrate central policy with contextual reality – what one deputy head described as 'operating in parallel universes'. We have had to reflect seriously on our own research protocols when some interviewees (men and women) have dissolved in tears while describing the ways their contributions have been marginalised and their sense of professionalism obliterated. At other times the humour with which people have described their strategies for resolving policy tension has left us rocking with laughter. At no time have we felt indifferent to the issues at stake or hardened to the impact of 'hard times' on those trying to make policy work.

Through all of it, however, we have had tremendous support from our Steering Group, Roy Beardsworth, Des Malone, Ian Menter, Erica Pienaar, Mary Russell, Susan Sidgwick, Meryl Thompson and Claudette Williams, whose encouragement and experience guided us through some difficult issues and whose wisdom and constructive guidance enabled our research to be better than it would otherwise have been. We are indebted to Penny Scuffil, who transcribed our interviews with energy and good humour, and to Chris Devereux, whose creativity and expertise helped us to interpret and present our data. We are grateful to all those who returned our questionnaires, gave generously of their time in talking to us and enabled us to gain wider national and international perspectives by inviting us to speak at their conferences. Thanks go to the University of Surrey Roehampton, which provided the enormously supportive context in which our work took place and to former colleagues and students at Goldsmiths, who will recognise their influence on our arguments. The contributions of our respective partners and families while we were writing this book were immeasurable – they have helped, encouraged and sustained us throughout. Finally, our thanks to each other for what has been a memorable and exciting four years that has left our friendship not just intact but richer than it was. Throughout our working lives we have gained immeasurably from the experience and insights of practising teachers – this book is dedicated to them.

Pat Mahony and Ian Hextall

Introduction

... critical policy analysts have an important role to play in relation to educational change. If policies are judged to be progressive then critical policy analysis can contribute to enhancing people's understandings of the origins of the policies, of their political context, of their moral bases and of the ways in which they relate to the progressive purposes of education in creating a more equal and caring society. If, on the other hand, policies are assessed to be regressive then critical policy analysis can help provide intellectual and political resources with which to establish patterns of opposition and resistance. If, however, policies are an amalgam of progressive and regressive elements, as is so often the case, then the task of critical policy analysis is to help to develop strategies to harness their progressive potential.

(Taylor *et al.* 1997, p. 156)

This book is concerned with teaching and teacher education. Although our story begins with the establishment of the Teacher Training Agency in 1994, our orientation has undoubtedly been shaped both by our own experiences of becoming teachers in the 1960s and 1970s and by the twenty years we spent working together with colleagues and with beginning and experienced teachers in developing programmes of teacher education. We were privileged to work in a context (a university in South East London) that gave us access to inspired teachers whose passion for teaching coupled with deep understanding of its challenges were influential in the development of our own learning. We were also galvanised (albeit differently as a white woman and a white man) by the 'new' social movements and by the growing volume of critical educational research (in some of which we took part). This drew attention to the material impact on young people's lives of teachers' negative attitudes and practices in reconstituting social divisions based on social class, disability, gender, 'race' and sexuality. These twin influences led us to be critical of the overly practical nature of a preparation for teachers which concentrated almost entirely on the mechanics of teaching whilst paying scant attention to debates about the purposes of education or the significance of research on human learning, and which provided little access to ways of understanding the dynamic relationship between schooling and the wider society. On the other hand, we were equally dissatisfied with the opposite tendency to concentrate on 'theory' at the expense of practical preparation.

In our own attempts to integrate theory and practice, we were part of an enthusiastic team that tried to develop a programme of initial teacher education which moved back and forth between explicit principles, general statements of expected performance and the specifics of practice. Teacher education became for us a process through which practitioners develop an underlying knowledge, principles and values base, acquire an expanding repertoire of potential strategies from which to choose, and can justify and defend their choices as being appropriate for particular contexts and purposes. It is with these orientations that we come to write this book, and we make no apologies for them. Indeed, it would have been illuminating had the originators of the policies which form the substance of our book made their value positions explicit, described the contexts in which these were formed and the grounds on which they were founded.

From the mid-1980s teacher education was characterised by a number of changes introduced by successive Conservative governments. These included: the setting up of CATE; the establishment of alternative routes into teaching (including licensed and articled teachers); the introduction of competence- or outcome-based approaches to the assessment of students; the abolition of the probationary year and the devolution of responsibilities for induction to schools; the introduction of partnership arrangements between HEIs and schools (with locally negotiated payments) and the establishment of SCITT schemes, without necessarily involving HEIs (Sidgwick *et al.* 1994). Thus in 1994 when the Teacher Training Agency was established, it was but one in a long line of initiatives designed to 'reform' teacher education, or 'teacher training' as it had become known. We have spent the last five years trying to grasp the nature and significance of what continues to be a changing scene in relation to teachers and teaching, an endeavour which has taken us far beyond England, beyond teacher education, and beyond the broader world of education to the even broader world of the public sector.

Our work has been made possible by two research grants from the Economic and Social Research Council. Our first project *The Policy Context and Impact of the Teacher Training Agency* (R000 22 1642) ran from September 1995 until November 1996. The second, on *The Impact on Teaching of the National Professional Standards and Qualifications* (R000 23 7382), began in December 1997 and was completed in December 1999. Taken together, funding for the two projects amounted to £100,300. As well as providing funding for ourselves and our administrative and technical colleagues, this has enabled us to analyse relevant national and international documentation from government bodies, professional associations, educational and non-educational organisations. We have also been able to keep a running review of educational and social policy literature from the UK and elsewhere, as well as maintaining professional dialogues via email with colleagues in Europe and Australia who are engaged in work similar to our own.

During the course of the two projects we have circulated over 800 postal questionnaires to HEIs, LEAs, schools, professional associations and unions, NPQH Training and Assessment Centres, and members of TTA Working Groups on Standards. Across both projects taken together we have received approximately 40 per cent response rates. We have interviewed ninety-six individuals, including schoolteachers and headteachers; school governors; union and professional association officers; LEA personnel; HEI staff; officers from teacher education umbrella organisations; private consultants; politicians; civil servants; inspectors, both lay and HMI; policy analysts within and outside education, at home and abroad; TTA officers, committee members, working group members and Board members. In addition we have conducted focus group interviews with two groups of student teachers, following a four-year undergraduate teaching degree programme and a one-year postgraduate programme respectively; one group of teachers in their first year of teaching and a group of experienced teachers undertaking a part-time Masters degree. Our presentations at conferences and seminars, of which twenty-one of the fifty-two (to date) have been in countries outside England, have also enabled us to gain access to a broad range of perspectives and experience.

Throughout the period of our research, the TTA has played a central role in the redefinition of teacher education. At present the significance of the TTA appears to be diminishing before our eyes as its purposes become displaced either to the GTC or relocated at the DfEE. We also find that many of the dominant strands which have characterised thinking about teacher education and development in this country have made their appearance in a whole range of other countries and locations without the 'benefit' of an agency such as the TTA. For these reasons, although the history and practice of the TTA figure at various points throughout our argument, we believe it is more interesting to see the Agency as symptomatic of a constellation of tendencies which has both generated and will survive the particularities of the 'TTA experience'. In our writings and our discussions we have been drawn back time and again to certain key themes, and it is with these and their interactions that we want to engage in this book. So while we see the Agency as having been strategically central in shaping teaching and teacher education, we shall also be endeavouring to hold a balance between grasping the nature of the 'big picture' within which policy can be understood, and the specificity which gives policy its character and bite.

The story we shall tell is, briefly, as follows. What has been happening to teaching over the last decade or so bears a close family resemblance to what has been happening in other areas of the public sector, nationally and internationally. Health provision, housing, employment and welfare services have experienced a period of restructuring, driven by many of the same impulses and arguments as those which have become well known to people involved in education. Although given different names in different contexts, we shall describe this restructuring as *new public management* or *managerialism*. We shall return to this in fuller detail in Chapter 1, but for the moment we need to stress that this development has been internationally based on the idea of taking managerial and organisational approaches developed within the private sector and applying them to *public policy*. This drive provides one way of understanding the enormous significance being attributed to the concept of *standards*, the subject of Chapter 2. There is much confusion and debate about how to grasp the idea of 'standards', but they do appear to hold out the promise of calculability. This is perceived as vital if it is considered important to construct some kind of firm basis on which the performance of the public sector can be judged or measured – clearly no small matter given the scale of expenditure on public services, its impact on private and commercial tax levels, and the extent to which these services fall largely outside the realm of private profit. Standards provide a central part of the technology which is used both to deliver and legitimate the culture of performance which has become so ubiquitous within the whole public sector, not least in relation to schools and teachers.

Performance management, explored in Chapter 3, is the term which binds together managerialism and the culture of performance in both the private and public sectors. A whole language and set of assumptions about motivation and human behaviour are embedded within this term. There are also many different methods and techniques which are used to deliver it and to ensure that it is being properly applied. Its significance for us is that teaching is currently being subjected to reorganisation on the basis of performance management principles. This will lead to changes in the structure of teaching as an occupation and will impact on the nature of teaching as an activity. As people in other public sector occupations have found, and as we discuss in Chapter 4, such transformations have significant effects on their *work and sense of 'professionalism'*. Such changes are not trivial, since they have broad implications for the ways in which teachers relate to one another, to the learners with whom they work and to the wider communities within which their activities are conducted.

Considerations of the reformulations of teachers' work will lead us in two intertwined directions. First, we shall ask in Chapter 5 what the implications of these new relationships within teaching will be for questions of *social justice*. Given the new 'standards' within and towards which teachers are expected to work, we shall consider the models of social relationships and assumptions about society which are built into them. Second, as teaching is being reorganised and redefined, we shall explore the consequences for different categories and groups of teachers. These are important issues, though they have received little direct attention within the recent policy developments, despite the rhetoric of social justice. This leads us on to Chapter 6 and to the heart of discussions on *governance and accountability*. As we have been researching the development of teacher education policy, we have become increasingly aware how 'thin' is the democratic basis on which decisions of enormous social significance are being made. Sometimes the democratic deficit is quite specific, for example, we have become progressively concerned about the nature, purposes and form of 'consultation' as an exercise in policy formation. More generally, we have found ourselves asking just who should be involved in policy formation and on what bases. These are not easily resolved issues, but they are questions which take us directly to the centre of contemporary discussions on democracy and focus our attention on the criteria by which we would wish our societies to be judged *in the future* and the processes through which these might be established (Chapter 7). Throughout the book we question whether the changes that have occurred in recent times have been the right ones, initiated by the right people for the right reasons and in the right ways. While our conclusions are sometimes negative, we are not. To be so would seem self-indulgent given so many 'lives at stake' and 'futures at risk'. There are many lessons waiting to be learned by those open to learning them and we hope that in presenting our evidence and arguments we have made clear enough what some of these might be in relation to policy-making.

1 The reconstruction of teaching in context

Our research on the TTA began at a time when there was relatively little debate about the relationship between education and broader definitions of social policy. Most texts about what was then called the 'Welfare State' paid perfunctory attention to education. Similarly, few analyses of education placed it within the field of public policy. How much has changed. It is now broadly recognised that it is only through connecting the broader contexts of public policy and education policy that we can begin to understand the trends which are reshaping the nature of teaching and restructuring the teaching profession. In many ways we have the Conservative administrations of 1979–97 to 'thank' for this heightened awareness, and certainly for the genesis of the TTA, which is the touch-paper of our research. We shall, however, argue that whilst the TTA has played a pivotal role in the reconstruction of teaching in England, it would be parochial to concentrate solely on this body, given similar tendencies evident both in the reshaping of teaching in other countries and in experiences in the public sector more generally.

Public policy

The past two decades have represented a period of dramatic transformation across the public sector, not only in the UK but internationally. In movements variously described as involving 'New Public Management' (NPM), 'corporate managerialism', 'managerialism' or 'new managerialism', principles drawn from the private sector have been imported into the public sector of most advanced Western economies (Shand 1996) and increasingly introduced to developing countries through the influence of supranational organisations such as the OECD (Lingard 1999a) and the World Bank (Smyth and Shacklock 1998). That these developments have had direct impact upon and implications for educational policy and provision in this country and other developed and developing nations is now well documented (Bottery 1998; Elliott 1999; Hartley 1997; ILO 1996).

A variety of reasons have been given at different levels for the transformations that have occurred (Exworthy and Halford 1999). First, analysts have referred to the 1970s and 1980s as a significant period in which a number of material and political factors came together to provide a new context for governments. The power of Western governments to deliver prosperity, security and opportunity to their citizens within 'walled' economies controlling the movement of capital, goods and services was undermined by a world recession created by escalating fuel prices following oil crises in the 1970s (Halsey *et al.* 1997). Falling profits motivated multinational corporations to seek new markets, with increasing deregulation of the world economy and financial markets in the 1980s and 1990s making it easier for them to do so. This was sustained by the increasing political influence of the New Right and their mobilisation of reaction against Keynesian economic and welfare policies. At the same time new technologies have made it increasingly possible (but not inevitable) for production of goods to be relocated in areas where costs are lower. In this context the 'competition state' was born, pressuring governments to seek reductions in public expenditure (in order to attract inward investment) and to secure maximum returns from public-sector resources.

> As the world is characterised by increasing interpenetration and the crystallisation of transnational markets and structures, the state itself is having to act more and more like a market player, that shapes its policies to promote, control, and maximise returns from market forces in an international setting.
>
> (Cerny 1990, p. 230)

In an influential text from the USA, the age of 'reinvented government' and 'entrepreneurial governance' arrived, advocating a 'steering not rowing' role for governments and recommending that public services be reorganised.

> … entrepreneurial governments promote *competition* between service providers. They *empower* citizens by pushing control out of the bureaucracy into the community. They measure the performance of their agencies, focusing not on inputs but *outcomes*. They are driven by their goals – their *missions* – not by their rules and regulations. They define their clients as customers and offer them choices – between schools, … They *prevent* problems before they emerge, rather than simply offering services afterwards. They put their energies into *earning* money, not simply spending it. They *decentralize* authority, embracing participatory management. They prefer *market* mechanisms to bureaucratic mechanisms.
>
> (Osborne and Gaebler 1992, pp. 19–20, emphasis in original)

While different historical, political and cultural traditions have influenced both the forms of the transformations and the ways they have been introduced within various countries, the winds of change have blown either as relatively minor gusts or as full-force gales (Clarke *et al.* 1994; Dunleavy and Hood 1994; Eliassen and Kooiman 1994; Ferlie *et al.* 1996). Trends being identified as common by the EU project on Educational Governance and Social Integration and Exclusion (Lindblad 2000) include: increased competition, the pursuit of efficiency and effectiveness through employee-performance measurement, increased demands for public accountability in achieving goals, targets and other outcomes (often specified centrally), and increased regulation by central government at the same time as decentralisation or devolution of responsibility for local management (sometimes termed 'deregulation'). It has been suggested that these tendencies lead to a version of 'managerialised politics' which

> ... does not just concern the effectiveness of institutions, but involves the managerialisation of the policy domain itself, which influences not only the structures and institutions, but the discourses and frameworks within which deliberation and evaluation take place. Managerial discourse offers particular representations of the relationship between social problems and solutions. It is linear and oriented to 'single goal' thought patterns. It is concerned with goals and plans rather than with intentions and judgments. It is about action rather than reflection. It draws on analysis (breaking problems down) rather than synthesis. It sets boundaries between 'policy' and 'delivery', 'strategy' and 'implementation', thought and action. It offers a technicist discourse which strips debate of its political underpinnings, so that debates about means supplants debate about ends.
>
> (Clarke and Newman 1997, p. 148)

A current expression of this in the UK can be seen in the Labour administration's determination to 'modernise government'. This is a textbook expression of such a managerial modelling of politics and policy-making (Cabinet Office 1999a).

Whether or not such developments constitute the emergence of a new global paradigm remains a matter of considerable controversy. There are certainly differences between countries, one of which is the emphasis and interpretation that have been given to the 'virtuous three Es: economy, efficiency and effectiveness' (Pollitt 1993, p. 59) underpinning the 'value for money', calculative measurement of the public sector in the UK compared, for example, to the Scandinavian countries (Ferlie *et al.* 1996). Such differences suggest that policy development is not simply a question of reacting to the supposedly deterministic imperatives of the global economy. Although restructuring has been widespread and common tendencies evident, there are still value judgments and political calculations to be made in the shaping of social policy. As Lingard and Rizvi (1997) argue,

> ... in the construction of policy, globalization works as an ideology just as much as it refers to direct empirical effects. Thus there is a way in which governments argue that certain policy developments are the only possible options in response to global imperatives. This is a hegemonic policy device ...   (p. 258)

The recognition that different forms of NPM and managerialism have been introduced in a variety of ways and with different motivations is important for analysing and comparing their progressive or damaging effects. In the UK context the ideological hue of the Thatcher government was fuelled, according to Taylor-Gooby and Lawson (1993) by

> ... antipathy to large bureaucracies and the structured planning of services: an ideological commitment to privatisation and the extension of market systems:

the vigorous endorsement of monetarist economic theory ... and the determination to cut taxation for electoral advantage.   (p. 1)

In addition the introduction of NPM was justified by questioning the motivations and efficiency of public-sector workers to an extent not experienced elsewhere. Education, in particular, was seen as epitomising

> ... much that was seen to be wrong with burgeoning state power. It was construed as expensive, not self-evidently adequately productive, insufficiently accountable, monopolistic, producer-dominated, a bastion of an entrenched professional elite, resistant to consumer demand and, at worst, self-generating and self-serving.
>
> (Fergusson 1994 p. 93)

As well as being framed by this wider context of public policy and subject to the transformations outlined above, education policy has been given its own particular role to play within the 'competition state'.

Education policy

The imperatives emerging from the school effectiveness and improvement movements have been profoundly influential in defining 'effective' teachers and leaders as the key to 'effective' schools, defined predominantly in terms of raising standards of academic achievement. Key to these movements has been the 'standards' debate which has been strongly foregrounded in recent times, referring sometimes to the academic achievement of school students, while at other times being used to denote a framework of criteria or specifications defining what teachers should be able to do.

In the first sense, the history of state education could be written from the perspective of the concern with 'standards', with the last three decades witnessing an increasingly detailed preoccupation that has transcended party lines and educational philosophies. But while everybody has claimed a commitment to better educational standards (by definition only a fool would want worse standards or ineffective schools), the debates have centred first, on how these terms are defined, second, by whom, and third, on how improvement or effectiveness is to be achieved.

The former Conservative government's strategy for levering up standards of achievement in schools is well known, embracing: greater centralised prescription of the curriculum allied to reform of the examinations and assessment system; devolution of financial management to schools and a weakening of Local Education Authority (LEA) powers; the introduction of competitive quasi-market policies that exerted pressure on schools through published league tables of exam performance and inspection reports; open enrolment to deliver parental 'choice', and the reintroduction of differentiated schools. The extent to which the Labour government's policies of 'standards not structures' represent a continuation or even an extension of what the Conservatives began, and the extent to which we are witnessing superficial or significant discontinuities are matters of considerable debate in the educational and academic press (Demaine 1999; Docking 2000; Hill 1999; Power and Whitty 1999). We cannot pursue these discussions here except in one important respect, and that is to note the continuities across time in the way that the drive for 'effective schools' has been tied to the needs of UK Ltd to become more competitive in the global economy.

The claim that national prosperity depends on high levels of knowledge and skill is one surrounded by controversy. For example, Ashton and Green (1996) devote an entire book to challenging the 'simplistic consensus' from which 'policy debates and much scholarly discussion begin' (p. 3) that more and better skills necessarily lead to improved economic performance, and Robin Alexander has been quoted as claiming that

> ... there is no direct and causal link between pedagogy, attainment in literacy and national economic competitiveness ... dominant values underlying Britain's obsession with literacy and numeracy targets are the same now as they were in the 1870s – economic instrumentalism, cultural reproduction and social control ...
>
> (Budge 1997, p. 17)

Furthermore, although high educational attainment may help individuals in the competition for jobs (as long as employment opportunities are available in the first place), one cannot conclude that this logic automatically operates at the level of the global economy. Companies are attracted or deterred from locating their operations by factors that may include the local availability of appropriate skills, but that also relate to levels of taxation, labour costs and flexibility, degrees of social stability and a social infrastructure relevant to their needs.

As with public policy, the significance of education policy as an element of effective economic policy has been weighted differently in different countries. In a speech given in Soroe in August 1997, Ole Vig Jensen, Danish Minister for Education, said

> Our educational system shall not be a product of a global educational race without thinking of the goals and ideals we want in Denmark.

The 'goals and ideals' in this case revolved around the role of schools in educating citizens for democracy. The Danish minister went on to explain

> A democratic challenge to education is the way to go if we want to develop our democracy. If an education must prepare for democracy it must be democratically organised. ... We don't suggest a connection between democracy and education. We insist on it.

In recent study of school leadership across four countries, strong differences emerged between England and Denmark (Moos, Mahony and Reeves 1998). The rhetoric of competition was only weakly present in Denmark and devolution of powers and responsibility had occurred to some extent along with an increased emphasis on leadership and management of schools. However, compared to England, conceptions of 'leadership' were rather different in Denmark, where there has been a long tradition of flat structures consisting of the leadership team (head and deputy) and teachers. School 'leaders' had often emerged from the once-powerful Teachers' Council imbued with values which accorded high levels of trust to their colleagues' professionalism. This 'flatarchy' is gradually being transformed in many schools because of the difficulties in 'leading' so many staff. However, rather than what is seen as the 'UK-hierarchy', Danish heads, parents and teachers seem to be favouring the project-group structure of the 'starburst organisation' because it is consistent with collaborative, democratic traditions and culture. There are requirements for teachers to work collectively, at times in cross-curricular ways, and to teach and assess students through project work. Such diversities in tradition and culture do therefore appear to bear on the different English and Danish interpretations of both NPM and the role of schools within it. The less centralised, less tightly framed, less regulatory framework would seem to fit within the Danish tradition of democratic participation which, throughout the school leadership project, was reiterated by Danish heads as something to be valued and retained.

Despite its controversial status, the redefinition of education policy as one element of economic policy has been reiterated time and again. It was evident in the former Conservative government's aim 'to support economic growth and improve the nation's competitiveness by raising educational achievement' (DfEE 1995), and in Labour's pre-election policies.

> ... after more than a decade of turmoil, we are slipping even further behind – all the way to 35th out of 48 in the education league ... We know what makes a good school: high expectations; strong leadership ... and a vision of the future that motivates pupils and teachers alike ... The rewards will be enormous – a thriving and united Britain, competing with the cutting edge of the global economy.
>
> (Labour Party 1995, p. 35)

It has formed a continuing theme underpinning the Labour government's policies.

> We are talking about investing in human capital in the age of knowledge. To compete in the global economy, to live in a civilised society and to develop the talents of each and every one of us, we will have to unlock the potential of every young person.
>
> (DfEE 1997, p. 3)[1]

Inevitably, government attention has focused on teacher 'training' where the winds of change have generated varying degrees of reform in different countries. The responsibility of the education service (or business) for producing a workforce geared to meeting the demands of the global economy has been seen as paramount in the UK, focusing a spotlight on what constitutes teacher effectiveness and how best to achieve it. What counts as good teaching and how to reward it are increasingly being underpinned by 'teaching standards' or competence-based models of teacher education which are well advanced in Australia, USA and the UK (Ingvarson 1998; Mahony 1998). The establishment and subsequent work of the TTA, in laying the foundations for the future shape of teaching, can be seen as exemplifying both the particular ideological stance of the former Conservative government and more general global trends. Under the Labour government, the continued managerialisation of teaching could be seen as an extension of these trends.

The establishment of the TTA

From the mid-1980s there was increasing centralised control over the definition of teaching and the structuring of the teaching career. Much of this was carried through by CATE via its criteria for course approval and by OFSTED through its procedures for the inspection of schools (for a detailed account of the period up to 1994, see Hoyle and John 1995). September 1994 marked a highly significant extension of this process with the establishment of the TTA by John Major's government.

The intention to establish the TTA first entered the public domain via a document entitled *The Government's Proposals for the Reform of Initial Teacher Training* (DFE and Welsh Office 1993). It appeared with little warning in a context where some of us had naively believed that ITT[2] had already been 'reformed' through the long line of Conservative government interventions which had already occurred.

The Proposals gave two main reasons for the establishment of the TTA: first, to improve the quality of teachers and teaching so that the quality of pupils' learning would be enhanced; second, the need to make arrangements for the funding for SCITT schemes since HEFCE could not (by definition) do this within its existing powers.

There ensued a period of considerable controversy which generated a range of issues. First, the evidence cited as indicating the need for reform, namely ' ... recent evidence from the OFSTED that around a third of lessons taken by new entrants were unsatisfactory' (para. 5, p. 1) produced a storm of protest. The then Director of the Institute of Education, London, spoke for many when he said

> Even by the standards to which we have unhappily grown accustomed lately, the Government's *Proposals for the Reform of Initial Teacher Training* is a singularly dishonest document ... the opening words of HMI's own summary are: 'In 1992, over 90 per cent of headteachers considered their new teachers to have been adequately prepared for their first teaching post and over 70 per cent of lessons taught by new teachers were considered by HMI as satisfactory or better.'
>
> (Newsam 1993, p. 4)

Newsam went on to point out that new teachers in the survey were judged by the same standards as their experienced colleagues. He claimed that an alternative reading of HMI's findings might have been that the training system was improving, albeit with some way yet to go.

Baroness Blatch, in a subsequent House of Lords debate on the establishment of the TTA, apologised for the error in interpretation within the Bill (Education Bill (HL)

1993, p. 922), and a senior civil servant in the DfEE whom we interviewed personally claimed the mistake:

> ' ... there was so much fuss about it and there was no absolutely no element of evil external political pressure on this. I got it wrong ... for which I am entirely willing to be personally crucified.'

A second indication of the level of controversy provoked by *The Proposals* was the campaign coordinated by the Teacher Education Alliance.[3] This was a non-party-political coalition of organisations involved with education, including parents, governors, schools, colleges, teacher organisations, researchers, universities, local authorities and churches. The Alliance produced a number of briefing papers; its main arguments were that

- no reasons were given as to why the Government's objectives could not be achieved within the existing framework;
- teacher supply and the future of university departments of education would be threatened;
- the TTA would represent yet another government agency accountable only to the appointing Minister.

The Alliance emphasised in one briefing paper what was at stake in the establishment of the TTA:

> Is it healthy in a democracy to have so much of the education system under the control of a QUANGO answerable only to the secretary of state?
>
> (TEA 1994, p. 2)

We shall subsequently see that this is a question which continues to raise concern.

Third, following *The Proposals* and notwithstanding the protest which had ensued, *The Education Bill* was drafted and hotly debated in the House of Lords (Education Bill (HL) 1993). Beginning its second reading on 7th December 1993, Baroness Blatch claimed that the Bill ' ... rests on fundamental principles which have inspired so many of our reforms: quality, efficiency, choice and accountability' (p. 819), terms which could be echoed in many other public-sector areas. She reiterated the objectives for the TTA which were later enshrined in the Education Act 1994. These stated that the Agency had responsibility

- (a) to contribute to raising the standards of teaching;
- (b) to promote teaching as a career;
- (c) to improve the quality and efficiency of all routes into the teaching profession; and
- (d) to secure the involvement of schools in all courses for the initial training of school teachers.

(Part 1 1.(2))

She also claimed that the TTA would 'encourage diversity by supporting courses run by schools as well as by higher education' (p. 820).

Some noble persons, however, were not persuaded by the discourse of 'support':

> I estimate that this Bill and accompanying measures are of major importance. It is a crucial part of the drive to ensure centralised control over all aspects of education and, in particular, to destabilise and threaten the role of the universities within that system ... I see it also as another attempt to destroy what the Government are pleased to call the 'education establishment'; that is, those who know about education.
>
> (Baroness David, Education Bill (HL) 1993, p. 919)

Others complained about the

> ... haste to legislate [which] clearly indicates that the statutory gesture towards consultation was made with minds already closed rather than with a desire to reflect on the considerable and weighty advice received.
>
> (Lord Judd, Education Bill (HL) 1993, p. 826)

Through all this debate and controversy, and from our interviews with people close to the policy process, a number of points emerged about the various motivations for setting up the TTA. Some saw it as an attempt to introduce coherence into the system, arguing that the wide array of bodies that played a part in the organisation and administration of teacher education (one body for recruitment, another for allocation of numbers, another for funding, another for accreditation of courses and so on) created confusions over who was responsible for what, led to inadequate coordination and the fragmentation of policy, and spread accountability too thinly. It was argued that the education of teachers and of children in schools was being hindered by these disparities, especially since the National Curriculum required greater coherence in teacher education. As one of our interviewees said,

> I suspect that any Secretary of State might sensibly say, why don't we bring these functions together, why not bring recruitment, initial training, induction and in-service training of teachers together and put it all under one umbrella ... if you're interested in school improvement – in improving teachers, ... improving teaching, improving teaching qualities, improving initial training, improving induction and improving recruitment, improving Continuing Professional Development ... it is a short step from that ... to say, well it is stupid to have these various functions separated out and some of them not functions allocated to anybody.
>
> (TTA officer)

For others, the establishment of the TTA provided an answer to the problem of quality control. A number of people, from diverse contexts, drew attention to the argument that it was very difficult to provide an adequate 'quality steer' to teacher education – that a gap existed between directives *designed* to improve practice and the translation of these into *actual* improvements. 'The teeth were not there to make them bite', as one person put it.

Others viewed the TTA as one of a long line of initiatives designed to reduce the influence of higher education in the education of teachers. In relation to the legal problem of funding arrangements for SCITT schemes, for example, it was acknowledged that the powers of HEFCE could have been extended, as they were in Wales, but that would have impeded change.

> Well I mean in legislative terms you could do anything ... But if part of the shift of responsibility and power is out of Higher Education into school ... you know I think it didn't appeal ...
>
> (Senior civil servant)

These arguments often slid into accounts which emphasised political or ideological reasons for the establishment of the TTA. The TTA was seen as one of a long sequence of endeavours on the part of the Government to 'break the education establishment's hold on teacher education'. One meeting with Conservative politicians was described as follows:

> Baroness Blatch did use the argument about teacher training being dominated by a single philosophy – we actually raised that in our first meeting with her, ... Do you think that academics in any institution would simply clutch on to a single philosophy? ... she did feel that ... We did have meetings followed by working lunches with some Conservative MPs and I think we were more or less warned not to underestimate the strength of the view and the passion with which the Conservative MPs detested educational theory – it's not just useless, it is positively dangerous and it's all pervasive.
>
> (Former officer of UCET)

Another of our interviewees confirmed this view:

> ... if you read through the Debates on the TTA Bill, ... the depth of the hostility to teacher education amongst the Government back-benchers, ... they talked incessantly about 'Training Colleges' ... staffed fully by people from the 1960s who were all raving Trots and that is still there, that hasn't changed. ... all these opinions are still there.
>
> (Member of Parliament)

Over the preceding months HEIs had been pilloried in the press and by politicians for filling lecture halls with captive audiences of student teachers and indoctrinating them with woolly, left-wing, child-centred propaganda. Sometimes interviewees referred directly to this as the backcloth against which the ideological modes of argument were formulated. Furthermore, some saw the SCITT proposals as a device for putting the 'frighteners' on HEIs by teaching them that they had no reason to rely on the certainty of a natural monopoly and that the government was willing to encourage the introduction of new 'suppliers' or 'producers', echoing the assault on 'producer-capture' found elsewhere in debates on the public sector. Through all this, some critics of *The Proposals* also took pains to dissociate themselves from 'a professional autonomy model' of governance and from the elitist attitudes expressed by a few of the HEI staff whose vested interests were undoubtedly being threatened. In addition it was noted that the voices of classroom teachers were largely absent from both sides of the debate. As one deputy head put it, 'We'd got our own problems. In any case, when it had been our turn to be bashed where were the university professors then?'

These different perspectives both illustrate and reflect one of the key difficulties in accounting for policy change. Multiple accounts that may be historical, political, administrative, ideological, economic or a mixture of all of them, offer a range of possible motives and reasons why particular developments may have taken place. Clearly this is by no means limited to the issue of the genesis of the TTA. Contained within each and every account of its origin, is an array of values and presumptions as to what the problem was to which the establishment of the TTA provided the answer. Though other elements of education policy were referred to frequently by our interviewees, largely absent from their accounts were references to the wider context of public policy concerning the purposes, nature and functioning of government and the broader restructuring of the public sector. It is for this reason that we began this chapter with a brief account of that wider context, for it is at this level that we can begin to understand the nature of the TTA and the continuities that have occurred over time and despite a change of government. Such continuities suggest that it is not the TTA itself that should ultimately preoccupy us but rather what it did, the parameters it established for the future and what it reveals about modes of policy-making within re-invented government. It is at this level too that comparisons can be made with changes in other areas of the public sector in England and with the 'remaking' of teaching occurring in other countries.

QUANGOs and the TTA

Under the Conservative government, part of the radical transformation of the public sector expressed itself in an explicit move towards what has been called 'consumer democracy'. William Waldegrave who, as Minister of the OPSS, had Cabinet responsibility for the implementation of the Next Steps programme of developing Agencies in the public sector, was very clear about the Conservative government's orientation in driving forward this policy.

> The key point is not whether those who run our public services are elected, but whether they are producer-responsive or consumer-responsive. Services are not necessarily made to respond to the public by giving our citizens a democratic voice, and a distant and diffuse one at that, in their make-up. They can be made responsive by giving the public choices, or by instituting mechanisms which build in publicly approved standards and redress when they are not attained.
>
> (Waldegrave 1993)

He also claimed that the restructuring of central government policy and administration was no less than 'a revolution in Whitehall' and, with direct reference to Osborne and Gaebler (1992), that the Conservative government was in the process of 'reinventing government'. The general issue of standards in public life consequent on this transformation in public administration and governance was thrown into high relief by the work of the Nolan Committee (Nolan 1995). Although much of the media attention focused on the issues of 'cash for questions', declarations of MPs' business and commercial interests, and, more salaciously, the moral (sexual) behaviour of politicians, the Committee raised serious questions not only about the effectiveness of the democratic process but about the nature of democracy itself in Britain. On the effectiveness of the processes of government, a major concern has been the effect on democratic accountability of the spread of QUANGOs at all levels of society (Weir and Hall 1994).

Before moving into the particularities of the TTA, the QUANGO[4] in which we are particularly interested, some general points need to be made. First, the UK is not alone in its use of QUANGOs or their equivalent.

> Governments in all modern democracies use quasi-public bodies, regulatory agencies, tribunals and other extra-governmental arrangements to assist them in the conduct of public business, to manage a mixed economy and to regulate all manner of public and private activity.
>
> (Weir and Hall 1994, p. 6)

Second, QUANGOs have long been present on the political landscape in the UK. Their growth, according to Weir and Hall, was a matter of considerable concern to two Conservative MPs, who complained in 1978 about the number of prominent trade unionists occupying positions on these bodies.

> Ministers have discovered that the system can be used for shedding personal responsibility, rewarding friends, expanding the corporate state, diminishing the authority of Parliament, and enabling themselves to retain a measure of control over the interpretation of their own statutes. On its present scale, the vast and complex network of QUANGOs encourages an abuse of patronage and invites corruption.
>
> (Weir and Hall 1994, p. 6)

Third, they possess considerable power and control over large swathes of public resources. Weir and Hall, for example, claim that on their calculations there were 5,521 QUANGOs in 1993 (recently updated by Weir and Beetham (1999) to 5,681 as of 1997) which were responsible for spending approximately £46.65 billion, amounting to nearly a third of total central government public expenditure. When such responsibility for public services is shifted from elected government to unelected QUANGOs, issues of democratic accountability are raised which need to be opened up to public scrutiny.

The size of this expenditure on public goods is not in itself a cause for reproach; ... The point is that the bodies spending this huge tranche of public money are under the control of an appointed and self-appointing magistracy in a multiplicity of public bodies. None of them are directly responsible to the public; and ... the mechanisms of accountability which do seek to direct and scrutinise their activities are inconsistent and defective.

(Weir and Hall 1994, pp. 9–10)

It is within this wider concern for democratic accountability that issues emerging from our research can be located. Some of the areas upon which the Nolan Committee deliberated are directly pertinent to issues we have encountered in that element of our project which has concentrated on the structure, dynamics and working procedures of the TTA. There are also other issues being raised in the wider social policy literature about the workings of 'reinvented government' which we found echoed in the practices of the TTA. To this extent the TTA can be viewed as providing a symptomatic context for engaging with a range of concerns of relevance to an understanding of current education policy and its location within the wider setting of public policy.

Many political analysts and commentators argue, for example, that far from a new form of democracy emerging, what we are witnessing is a growing 'democratic deficit' (Mahony and Hextall 1997a; Ranson and Stewart 1994). Such issues spread far beyond the UK, for if such a deficit is consequent upon the competitive-economic models increasingly dominant (often at the cost of welfarist/equity-driven approaches) in the various European (and non-European) nation states, then the future of democracy and the forms that it takes in our complex societies are issues for all those undergoing the transformations outlined above. Experience in a range of countries of a shift in the locus of control away from the 'professionals' undertaking teacher training and towards greater centralised control by the state is bringing to the fore a whole host of questions about who, in any democratic society, ought to be involved in decisions about teaching – an occupation which not only has to deliver its 'targets' today, but which also has a key role in shaping the future for individual children as well as the political and cultural texture of societies.

Such issues, to which we shall return in Chapter 6, pick up more general concerns that the work of accountability that was once borne by subjecting decisions to democratic scrutiny is now mediated through contractual relationships within the newly framed purposes, organisation and delivery of public-sector services. It is often difficult to detect the boundaries between the government department framing such contracts, and the organisations (in the UK often from the private sector) successful in the competitive bidding process through which they are awarded.

The workings of the TTA

As we write, the TTA has a budget of over £242.2 million, a staffing complement of over 100 people, a Board of ten members and a range of responsibilities in relation to the occupational and professional lives of teachers. Few would question the dynamism and energy which the TTA brought to its activities, but concern has persistently been expressed about the procedures through which these initiatives have been established and implemented. Whilst compared with some of the health or social-security QUANGOs there is not a great deal of financial honey in the TTA pot, its strategic location in the shaping of teachers' work and in restructuring the teaching profession has provided it with access to power structures which distribute and control considerable 'cultural capital' within the educational system.

It is in the light of these considerations that we shall explore some of the key aspects of the structure and working practices of the TTA which are of relevance for the rest of the book and in particular for issues of accountability and governance.

Appointment to the Board of the TTA

One feature of QUANGOs is that membership is generated not through election but through appointment by ministers; in the TTA's case by the Secretary of State for Education and Employment. Thus the Board could not claim to be a representative body even though certain constituencies may be present in its membership. In our interviews concern was expressed that whilst some members of the Board are connected with particular HEIs, the sector as a whole is not formally represented. When the original Board was appointed in 1994, commentators remarked on the particularly controversial nature of two appointments who were identified as having explicit connections with 'New Right think tanks'. From its inception this rendered the TTA vulnerable to the general concern about 'patronage' and lack of representation in the governance of the public sector.

> There is nothing new about patronage. It has oiled the wheels of politics for centuries. In Britain's unregulated state, what control there is has largely been a matter of discreet and high-minded 'cronyism' which relies heavily on the good faith of ministers and their willingness to obey the informal 'rules of the club'. Patronage has never been governed by formal rules of procedure or laid open to democratic scrutiny … The growth of government by appointment has greatly magnified the scale of political patronage.
>
> (Weir and Hall 1994, p. 16)

This was one of the areas of direct concern to the Nolan Committee, which recommended that

> Appointments to the boards of executive NDPBs and NHS bodies should be made on the basis of merit, to form boards with a balance of relevant skills and backgrounds.
>
> Responsibility for appointments should remain with Ministers, advised by committees which include independent members.
>
> A Public Appointments Commissioner should be appointed, to regulate, monitor and report on the public appointments process.

The process should be open and departments should have to justify any departures from best practice. Job specifications should be published, and a wide range of candidates should be sought. The suitability of each candidate should be assessed by an advisory committee.

(Nolan 1995, p. 65)

In the case of the initial Board, which was so influential in establishing the ground rules within which the TTA conducted its activities, neither the appointment procedures nor the criteria for appointment were ever clear. This hardly generated confidence in the Board and it was a matter highlighted in considerations of the emergent GTC. Procedures for appointment to the TTA Board have recently been amended in line with the Nolan procedures; vacancies are now advertised and applicants are sent brief outlines of the role of the TTA and job and person specifications. Whilst the press adverts make reference to equal opportunities, this 'commitment' finds no echo in any of the materials which are actually circulated to applicants, an only too familiar 'slippage' between statement and action (Gillborn 1999).

Organisational structure of the TTA

The working structure of the Agency is both clear and complex at the same time. There is a well-established model of Chair, Board, Chief Executive and Officers however, as with many other public bodies, the clarity of the framework clouds once one tries to grasp the interactions between different elements and the power flows and dynamics of policy steering.

In addition to the senior management level there are also staff who work within groups or sections and are answerable to more senior officers within their divisions. The precise composition of this cohort is somewhat less clear. There is a core of staff who are experienced civil servants at different levels and with diverse ranges of prior experience. Some are deeply rooted in the DfEE; of these, some may have moved across 'permanently' to the Agency, while others may be there 'on loan'. There are also people who have been brought in from 'outside' (for example, from OFSTED, LEAs or HEIs), sometimes on part-time contracts, sometimes on secondment, sometimes on loan. There are other staff, some on part-time contracts, with, according to our interviewees, 'relatively' or 'debatably' little experience of working in education or teacher education. In respect of its employment practices, the TTA is a typical example of an organisation run according to the principles of NPM (Hood 1991), with a restructured, unstable, high-output labour force. In some areas of the public sector this structure of employment has given rise to the concern that employees can be more easily exploited and that job insecurity generates an unhealthy fear of 'whistle-blowing' (Hoggett 1996).

Within the Agency, team working has from the beginning been a preferred model of operation where specific groups are composed from within the staff to work on particular projects and then disbanded once that activity is over. Team working, however, is not without its critics. Amanda Sinclair (1995), for example, argues that 'teams are a time-honoured device for displacing responsibility ... And teams are frequently used to diffuse accountability' (p. 57). Trying to keep track of who had been working on what, and who was directly responsible for which particular activity (and hence could answer detailed questions) was described to us as 'perplexing'. Richard Sennett (1998) generalises these criticisms in his comments on the 'fictions' of teamwork in the working practices of 'New Capitalism'. He puts it in the following way:

> ... power is present in the superficial scenes of teamwork, but authority is absent. An authority figure is someone who takes responsibility for the power he or she wields. ... this absence of authority frees those in control to shift, adapt, reorganise without having to justify themselves or their acts.   (pp. 114–15)

Committees and groups

From the Board downwards the TTA works through a plethora of Board Committees, sub-committees, working groups and advisory groups. The Board Committees have clear and publicly identified memberships, albeit with no clarity as to the basis on which they have come to be composed, nor with any public access to their agendas, minutes or proceedings. Weir and Hall compare this situation, which is typical of QUANGOs, to that of local authorities, where the public have access by law to all council meetings, including committees and sub-committees, and to all relevant agendas, minutes and background papers.[5]

Aside from the Board Committees, the range, composition and purposes of the other groups operating at any one time is not transparent. This has important implications for issues of responsibility, accountability, transparency and policy attribution. Our early research revealed that the range of working groups is substantial: these groups are established for a purpose, with a given brief, and then disbanded. Mostly, though not always, it is not known publicly who is involved in a particular group or indeed that it exists at all. The process of appointment seems entirely mysterious and even working-group members we interviewed were not clear how or why they had been chosen. There is a whole range of people who are 'used' by the TTA in various aspects of its activities but who have no formal relationship with it. These include HEI, LEA and school staff and individuals from unions and professional associations who work under the direction of TTA officers (Mahony and Hextall 1997b). The opaque nature of the TTA's procedures for appointing to its various bodies, and its avowed denial of explicit representation, were issues to which many of the people we interviewed made reference. It may well be that a particular member of a group happens to be, say, a member of a teacher education organisation, but that is not why they are there, nor does that organisation necessarily have any say in their membership. This problem is exacerbated by the fact that it is not clear to all participants what the conventions are governing issues of confidentiality and secrecy in relation to the deliberations of these groups. This was reported to us as giving rise to the intertwined anxieties of 'collusion' on the one hand and 'fear of whistle-blowing' on the other, an issue to which we shall return in the next chapter in relation to the Working Groups on Standards.

There are also powerful resource implications involved in these working procedures. In hard times and with an eye to the efficiency of the organisations from which this expertise is drawn, it means that the TTA has been able to utilise a valuable 'professional' resource without having to meet its labour costs. It would, of course, be possible to refuse an invitation to be a member of a working group, and perhaps some people have. However, given the opportunity to participate and given that the TTA is potentially so powerful, some interviewees were not 'inclined to make waves'. In this sense the power of the TTA was described to us as both 'seductive' and 'threatening' at the same time.

The difficulty of 'deciphering the map' makes centralisation of power inescapable. No-one outside the TTA really knows who is working on what, with whom, with what remit, through what procedures, reporting to whom or with what recording procedures. Indeed, as we have indicated, merely getting an overall view of the nature and scale of this activity is difficult to achieve. All of this is made even more complex by the practice of external contracting.

Contracting out

The TTA has contracted out some substantial and highly significant aspects of its activities. These vary from conventional academic contracting, instances of which were the work of SCRE and the University of Northumberland on the evaluation of the Career Entry Profiles pilot, or NFER in relation to monitoring NPQH provision, through to the use of large-scale private sector organisations to conduct reviews and undertake specifically designated areas of activity. Some of the most substantial and widely known collaborations have been: Coopers-Lybrand's involvement in the Funding and Allocations strategy; Hay-McBer's development, in conjunction with NAHT and the Open University, of the Leadership Programme for Serving Heads and now heavy commitment to the performance-management procedures; and Hill and Knowlton as contractors for developing the recruitment strategy, including the much-disputed 'No-One Forgets a Good Teacher' campaign. Now extensively applied across wide areas of public activities, such external contracting makes it difficult to chart the boundaries between what is government and what is not. The significance of such contracting should not be underestimated. It represents within education an example of what is being debated within the wider public policy literature as an extension of the contract state, where, it is argued, commercial-style contracts are becoming a major mechanism for displacing traditional forms of accountability (Yeatman 1996). Most of the work on the contract state is based on a range of case studies from the public sector. A number of concerns are being expressed in the literature:

- The difficulty of writing adequate contract specifications for complex, professionally-based activities (Deakin and Walsh 1996).
- The increasing administrative and bureaucratic costs of managing and monitoring contracts, linked to the related problem of responsibility for attendant transaction costs (Hoggett 1996; Kirkpatrick and Lucio 1996).
- The problems around contract breakdown and the need to rely on persuasion,

mutual understanding and trust, not penalty clauses. In such cases the status of contracts comes into question (Deakin and Walsh 1996).

- The confusions around varied types of contract and their appropriateness for specific sectors (Bennett and Ferlie 1996).
- The extent to which a tendency is emerging for purchasers to shift risk onto providers and to cut resourcing in the second year when they know that providers are locked into the arrangements (Deakin and Walsh 1996).
- The high level of performance monitoring to which contracting between central purchasers and devolved providers leads (Hoggett 1996). This, according to Paul Hoggett, constitutes a new form of labour control which is responsible for creating a 'high output/low commitment' public-sector workforce.

Whilst our projects could not focus on the details of such transformations, it became clear that the TTA was taking on some of the characteristics of a super-purchaser and that this provided a material foundation to what is often viewed as an ideological restructuring of teacher education. Issues arising from contracting have considerably wider ramifications once we take account of the progressively more 'contractual' nature of the relationship between the TTA and 'providers' of teacher education, and the ways in which partnership relationships with schools are increasingly being bureaucratically framed through documentation and 'partnership agreements' (Whiting *et al.* 1996, Sidgwick *et al.* 1999). The extension of such approaches into Continuing Professional Development arrangements has also been explored in Graham *et al.* (1999).

Consultation

One very concrete expression of the tensions and dilemmas involved in procedures for policy determination resides in the TTA's espousal of consultation as a 'preferred' style of operation (TTA 1996a, p. 2). The Agency has relied heavily upon the process of consultation in developing and legitimating aspects of its strategic policy directions. In our research we found that the majority of our respondents in HEIs, schools and LEAs were very appreciative of the fact that consultation was taking place. Most people also expressed appreciation of the logistical quality of the consultations and, even though it added markedly to their workloads, there was a noticeable appetite for involvement. At the same time, however, in both questionnaire returns and interviews, many reservations were expressed about the quality and significance of this involvement. For the purposes of this argument we shall limit ourselves to three broad areas of concern.

Agenda for consultation

The TTA has gone out to consultation on an extremely wide range of issues. The criticism coming from our questionnaires and some of our interviews was that the agenda for consultation has itself not been negotiable. Two quotations from our questionnaire responses illustrate this concern.

Consultation means 'talking with'. For the TTA it means 'talking to' – i.e. we're asked to *respond* to elaborate schemes, not to help in devising them.

(HEI respondent)

We would have preferred genuine consultation rather than views to a pre-set agenda.

(LEA respondent)

This point was put to a member of the Board early on in the TTA's history:

IH: Do you think that it [the TTA] should have included the possibility of the wider community establishing what the consultations should be about?

TTA BOARD MEMBER: No, I think Dearing[6] taught us that. If you're going to have consultation in a time frame that gives you results before people get bored with the whole process you have actually got to railroad some parts of it and, in particular, the process of consultation. We decide and we impose it on people.

PM: But the subject of consultation – where should that agenda be set up?

TTA BOARD MEMBER: Yes, yes, well people do write to us all the time and if enough people wrote, or somebody wrote sufficiently powerfully about an issue and it was the sort of issue that we would consult but, yeah I think that mechanism would work fine. I don't think we can send out a questionnaire which says, what are the problems because we wouldn't be able to handle the response.

Some time later in the interview the issue was raised again regarding the context in which debate would be possible over the agenda for consultation.

PM: … a consultation document comes out, people write back to you, that isn't the same as a debate.

TTA BOARD MEMBER: Okay, but if you and your friends felt strongly about that you could organise a debate in the Queen Elizabeth Hall and Gillian Shephard would come and open it and so on – so you can have a debate. On the other hand, the Training Agency has this constituency that it feels it needs to consult which is CBI, DFEE, Training Institutions, yes and a list of schools – sometimes we write to all of them … I'm not saying there aren't other ways but that's how we do it.

PM: But what would give the push for a consultation which might be called, 'what we're not thinking about but maybe ought to be'?

TTA BOARD MEMBER: Oh! Some of the Board Meetings and one in particular where we went off to a hotel for two days was precisely that – very open agenda and what happened we talked about questions. But there are other bodies … and if they come up with something they communicate it.

The point was repeatedly made that the TTA operated in the context of a set of political definitions outside of which they would/could not stray.

The TTA works, not surprisingly, to government policy steers, consultation is often marginal.

(HEI respondent)

Consultation constituencies

That there is a political agenda in the circulation and distribution of Consultation Documents was highlighted by the lack of awareness about the TTA and its operations. Amongst the schools we surveyed, for example, the majority of the Consultations had been received by fewer than 25 per cent of those schools which responded to our questionnaire. This marginalisation is somewhat ironic given the importance the TTA claims to attach to schools' involvement, especially within the partnership context.

> The TTA's responsibilities relate closely to the work of schools and involve seeking ways of ensuring that most schools become involved in the initial training of teachers. Schools now have a significant involvement in helping to provide that training, in partnership arrangements with higher education institutions to provide a school-based experience for trainee teachers.
>
> (TTA 1995, p. 12)

Bob Lingard has pointed to a comparable phenomenon in the Australian context in what he calls 'the silencing of teachers' voices in policy production' (Lingard 1995, p. 15). He expresses a view with which we would agree when he says

> … the call for a reinstatement of teachers' and teacher educators' voices in the relevant policy production process, … is not about establishing professional barriers, but about providing a more inclusive and socially just form of education for all.
>
> (p. 3)

Perhaps the TTA's presumption was that HEIs and LEAs would circulate their partnership schools with the consultation documents. If so, this would indicate a reliance on traditional hierarchies of communication and power, which would then be at odds with one of the reasons suggested to us for the establishment of the TTA, namely to deliver teacher training from the grip of producer capture. It would also constitute a significant material cost for HEIs and LEAs, in their currently straitened circumstances.

This issue of school involvement and awareness became even more significant in our first research project when we considered the responses of SCITT schools to our questionnaire survey. These had a much higher awareness of the 'consultations' distributed by the TTA, over 75 per cent of such schools had received most of the Consultation Documents, which enabled them to play a more active part in policy discussion than other schools. Across the full range of the questionnaire they also made more positive interpretations of the activities and working practices of the TTA than did schools in partnership with HEIs. In our second project on the

National Professional Standards we have found a similar pattern of positive responses emanating from the NPQH assessment and training centres which have been directly contracted to translate TTA policies into practice. Clearly, there are important issues of representation and sponsorship embedded in this pattern of asymmetrical information which would justify fuller exploration than we can provide in this chapter.

Interpretations of consultations

The TTA leans in the direction of 'open government' and has explicitly linked itself to the ideas of 'Charter politics', especially in relation to questions of responsiveness, accountability and transparency (TTA 1995b, p. 9). In reviewing various models of open government, David Clark distinguishes between managerial and legal forms. His argument links back to our earlier discussion of models of accountability, with the managerial style committed to 'the release of categories of information that promote greater transparency in the aims, performance and delivery of the public services'. (1996, p. 24) However, of the legal model he has this to say:

> The test of open government here is whether the public is enabled to know the (real) reasons for (actual) policy and administrative decisions … this would seem to involve the presumption of a right of public access (not necessarily with attribution of views to individuals) to the written record of considered views, advice and recommendations … once the policy to which it relates has been announced. The legal model connects with a normative language of democratic citizenship … best described as 'deliberative democracy'. This refers to an approach … which legitimates policy outcomes because they are seen to reflect the discussions that precede them and to be the product of open and reasoned debate.
>
> (1996, p. 26)

Many of our respondents expressed concern over the procedures which were adopted by the TTA in making interpretations on the basis of the consultations. These concerns were variously expressed in terms of the quality and clarity of the questions being asked in the consultations, the procedures being adopted for the interpretation of the responses and the difficulties involved in knowing how the policy outcomes were generated. It was claimed that these lacked the transparency which was needed for people to have confidence in the whole consultation process. At the most basic level, people did not know who was dealing with the consultation responses, how the different responses were being interpreted and weighted, what the overall patterns of responses were, what priority was being accorded to consultations in policy determination, and other comparable concerns. In short, many of our respondents felt very unsure as to how 'outcomes' had been generated and on the basis of what analysis. As Ian Kane (1996) put it: 'one assumes that the Board acts with integrity but it cannot be right in these Nolan times that there is no way to check' (p. 1). There is a sense in which it is quite appropriate for officers (hands-on managers) to keep a careful eye on the direction in which 'their lines' are developing; some would argue that this is what managers are paid to do. It becomes contradictory, however, when, in 'consultation mode', such a tight hand is kept on the format of the consultation, or on the interpretations of subsequent policy formulations, that there remains little room for democratic debate, difference or disagreement.

> Government in Britain undertakes a good deal of consultation when making policy, ... But consultation is not governed by formal rules and the processes are not as consistent, open or pluralistic as in many other advanced democracies. There is a variety of 'policy networks' and corporatist practices, most of which normally remain 'closed'. Frequently, even the comments and evidence received from interested parties are not published or made available for inspection, or they are inadequately summarised. The responses to consultation by government, government departments and agencies are rarely published alongside their decisions, except in quasi-judicial cases.
>
> (Weir and Hall 1994, p. 30)

In recent consultations the TTA seems to have moved beyond the position described by Weir and Hall. Consultation responses are now deemed to be public documents (apart from those which claim confidentiality). It was precisely in pursuit of some of these critical points that we undertook the analysis of one particular consultation which we report in Chapter 2. Whilst it is clearly to be welcomed that we were able to make such a detailed analysis, nonetheless it is clear that anxieties remain concerning the purposes, accountability and transparency which accompany the consultation process. A major theme in the rest of the book will be how such working practices cannot be disentangled from the policies that have emanated from the TTA.

The work of the TTA

At its inception, it was widely assumed that the TTA would be predominantly concerned with ITT. Only with the benefit of hindsight can we now interpret the 1994 Act and some of the early policy documents as signalling the potential for the TTA's much more extensive involvement in the whole of teacher education and professional development. Between 1995 and 1999 the TTA's functions were systematically broadened to the extent that it became difficult to think of any stage of teaching or area of teacher education which remained outside its remit. Its functions in relation to ITT included: promotion of teaching as a career; improving the quality and efficiency of all routes into teaching; funding and accreditation; developing and advising on national requirements for ITT; developing a national curriculum for ITT, and involving schools in all ITT courses. In addition, its remit had been progressively extended to develop and implement proposals for: a framework for CPD; induction arrangements; headship training and teaching assistants (DfEE 1999a). It also undertook a review of appraisal and initiated schemes to support teacher research. In addition to all this, a major element of its work has been to develop a framework of 'National Professional Standards' that has centrally defined the nature of teaching and subsequently laid the foundations for a restructuring of the 'profession'. Through all of it, unsurprisingly, a dominant theme underpinning the TTA's activities has been the determination to produce 'effective' teachers for 'effective' schools, geared to the needs of UK Ltd in the global economy.

> ... everyone is now agreed that the top priority in education is the need to raise pupils' standards of learning. ... And there is a widespread awareness that, in a competitive world, constant progress is necessary just to maintain parity with other nations.
>
> (Millett 1996a, p. 2)

In opposition, the Labour Party initially committed itself to the abolition of the TTA, though in its pre-election 'crusade to raise standards' (Labour Party 1995), this became muted to a commitment to reform it. In the Spring of 1999 a Quinquennial Review of the TTA was undertaken by the Department (DfEE 1999a). The review team, in conducting its enquiry into the TTA's current functions, powers, remit and activities as well as its efficiency and effectiveness, was asked

> to have particular regard to the establishment next year of the General Teaching Councils (GTCs) for England and Wales, and of the National College of School Leadership; and to the major agenda for modernisation of the teaching profession as set out in the recent Green Papers ...
>
> (DfEE 1999a, p. 3)

The review concluded that

- there is no case at present for abolition or privatisation. There will continue to be a need for the core functions of the TTA. But the TTA's responsibilities should be redrawn to take account of the GTC and the National College of School Leadership and the need to bring some elements of the Green Paper agenda closer to the Department.
- The TTA's current remit is too wide. The future remit should concentrate substantially on the two initial priorities it had when it was established in 1994, namely teacher supply and recruitment and initial teacher training ...

  (p. 1)

The Review represented a drawing back into the DfEE of responsibility for strategic policy-making and development, including that for CPD and research. Matters relating to headship/leadership became the responsibility of the leadership college, while the GTC took on responsibility for the registration of qualified teachers and for advising the Secretary of State on a range of professional issues (such as teaching standards and induction). The Review commended the TTA for its work in improving standards in teacher-training provision and for implementing the Leadership Programme for Serving Heads (contracted out to Hay/McBer, NAHT and the Open University) though it reports criticism of the process through which the NPQH was introduced and managed. The TTA was also criticised for some aspects of its funding and accreditation approach, its style of management and the abrasive quality of its relationships with partners and stakeholders. On the retirement of the Chief Executive, Anthea Millett, the appointment of Ralph Tabberer as her replacement was seen as demonstrating the Government's rejection of 'a confrontational style with training providers'. Mr Tabberer was quoted in the *Times Educational Supplement* 17 December 1999 as saying he wanted to 'listen to teacher trainers' (p. 3). Our evidence suggests that this would mark an important change in the policy process.

With the powers of the TTA significantly reduced, what are the implications for different policy actors? The TTA itself presented a dignified public face, continuing to describe its new role as a 'key' in the Government's crusade to raise standards. Clearly the jury is out on whether the GTC will take over some of the responsibilities of the TTA. A TTA Board member whom we interviewed seemed sanguine about this possibility.

> I think in the very long run obviously there are big questions like, will the GTC as it were, have handed to it by government, much greater responsibility for setting and maintaining standards, professional standards. A bit like, you know, an autonomous Royal College of whatever in Medicine or Engineering Council – does at the moment. And it is obvious that Ministers have wanted to proceed cautiously. They've been nervous about the possibility that the GTC will be, you know, kind of hijacked by special interests ... I said when I was first appointed that I thought that the ultimate goal of the TTA should be to do itself out of a job and I still believe that but I don't think we're actually within five years of doing it. ... I think if your ultimate model is a profession which is of very high status, and achieving very high standards by any kind of international comparisons, then the only appropriate model for that is a very high degree of self-government and self-regulation. But you know, that also requires a very high level of political trust and I don't see any politician around at the moment who is willing yet to hand that over.

It is as yet much too early to foresee the evolution of the role of the GTC and how its activities will be articulated with the Department, the TTA and other educational agencies. It is certainly clear that from a political point of view, the TTA continues to serve as a useful lightning rod that deflects 'professional flak' away from its parent department in a major area of impending crisis, namely the recruitment of teachers.[7] At the same time, the DfEE has taken a much more assertive stance by pulling control and definition of policy-making back to the centre, thus making it easier to pursue its political priorities. A key strand of these policies lies in the performance management frame within which teaching is being tightly 'modernised'. As we have already implied, such a performance-driven approach to the shaping of occupational behaviour in other public and private sectors is heavily dependent upon criteria and standards through which effective outcomes can be defined and regulated.

2 Standards in teaching

Between 1994 and 1998 the TTA was active in developing a framework of National Standards for teaching which would 'define expertise in key roles' (TTA 1998a, p. 1). The Agency focused its attention on Standards for:

- the award of qualified teacher status (QTS);
- expert teachers (developed but never published);
- subject leaders;
- special educational needs coordinators (SENCOs); and
- headteachers.

Standards for special educational needs teachers (SENs) were published later in 1999. This framework was intended to form a central plank in the TTA's strategy for achieving its purpose of raising 'standards in schools by improving the quality of teacher training, teaching and school leadership, and by raising the status and esteem of the teaching profession' (TTA 1998a, p. 3). In the Green Paper *Meeting the Challenge of Change* (DfEE 1998a; DfEE 1999), the Labour government laid out its own proposals for 'modernising the teaching profession'. These included the utilisation of National Standards for: the award of QTS; completion of an induction period; movement through the performance threshold, appointment as advanced skills teachers (ASTs) and headteachers (see Table 2.1). In part these proposals build on the TTA framework, in part they constitute a new formulation. Certainly they continue the binding together of standards in schools with standards in teaching, even though these do not always appear to be being 'steered or rowed' in the same direction.

Although these particular developments have occurred within a relatively short space of time, the history of occupational standards is rooted in a movement that has grown internationally over the last thirty years. This movement has involved the specification of outcomes of vocational and (later) professional education and training designed to guarantee that individuals have achieved required standards of competence. There is now an enormous literature and research tradition in which the history, philosophy, politics and practicalities of this standards movement have been debated across a range of ideological perspectives (see Hodkinson 1995; Hyland 1994; Pring 1992). This work has been extremely varied and has focused on different

Table 2.1 National Standards for teachers

Original framework	Added later	Green Paper
Award of QTS		Award of QTS
Expert teacher (never published)	SEN teachers	Induction
Subject leaders		Performance threshold
SENCOs		Advanced skills
Head teachers		Head teachers

phases of education and training (Wolf 1995) and different occupational areas, including teaching (Eraut 1994; Hustler and McIntyre 1996). If greater attention had been paid to this literature perhaps some of the problems emerging in relation to teaching standards could have been foreseen. The public money saved could then have been invested in an activity representing more value for money than reinventing a (wobbly) wheel.

Approaches to standards

There are a number of ways in which standards can be approached. Particular sets of standards can be analysed for their clarity, consistency and coherence, and in terms of the values, principles and assumptions which underpin them. They can also be considered in terms of fitness for their purpose – are they capable of doing the work they are intended to do? And is this consistent with the wider purposes of their institutional setting? Procedurally, standards can be investigated in terms of their mode of establishment and formation, with all the questions of accountability and transparency that this entails. They can also be questioned in terms of the manner in which they are translated into practice and the consequences, both manifest and latent, which follow. More broadly, there is a set of issues to consider in relation to the culture and ideology of standards as a widespread phenomenon operating across both the private and public sectors in England and elsewhere. As we explored some of the major issues that emerged in our research on the aims, development, content, use and impact of the National Professional Standards (NPS),[1] we found ourselves making use of these different elements of analysis and attempting to untangle the relationships between them. Before moving into a more detailed consideration of the NPS, we shall broadly identify two competing orientations to standards. These underpin much controversy and misunderstanding, and make their presence felt in the competing claims and counter-claims with which the whole standards debate is bedevilled.

Along with other people, we are entirely supportive of attempts to make what is required of teachers more open and explicit. Indeed, with colleagues and teacher partners we were involved in our own attempts to develop such practices with beginning teachers some years before outcomes-based approaches to the assessment of student teachers were formally introduced by the Conservative government in 1992 (Mahony and Harris 1994). The profile of 'criteria for good practice' we developed locally was motivated by what we understood to be a progressive attempt to be

- transparent (and therefore open to challenge) in relation to the guiding principles underpinning the organisation of our ITT course;
- inclusive in the development of an account of good practice which involved class-room teachers, student teachers and pupils and which attempted to reconcile their perspectives;
- supportive of student teachers' professional development by enabling them to participate in negotiating the agenda for their own learning;
- open about the basis on which student teachers would be assessed, which we hoped would lead to greater transparency, consistency and fairness in the application of assessment procedures; and
- more widely accountable and responsive within a public education system: an approach founded on a rejection of 'trust me, I'm a professional'.

These experiences would lead us to support a *developmental approach* to standards, which can provide structured opportunities for teachers' further professional learning, aimed at improving the quality of their teaching throughout their careers. Within this approach, we would also want to emphasise the importance of making explicit norms of professional conduct and practice to which pupils ought to be entitled and of which a wider public has a legitimate right to be assured. We are also entirely in favour of ensuring that membership of an occupation or promotion to positions within it are based on validated capacity to do the job rather than on nepotism or accidents of birth or inadequacies in institutional procedures.

However, as well as having progressive potential, standards can also be used within a *regulatory approach* as a managerialist tool for measuring the efficiency and effectiveness of systems, institutions and individuals. As Hyland points out, the immediate origins of outcomes-based approaches to education and training are to be found within this ideology. In the 1960s in the USA, a performance-based teacher education movement rose to prominence because it offered administrators the wherewithal to control and regulate teachers. It is motivations such as these that, according to a number of analysts, underpin 'trends that frame the current worldwide infatuation with outcomes' (Smyth and Dow 1998, p. 293). For example, as a key element of the restructuring of the public sector in England, commentators have pointed to the development of a raft of controlling and regulatory technologies designed to enhance the ability of government to steer policy from the centre.

> In virtually all sectors operational decentralisation has been accompanied by the extended development of performance management systems. Such systems seem designed to both monitor and shape organisational behaviour and encompass a range of techniques including performance review, staff appraisal systems, performance-related pay, scrutinies, so-called 'quality audits', customer feedback mechanisms, comparative tables of performance indicators including

'league tables', chartermarks, customer charters, quality standards and total quality management.

(Hoggett, p. 20)

Within this general context of public-sector reform, we have already noted that education policy has been subject to the stringencies of both 'efficiency and effectiveness', and in addition, that effectiveness has been predominantly defined in relation to the nations' competitiveness in the global economy. Smyth and Dow (1998), making a similar observation from an Australian context, describe how

> ... the balance has shifted from schools for the betterment of society through a more educated citizenry, to how best to control education by making it do its economic work through greater emphasis on vocationalism ... the work of teachers is reconfigured so they become deliverers of knowledge, testers of student outcomes and pedagogical technicians ...
>
> (p. 293)

In these wider settings of education policy and public policy there has occurred a drift from developmental to regulatory orientations towards standards. In the latter sense the development of NPS can be seen both as providing a centralised specification of 'effective teaching' and as the codification of relations between managers and managed. This takes place in the context of a centralisation/decentralisation nexus where 'policy steering' is achieved through much tighter regulation by the centre and managers become locally responsible for staff compliance. In this ideology, 'standards' often obscure the ways in which evaluation processes are inescapably mediated through human subjectivity. They emphasise what can be 'measured' at the expense of the immeasurable (Broadfoot 1999), which leads to an over-concentration on the 'operational' (Devereux 1997) and patrols the boundaries of what is to be allowed to count as 'quality'.

In what follows we shall see both approaches to standards at play in the range of competing claims made about the role and function of the NPS and the diverse ways they are being used and justified. In consequence there is no neat and tidy story of the NPS in terms of their purposes, functions or impacts. In view of the significance of standards in the development of past and current government policy, we shall explore in some detail major issues that have emerged in our research on the development processes, purposes and aims, content, use and impact of the NPS. We have discovered that, in line with other policy areas, the ways in which 'standards' are translated from policy text to practice varies across the system, depending on the groups for whom particular sets of them are designed, who is responsible for their translation into practice and the contexts within which they are being implemented. 'Standards' in the sense of some essentialist Platonic ideal of what teachers at different stages of their careers can do, simply do not exist and whatever else they do, 'Standards' do not guarantee standards.

Purposes of National Professional Standards

The original aims or purposes of the framework of NPS were linked with concerns to produce effective teachers for effective schools.

> ... A principal aim of the TTA is to promote effective and efficient professional development for teachers and headteachers, targeted on improvements in the quality of teaching and leadership which will have the maximum impact on pupils' learning. The cornerstone of this work is the development of national standards for the teaching profession to define expertise in key roles ...
>
> (TTA 1998a, p. 1)

In relation to the connections between the original formulation of the NPS by the TTA and their subsequent application and transformation in the Green Paper, a TTA Board member we interviewed took the following evolutionary view:

> ... if you said – was there in 1995 a grand plan and all these things would happen and they would be linked to appraisal and performance thresholds – it wasn't like that, I don't think. What did emerge early was a realisation that you couldn't have a systematic approach to training and continuing professional development unless you had some notion of what the standards you were aiming for should be ... But with the wisdom of hindsight, it looks rather neat. You set up a body that has a training responsibility, it realises that you can't really have sensible training and CPD responsibilities without having standards. The Standards link naturally into monitoring people's professional development whether through appraisal or other methods and this may also have consequences for pay and so on.

Here we can detect the developmental and regulatory approaches clearly in play at the same time. The quotation points to the purposes of NPS as, on the one hand, providing an agenda for professional development and, on the other, as 'measuring' performance. The slide occurs in the phrase 'monitoring people's professional development' which could mean, first, determining what people need and ensuring they get it, second, checking the quality of provision and ensuring that it has maximum impact or, third, developing a technology that enables the 'measurement' of individuals against expectations. The last clearly slips into a conception of standards as a mechanism for differentiating performance for the purpose of reward (financial or otherwise) or for determining the boundaries for entry into the profession or occupation of positions within it.

Both conceptions can be found within the particular purposes being assigned to different sets of NPS and in an early justification for the overall framework given by the Chief Executive of the TTA. Contrary to the Board member's view quoted above, her comments suggest that rather than, as it were, *discovering* that Standards could be used to measure performance (and linked to reward), such an intention already existed.

We must find ways of recognising high quality teachers and rewarding them accordingly. ... That will inevitably be a major landmark in terms of recognition of teachers. And it provides a framework of opportunity for the whole profession. ... I have already been told ... that rewarding excellence with extra points is divisive and subjective. Is it beyond our wit to find a non-subjective and transparent means of doing so? I believe that a framework of professional qualifications, to which all teachers can aspire, will provide the means and opportunity to provide a better, more responsive system of rewarding our teachers for their work.

(Millet 1996b, pp. 11–12)

As was made clear in an interview with a TTA officer, the various NPS 'are very different animals' and a distinction needed to be made between the purposes of 'standards that are enshrined in statute which are the Secretary of State's requirements and regulations, the QTS Standards and the induction Standards', and those that are non-statutory such as Subject Leader and SENCO Standards. The latter are 'able to be used however teachers find them more useful'. As we shall see later, in practice, providers, employers, trainers and individuals are indeed creatively adapting and using the various elements of the NPS to meet a whole range of professional development purposes designed to enhance their professional practice. At the same time, Standards for the award of QTS provide an example of the control and regulatory function of Standards. From our research, four main reasons emerged for the introduction of Standards for QTS. These can be summarised as

- the difficulty of ensuring quality and consistency in a context where a variety of diverse routes into teaching had been established;
- the perceived desire for greater control by central government, fuelled partly by distrust of 'professionals' (accounting both for the establishment of the TTA and the initiatives it has subsequently undertaken);
- the increasing use of standards in other countries;
- the need for a procedural basis for external inspection of ITT.

The intention behind the QTS Standards was recognised as regulatory in two ways. First, within a context where a variety of routes into teaching have been actively encouraged,[2] QTS Standards claim to provide a quality assurance mechanism in relation to individuals entering teaching.

> ... part of the rationale behind it was to have this threshold of standards to say, whichever way you came, wherever you trained, whatever you did, would meet this minimum threshold which you would have to pass to qualify, so therefore there couldn't be a second-class route. There would just be different routes.
>
> (TTA officer)

That this rationale of consistency may be more dream than reality is revealed in the following interview extracts concerning the GRTP, which is an employment-based route into teaching.

Don't you think it's arguable that the QTS Standards are a sham? In terms of national assessment. I mean particularly when you come down to employment-based routes into teaching. You know they're a sham. You know there is no quality assurance. What's the moderating process between the quality assurance and the employment-based route and an ITT route?

(Union officer)

The following comments about monitoring and quality assurance were made by a trainer responsible for implementing GRTP.

… nobody has ever asked to look at any of my training materials … As far as I know nobody goes round and monitors the quality of the assessment from here. They haven't so far and I don't know where OFSTED comes into it.

And talking about the external monitoring of the candidates on the programme,

It has to be somebody externally going in and you know, observing the teacher, looking through their file. Now I've got somebody in … LEA doing that and he's just sent me the report but interestingly he's using the OFSTED framework for assessing … I can't tell him what he's got to do. He should be using the Standards but he said he wants to use the OFSTED framework. Fine, I can't tell him – he's actually not charging us. But do you see the hotch-potch?

Finally this trainer talked about the reactions of schools when they were given a QTS Standards assessment document to complete.

… you imagine being given this huge document to sort of use – I mean first of all it's just awful to ask them to do it but you have to be able to demonstrate that you have been very rigorous about this whole process. I know it doesn't happen in other places but that's irrelevant. So they say things like, bloody hell, what is all this for. What does all this mean? And will it really improve the quality of the training? … without a lot of input and in-service training I don't think they're going to work. People will just pay lip service to them and they'll start checking boxes which I think is the biggest fear that I've got about this graduate registered teacher programme that it will become a tick-box exercise rather than a real kind of interaction with the Standards, with the trainee you know, and some real kind of critical reflection on what they might mean.

Inescapably bound to this individual quality specification is the second regulatory function, which relates to institutions providing ITT. The question of whether ITT providers enable trainees to meet the Standards forms the basis upon which they are inspected by OFSTED. In what the House of Commons Select Committee (1999) described as a 'high stakes activity' (p. xlvii), the grades awarded to institutions during those inspections are materially critical because the TTA uses them either to reward ITT providers with increased student numbers or to penalise them (the ultimate penalty being closure). In both cases, for regulatory purposes to be met, consistency in applying the Standards is crucial – otherwise, what it means to have achieved them evaporates into a profusion of different expressions and claims to fairness within the system disappear. The issue of consistency raises two immediate questions – is there consistency in application and do Standards resolve the consistency problem? As we shall see later when we come to explore the way the Standards are being used, our evidence suggests that the answer is negative on both counts. Within a regulatory context this becomes highly problematic, whereas within a purely developmental orientation, flexibility in interpretation and application would be defined as a major source of strength. This remains an inevitable tension within the framework which is seldom addressed at an official level and leaves 'providers' and 'recipients' struggling to achieve their own reconciliations. Because this carries such high 'risks', both for individuals and institutions, it remains an issue of abiding anxiety and uncertainty. We have also found that the vaunted 'objectivity' and neutrality of standards melts away once one analyses in detail the dynamics through which they came to be established. Such analysis also reveals much more about the procedures through which governance is accomplished and the rigour or otherwise with which official procedures are conducted.

Processes used in developing the Standards

In the Autumn of 1998 we studied in some detail (see Table 2.2 for a timelined summary of the TTA's activities) the processes used in developing QTS Standards (TTA 1997a), paying particular attention to the consultation exercise conducted by the TTA in the Spring of 1997 (TTA 1997b).[3] Of all the National Standards on which an in-depth study would have been possible, we chose the Standards for QTS because, being the mandatory gateway into the profession, they are highly significant in shaping the professional orientations of new entrants to teaching. They also play an absolutely central part in the OFSTED inspection framework for ITT providers. Our decision later turned out to have been fortuitous, as it emerged that the significance of QTS Standards will increase through providing the base line on which the Induction Standards, the Performance Threshold Standards and the Standards for ASTs are built. They also form key elements of the performance-management model of the Green Paper.

The TTA began the process of developing QTS Standards by convening a group of people drawn from LEAs, HEIs and schools who were 'locked away in some hotel for a few days … brainstorming what a set of standards might look like, how they might be organised … ' (TTA officer). Subsequently Working Groups were established to move on with this developmental work. These were selected by recommendation, prior knowledge or familiarity through networking, a process that has been criticised as tending to sponsor 'people like us' (Kanter 1993). One Member of Parliament expressed concern with

> … their setting up of the four groups to come up with standards. Now we can't get at what the criteria are for setting up those Committees. A question was put

Table 2.2 Summary of process used in consultation on *Proposed Training Curriculum and Standards for New Teachers*

Date	Details
Early Spring 1996	Hotel brainstorming
March 1996	Working Groups established. Schedule of meetings and membership announced.
February 1997	Publication of Consultation document. Consultation document sought views on: Revised requirements for ITT; ITT National Curriculum for Primary English; ITT National Curriculum for Primary Maths; Standards for Award of QTS. Questions on Standards asked about: Level of standards; Additional standards for specialist courses; Assessment against Standards; Implementation (exemplification).
April 1997	Seven regional consultation conferences held. Consultation conferences sought views on: Revised requirements for ITT; ITT National Curriculum for Primary English; ITT National Curriculum for Primary Maths; Standards for Award of QTS. Questions on Standards asked about: Level of standards; Additional standards for specialist courses; Assessment against Standards; Implementation (exemplification) and 'any other issues'.
May 8th	End of the consultation.
May 9th	First draft of Interim Reports on Outcomes of Consultation.
May 10th–13th	Redrafting of 2nd and 3rd Interim Reports
May 14th	Board subgroup meeting to consider the results of the consultations.
June 10th	Special Board meeting to consider TTA recommendations to the Secretary of State.
June 13th	Executive summary report.
June 23rd	Fourth draft of Interim Report (excluding 107 responses that came in late).
June 1997	Full Report on the Outcomes of Consultation.
June 1997	Summary Report on the Outcomes of Consultation.
June 1997	Publication by TTA of Standards for Award of QTS.
July 1st	Fifth draft of Interim Report (including 107 responses that came in late).
October 1997	Publication by DfEE of Standards for Award of QTS (Circular 10/97).

down for Gillian Shephard on that very matter, what were the criteria and who were the people and they simply wrote back and said, we'll let you know when they are appointed. ...

Officers we talked to were well aware of the political nature of the debates which had already occurred around 'standards' and of the particular controversies which had surrounded equality issues. It was apparent that there were some members of the TTA Board ' ... who didn't want to have any mention of equal opportunities at all' – clearly an expression of the dominant politics of the time. In negotiating their political position the TTA talked to members of the 'New Right'[4]

> ... to find out what they thought and to keep them on board ... partly so that it could incorporate anything that seemed to be a good idea but also so that it knew exactly where the opposition would come from.
>
> (TTA officer)

Respondents from outside the TTA but close to the policy process reported to us that some TTA officers attempted to create covert pegs on which institutions could hang progressive interpretations of the Standards. While we support the intent behind this strategy, it does raise questions about the claims made for the Standards in ensuring consistency of interpretation and application across the system as a whole.

Working Groups on Standards

Our interest in the role of the Working Groups in the development of the Standards arose from our initial research which as we explained in Chapter 1, had revealed a whole range of questionnaire respondents' and interviewees' concerns, including

- lack of public knowledge about who was involved in a particular group or, indeed, awareness that it existed at all;
- lack of clarity about the process of selection for membership and confusion about status of members as individuals or representatives;
- lack of clarity about terms of reference of groups, e.g. in ratifying or generating policy;
- confusions about what happened to groups' deliberations, to whom groups were accountable within the TTA and whether or not members were 'bound' by principles of confidentiality (the latter giving rise to considerable anxiety about whether they could report back to other organisations or bodies with whom they were involved or contribute to research on the functioning of Working Groups).

In 1996, a press notice announced the formation of four National Standards Working Groups and gave details of membership of groups, schedule of meetings, the time-scale under which they were operating and when they were due to complete their work (TTA 1996b). Taking this to signal a move towards greater openness, we distributed a questionnaire to the fifty-five publicly named members of the four National Standards Working Groups. This sought information which would clarify the concerns raised above, and our covering letter explained that we were trying to gain an understanding of the 'formation and modes of operation of these groups' as part of our wider research project on the NPS. Unfortunately we were not able to obtain the data we sought. Because of the very small number of returned questionnaires we undertook a second follow-up exercise by telephone, in the course of which five respondents told us that they had received a letter from the TTA which they had interpreted as indicating that they should not respond to us. We did not pursue our telephone follow-up on the grounds that it was unethical to ignore people's clear sense of discomfort about where to position themselves in relation to our research. We did, however, write to the Chief Executive of the TTA asking for clarification of the letter in question. She sought to 'reassure' us that the TTA had not 'discouraged anyone from responding to your questionnaire. Indeed, it would be wholly improper for us to have done so'. However, the extract quoted below from the Head of Communication's letter to Working Group members perhaps explains why some could easily have interpreted 'the sub-text of the letter to be warning me off ... saying that the Working Group was confidential.' The letter said:

> ... The working group process was, as you will recall, a confidential one ... I am writing to let all members know that the research is wholly independent of the TTA.

It went on to claim that we had 'not sought to involve the TTA at all' in our 'review'. As there was no way of knowing whether the nature of the responses we had already received had been compromised by receipt of the letter, we did not analyse those questionnaires which had been returned. However, we do question the secrecy and defensiveness surrounding such groups: the Working Groups were publicly funded (as indeed was our own research) to contribute to policy production in relation to professional standards for teachers. While definitions of teaching embedded in the Standards are of considerable public significance, they are hardly matters of national security.

Consultation

In February 1997 the TTA began its formal process of consultation on *The Proposed Training Curriculum and Standards for New Teachers*. The written consultation was due to be completed by 8 May after which the TTA Board would submit proposals to the Secretary of State. Our reason for being particularly interested in the detail of this process of consultation was that since its inception in 1994 and in line with the 'managerial model of open government' (Clark 1996), the TTA has relied heavily upon the process of consultation as its 'preferred' style of operation (TTA 1996a). Also, when its policies have been publicly criticised it has often cited its consultation procedures in its defence. For example in response to a recent claim that the QTS Standards are 'unworkable',

> A spokeswoman said the standards had been well-received when they were introduced in May 1998 after extensive consultation.
>
> (TES 1999a, p. 2)

Consultation documents have been distributed on virtually every initiative, combined, in some cases, with regional consultation conferences because, according to a TTA officer whom we interviewed at the time the Standards were being developed, consultation is 'one way of securing public accountability'.

Given this heavy reliance on consultation we had, through the first of our projects, sought respondents' views about the TTA's consultation procedures Our evidence summarised respondents' concerns about

- the agenda for consultation being constrained within particular preordained parameters and not open to negotiation;
- the quality and clarity of questions asked in the consultation;
- the TTA's procedures for interpreting consultation responses and the lack of a clear relationship between consultation responses and policy outcomes;
- the lack of visible mechanisms for weighting the responses of representative bodies against those from individuals;
- the absence of some relevant bodies (e.g. the Commission for Racial Equality or Equal Opportunities Commission) on the formal circulation list;
- the fact that schools do not play a significant part in the consultations; and
- the lack of transparency concerning the influences on policy production in relation to the roles of Ministers, the TTA Board, officers and other groups or individuals.

This evidence has to be placed in the context of wider concerns about the state of democracy in England; concerns that have led analysts such as Weir and Beetham (1999) to undertake an audit of central political institutions and processes in which the quality of consultation procedures is used as one indicator of the democratic state of the nation. They raise a number of issues about consultation and conclude that

> Government consultation of interests and the general public is unsystematic and opaque. ... Overall, the absence of firm rules for consultation gives rise to concern. (p. 487)

The absence of firm rules for consultation

The TTA has undertaken various types of consultation but 'generally speaking the significance of the issue will determine the sort of consultation we're going for'. (TTA officer)

In other cases, 'if it is a very big consultation you might import somebody ... as in the MORI consultation ...' (TTA officer). The problem with contracting out public sector consultations to the private sector, is the lack of clarity over ownership of data and methods. This carries the attendant danger that they are not open to critical interrogation. Size, however, is not always the major driving force in determining the nature of the consultation process. Even where a consultation is 'enormous', the process is not 'standard' but rather 'intuitive' so that, as the TTA officer concluded,

'... in a way each consultation is slightly different', thus seeming to confirm Weir and Beetham's claim about the absence of 'firm rules for consultation'.

Consultation does not simply involve decisions on how to gather evidence but also on how that evidence is used and by whom. The TTA has always been clear that consultation functions in a limited way.

> We shall continue to consult widely, and listen and respond to what is said. That does not mean we shall pander to the lowest common denominator, or treat consultations as referenda.
>
> (Millett 1997, p. 12)

Nor is the strength of opinion expressed in consultation responses sufficient on its own to influence the direction of policy. The respective roles of the Board and officers are also important, with the added difficulty of distinguishing the boundary lines between them.

> ... where there's something that really upsets everybody, which you know that the Board doesn't actually mind about too much then you actually make a concession on that point. ... But I mean the art of consulting and coming to a consensus, not a consensus but a view that you can sell to the system is actually quite a difficult one ...
>
> (TTA officer)

Here it seems that it is not the Board that is the decision-making body but the officers, operating on the basis of their beliefs about what the Board wants. Also worth noting is the account of consultation as the art of arriving at a view that 'you can sell to the system'. This seems closer to the notion of persuasion than that of consultation with respected partners.

Dealing with responses

The actual mechanisms through which the consultation responses were presented to the Board at the time when the Standards were being developed, were described to us in the following way:

> ... the Board has access to the full responses, an analysis of what the responses are saying, an analysis of the responses in terms of what the issues are, and then it has a covering precis from us recommending what it should do. Then it makes its decision.
>
> (TTA officer)

It will become important, later, to have noted that such a process requires time: time after the end of a consultation for a 'complete analysis of the responses' to be undertaken; time for the Board to consider such analysis along with other documentation, and time to make its decision. The Board having made its decision, feedback is given to the system, accompanied by explanation where necessary.

There are some cases where you say: 'Following our consultation only 30 per cent of you said you wanted a) but we're still going to do a). The reason why we are going to do a) is because – x, y, z'. So one thing you can never do is pretend people haven't said to you what they did say to you ... better to come clean like that than to sort of pretend that your consultation proved that everybody wanted it.

(TTA officer)

There are a number of claims being made here about the procedures for dealing with responses: first, that a consultation is not a referendum and majority opinion may be ignored (though it is not clear whether it is the Board or the officers who steer policy in this respect); second, that the Board has access to the full consultation response; third, that feedback to the system is accurate and, fourth, that justification is given for decisions taken. Readers may be interested to consider these claims in the light of the following summary of our in-depth exploration of the TTA's handling of the consultation on QTS Standards.

Consulting on the QTS Standards

Having developed the draft set of Standards, the TTA proceeded to consult a wider constituency. The consultation on QTS Standards formed one element of an exercise which also sought views on three other reforms, namely

- the revised requirements for ITT;
- the NCITT for Primary English; and
- the NCITT Primary Mathematics.

The consultation was conducted through the distribution of 10,000 Consultation Response booklets (TTA 1997b), seven regional conferences, and meetings with various subject associations. In conducting our analysis we read the section relating to Standards in all the written consultation responses, notes from the consultation conferences and subject association meetings and details of the process used in analysing the data and redrafting the reports.

It is worth noting that a person whom we interviewed at the Equal Opportunities Commission (EOC) expressed considerable irritation at the Commission's lack of involvement in the process, which was seen as consequent on the TTA's failure to include the Commission on its mailing list.[5] This raises important general questions about the nature of the constituencies used as a basis for consultation.

I mean obviously we haven't been put on the mailing list because we haven't been getting them ... We've had to go back again and again and again. ... in fact we got to the stage where we thought, there's a list here of people they don't want to send their consultations to. I mean it's the sort of inverse of having a list of people to mail out to.

(EOC officer)

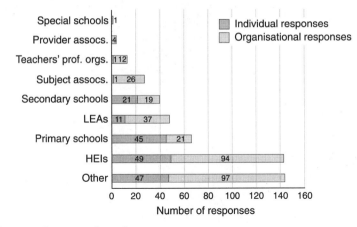

Figure 2.1 Responses shown by category.

The written consultation responses

Of the 10,000 consultation documents distributed, the TTA report received 487 responses (4.87 per cent). The TTA provided us with a copy of the spreadsheet they had used to record respondents' names, addresses and coding categories and from this we produced figure 2.1, showing the pattern of response by category.

The largest category, 'other', meant just that – everything that did not fall within the categories already listed (i.e. pressure groups, publishers, public-sector agencies, government bodies, associations and societies, church organisations and charitable trusts). The balance between individual and organisational responses is worth noting in relation to the issue of how responses should be weighted in consultation analyses. In addition, the relatively small proportion of schools responding (given their numbers) compared to HEIs can be seen within an increasing international concern about the marginalisation of teachers' voices from the policy process (Lingard 1995).

This initial reading of the documents enabled us to categorise the responses in terms of whether or not they could be said to have made a substantial contribution.

The responses which we deemed 'insubstantial' referred to brief comments made on the whole consultation document (i.e. all four sections). Such comments, of which there were fourteen, consisted of little more than 'looks okay to me' or 'no comments of substance to make'. A further 102 consultation booklets contained no comments on the Standards for QTS. Of those responses which did comment on Standards, we recorded sixty-six comments that we called 'cursory'. A negative example of this was 'insufficient attention to pastoral responsibilities' (School response), while positive examples included 'well organised balanced document' (LEA response), or

> ... it is good to specify personal and intellectual qualities required: teaching has for too long been a profession to drift into which tolerates poor standards of attitude and deportment. The demise of gowns is still regretted.

> ('Other' response)

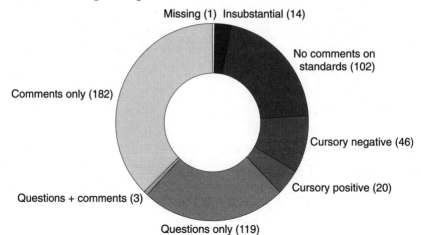

Figure 2.2 Responses on Standards.

The remaining responses, by definition 'substantial' in our terms, were analysed according to whether they kept within the question format as set out in the Consultation Response booklet, whether they had made general comments outside the format, or some combination of the two. The significance of separating the questions from the comments is that the questions posed as a basis for response were framed within limited parameters. Although the TTA said in the response booklet that it would welcome comments 'on any aspect of the proposals' the questions themselves only sought views on

- the level of the standards;
- whether additional standards were appropriate or necessary for specialist courses;
- whether the standards provided a basis for consistent and reliable assessment; and
- whether consistency of assessment would be improved by the provision of national exemplification materials.

(TTA 1997b, p. 8)

Respondents were not asked whether the introduction of professional standards represented a positive policy development nor whether these proposed QTS Standards represented an adequate account of a beginning teacher.

Having undertaken a content analysis of seventy-five substantial responses we compared our findings with a document entitled *First draft of Interim Reports on Outcomes of Consultation on New Requirements, Standards and the ITTNC for English and Mathematics* dated 9 May 1997, prepared by the team contracted by the TTA to undertake the analysis. We judged this interim report to be an accurate representation of the major themes emerging from the data and consistent with our own analysis. It pulled no punches in reporting that there was a great deal of critical comment, the detailed description of which we were able to verify.

We then moved on to a focused review of the school responses, not least because of the TTA's stated commitment (and remit) to improve the quality of teaching in schools. Of the one hundred and six school responses to the whole consultation[6] only sixty-one schools made more than a cursory response to the 'Standards' element within the consultation. Of these, fourteen were returned as identical photocopied sheets and thirty-two were sent as individual rather than organisational responses. Furthermore, we were able to identify only a tiny minority of the schools' substantive comments as wholly positive. Leaving these aside along with the responses we judged to be entirely negative (also a minority), the remaining responses (approximately 80 per cent of the substantial school returns) ranged along a continuum of concerns. Consultees often began with a 'we welcome'-type statement which expressed positive support for the broad principles underpinning the initiative or general approval of the 'intention to raise standards'. However, general statements of approval were followed by varying degrees of reservation, ranging from practical concerns to principled objection. Schools voiced concerns about the feasibility of school mentors being able to assess student teachers against the Standards in the time available and pointed out the variable circumstances and opportunities trainees encountered in schools. Concerns were also expressed about the attainability of the Standards.

> I am all for high standards, but one has also to be 'real'! It reminds me of the mistakes of the over-prescriptive, over-bureaucratic and over-detailed National Curriculum before Dearing trimmed it back to reality. ... those who drew it up are in danger of deluding themselves that the mere production of a high specification and wishful thinking will produce the desired outcomes.
>
> (SCITT coordinator)

Subsequently this has been reiterated in a survey conducted by NAPTEC, which has found that of the 51 per cent of providers who responded, 93 per cent 'agreed that it was impossible to ensure all the standards were met for every student' (TES 1999b, p. 3). At the other end of the continuum in responses to the consultation there were expressions of deep concern about the impact of the Standards on the nature of teaching and the account being given of the professional. We quote two examples to give a flavour of the kinds of critique being made by those schools expressing such reservations.

> It is obviously a good idea in principle to establish a framework for learning, training and practice for trainee teachers ... We are deeply concerned about the philosophical, sociological and theoretical settings in which skills are acquired, developed and selected as a part of professional practice. ... We need professionals not technicians, thinking and reflective intellects not insensitive bullish practitioners, flexible, developmental learning providers and not routine, systems-orientated instructors ... Unless they (teachers) can inspire the young

people they teach as well as instruct or direct them, they will end up as ... the teaching version of Mr Plod.

(Headteacher)

In the second example, the intentions of the Standards are welcomed, but

... the document ignores social and cultural context. It should include a requirement that trainees should demonstrate a commitment to the values of our diverse society and an understanding of the impact of equality issues on educational outcomes and achievement.

(Headteacher)

The substance of this comment was repeated many times over but as we already know, some members of the Board 'didn't want to have any mention of equal opportunities at all'.

The consultation conferences

Seven regional conferences were 'attended by some 630 teachers, headteachers, ITT providers from schools and higher education institutions, trainee teachers and newly qualified teachers' (TTA 1997c, p. 2). Participants were organised into groups and notes of forty-nine group discussions were made available to us. Discussion was organised, as in the consultation response booklet, around the four sections of the consultation and within this, we again focused our attention on the Standards. The first five questions were the same as in the consultation response booklet (see above). The last question, '(f) Are there any other issues about the new standards that you wish to raise?', was, from our point of view, the most interesting since it was here that the dominant 'how to' mode of consultation might begin to move into a more policy-orientated 'whether we should' type of consultation. Of the forty-nine groups, twenty-three discussed this 'other issues' question and, as far as we were able to understand the notes, it seems that the range of points raised were similar to those expressed in the written consultation response booklets.

In advance of the consultation conferences a document had been prepared entitled *Notes for Chairs: Some possible questions and lines to take.* Forty-four potential questions were identified under five main headings and though space does not allow us to reproduce these in full, a flavour is given below.

1 *General*
(j) Aren't you making teaching a career for technicians rather than for true professionals?

2 *Hobbyhorses*
(c) What are you saying in here about Special Educational Needs?

For each of these anticipated questions, a model answer was provided for chairs of the groups. Again we can do no more than give a sense of these.

Sample answers
(1j) That is rather like saying that once an artist has learned how to draw or paint he or she is only a technician. The reality is that mastery of one's craft releases creativity and potential, it does not stifle it.
and/or
We aim to equip trainees with a 'toolbox' containing the knowledge, skills and methods they need to be effective. Once trainees have learned how to use the tools they will be able to use them to their full potential to teach imaginatively, creatively and with flair.

There is nothing unusual or even necessarily wrong with an organisation ensuring that its staff are all singing from the same song sheet. However, it might be argued that such an activity begins to blur the distinction between 'selling' policy and consulting on it, thus giving credence to the view expressed in the written response by one primary school chair of governors that ' … this is less consultation than an elaborate public relations exercise designed to give the impression of participation'. In addition to this, the description of Special Educational Needs as a 'hobbyhorse' is hardly in keeping with moves towards greater inclusion.

Neither the consultation conference notes nor our review of schools' written responses enabled us to verify the evidence base on which the TTA subsequently claimed that '[M]any working in schools welcomed the standards as a useful tool for monitoring and support of both trainees and NQTs' (TTA 1997c, p. 8), although, as we shall see later, data from our own research shows that 74 per cent intended to use them for planning professional development. This again reveals the tension between developmental and regulatory orientations to standards.

Data, reports and feedback

Up to this point we had only compared our own analysis of the responses with the *First draft of Interim Reports,* and had judged this draft to constitute a fair representation of the major issues being raised. The significance of the *Interim Reports* cannot be understood without an appreciation of the timescale to which those undertaking the analysis were working. Thursday 8 May 1997 marked the end of the consultation and on Wednesday 14 May 1997 a Board subgroup met to consider the results of the consultations. With only three working days between the formal end of the consultation and the Board subgroup meeting, 'fast policy' seems to have taken on a new meaning. There would have been little alternative for TTA officers but to produce an *interim* report based on incomplete data with the result that the procedures for handling responses claimed by the TTA (see above) are unlikely to have occurred.

Having studied the detail of the written responses and the consultation conference material, we compared the *First draft of Interim Reports* with the final public reports on the consultation. There were two such reports, a full *Final Report*, available on request from the TTA (TTA 1997c) and a *Consultation Summary* (TTA 1997d).

The *First draft of Interim Reports* was subjected to a number of redrafts with amendments being based on handwritten comments from TTA officers. These systematically gave a more positive spin to the text. In the process of circulating drafts of the Report between themselves, officers sometimes wrote notes to each other.

> Some of the responses reveal so clearly the 'unreconstructed nature' of HEIs that their inclusion can only be helpful. I have however toned down the text …

> … and the changes I have suggested should strike the right note. On some points respondents are condemned out of their own mouths and these we can use with Ministers – on others they are right.

There is not space here to report the minute detail of this redrafting process. Our general point is that comparison between the *First draft of Interim Reports* and the full *Final Report* reveals first, the systematic deletion of the word 'criticism' and its replacement by 'comment' and, second, a more positive gloss on the evidence. For example, whereas the *First draft of Interim Reports* stated, 'The section on planning, teaching and class management attracted rather less criticism than the previous section', the *Final Report* reads: 'The section on planning, teaching and class management was generally acceptable' (p. 9).

While the *Final Report* does not misrepresent the *substance* of the main concerns arising from the consultation responses, the toned-down language in which these are expressed means that there is considerable under-reporting of disagreement or opposition. It is also worth noting that 'the very small minority' reported as having 'disagreed in principle' (para 1, p. 2) included the Committee of Vice Chancellors and Principals and the Association of University Teachers. This raises once more the issue of how responses are weighted, both in terms of numbers represented by the responses of collective organisations and in terms of the nature of the constituency they represent.

Unlike the full *Final Report*, only available on request, the *Consultation Summary* was widely distributed to all providers of ITT, all LEAs, all professional and subject associations, all respondents to the consultation and 'other interested parties'. It is worrying then to find that the *Consultation Summary* makes no mention of those concerns that are to do with the purposes of education or the kind of teacher who will be produced by the Standards even when these have been clearly identified in the full *Final Report*:

> the proposals lacked an explicit rationale   (p. 8)

> subject knowledge and the pupils' NC were over-emphasised at the expense of such matters as values, children's learning and development, and teachers' personal qualities   (p. 8)

there should be less emphasis on whole class teaching and more on other modes

(p. 8)

others noted the lack of references throughout to the various aspects of equal opportunities and to the diversity of a plural society   (p. 9)

several respondents were concerned that topics they judged important had been neglected or treated less fully than was appropriate. Among those raised most frequently were pupils with English as an additional language (EAL); pupils with SEN; equal opportunities; the pluralistic society; the teacher's pastoral and PSHE responsibilities; the teacher's interpersonal skills; and the role of the LEAs.

(p. 11)

Rather, the *Consultation Summary* does include much of the positive feedback.

There was general support for the *QTS Standards*. Many detailed comments were made about various aspects of the standards. Some respondents were markedly enthusiastic, seeing the standards as likely to improve the quality of ITT and the skills of NQTs. Many working in schools welcomed the standards as a useful tool for monitoring and support of both trainees and NQTs. Respondents generally welcomed a standards-based specification for QTS, and the requirement that all standards must be achieved, often on the grounds that the proposals would raise professional standards and status.   (p. 7)

While it is entirely accurate to describe as half full a jug which is half empty, it may not be the best way to produce policy text nor to ensure its acceptance by those who are crucial to its realisation in practice, namely, teachers. Evidence suggests that when teachers find themselves in opposition to policy they will ignore it where they can or reinterpret it within professional discourses that provide a greater fit with what they know and value (Smyth and Shacklock 1998). Others, believing they are in a minority, may simply accept with resignation policies to which they are not committed. Furthermore, in relation to the procedures adopted for developing the original framework of Standards, there seems to be considerable disparity between England and the countries from whom the TTA sought evidence (Australia and Canada). In terms of the scale, breadth and length of time allotted, it is not unusual for the processes of development elsewhere to have been conducted in much more inclusive and reflective ways, aimed at ensuring maximum participation by those with a legitimate interest in what counts as teaching and how teachers should be educated (Ingvarson 1998; Louden 2000).

A comparison between the draft Standards on which the consultation was based and those emerging as the final 'official' account (DfEE 1998b; TTA 1997a), also shows that very little change of the kind being advocated by consultees actually occurred. It is also worth noting that the Standards for QTS had actually been published (June 1997) before the results of the consultation had apparently been fully analysed (see Timeline, Table 2.2). This may in part explain why 'consultation', according to our evidence, is often perceived as little more than a legitimation exercise for policies already in train. As Terri Seddon (1994) has neatly put it: '[P]roposals for reorganization emerge in a neat glossy style as if they were finished documents' (p. 181). Yet we would still want to argue that care must be taken not to over-interpret the findings presented above. The consultation on the QTS Standards, embedded as it was within three other issues, is only one of many consultations under-taken by the TTA and by central government more generally. Our funding did not enable us to investigate others and we are therefore not in a position to generalise our findings. However, Weir and Beetham's conclusions suggest that there is nothing unusual about our findings in this particular case and we will return to their wider implications for democracy in Chapter Six.

Reflecting on the AST Standards (initiated by the DfEE directly), considerable alarm was expressed that however imperfect the TTA's procedures for developing standards, more recent 'fast policy' modes of operating had resulted in responses that were even more inadequate. A senior professional association official commented,

> ... We weren't consulted on AST Standards in the manner that the TTA have consulted on anything else. If we had been it would have been pointed out how reprehensible they are. They just stuck 'excellent' in front of six categories. It wouldn't be difficult to produce better AST Standards than that, after all pre-sumably the people handling ASTs must have done it. They must have got some concept of what this excellent skill is in order to differentiate, mustn't they? Oth-erwise they couldn't be judging who qualifies to be an AST.

This comment establishes very clearly that Standards are not only about entry into teaching but also progression within it and that procedures for developing them cannot be separated from either their purposes or their content.

Content of Standards

It would be misleading to talk of *the* content of any set of Standards as if there is just one. What emerges from our research is that a great deal of amendment and interpre-tation take place at the level of practice, even in relation to the statutory QTS Stan-dards. Thus, content that might be seen as problematic at the level of policy text, can disappear in the creative ways that some people are operating in the contexts of their own environments.

If we begin at the level of policy text, many of the issues raised in the consultation exercise resurfaced in our respondents' comments in relation to their levels of satisfac-tion with the QTS Standards. A basic omission which emerged strongly was the absence of any explicit account of how teaching is being conceptualised, any indica-tion that there are different representations of teaching or any justification of or rationale for the particular account of teaching implicit in the QTS Standards. As one HEI tutor said, '... [the] TTA's is only one definition of a beginning teacher'. How-ever, even in the absence of an explicit rationale, it is no surprise to find that the QTS

Standards are fundamentally grounded on achieving the subject knowledge and craft skills necessary to teach and assess the school National Curriculum. Thus some people have questioned whether today's new teacher might even be able to adequately achieve the Standards while at the same time being indifferent or ill-disposed to the young people they teach. This model of the teacher is to be expected if, as has been argued, one purpose underpinning the NPS framework is the demand for 'effective' teachers to 'produce' an up-skilled workforce able to enhance the nation's competitiveness within the global economy.[7] Yet in a recent study of schools across Australia, Denmark, England and Scotland, the relational and emotional aspects of teaching proved to be of crucial importance not only to young people but also to their parents (Moos, Mahony and Reeves 1998). Their absence from the QTS Standards is one example of the way that teaching and 'teacher skills' have been redefined predominantly in line with economic priorities – in ways that are not necessarily congruent with those of the communities that teachers serve.

> Being a teacher is not just a matter of having a body of knowledge and a capacity to control a classroom. That could be done by a computer with a cattle-prod. Just as important, being a teacher means being able to establish human relations with the people being taught. Learning is a full-blooded, human social process, and so is teaching. Teaching involves emotions as much as it involves pure reasoning.
>
> (Connell 1993, p. 63)

Teaching is also predominantly presented as an individualistic activity with no mention being made of the ability to work collaboratively with colleagues in countering the limitations of the 'egg crate school' where teachers are isolated physically and professionally (Fullan and Hargreaves 1992). The Standards do require 'effective working relationships with professional colleagues ...' (p. 16), but since these relationships are themselves in the process of being restructured in managerial terms, what it means to be 'effective' in this sense may well be precisely one area over which competing ideologies will be played out. The tension between the form of 'team work' that is the preferred mode of the 'new work order' and the individualised competitive relations being encouraged by the new reward structures (see Chapters 3 and 4) are clearly among the major areas that schools will have to negotiate.

Others argued that the social and political contexts and purposes of teaching and learning are inadequately framed within the Standards and as we have already seen, a major reason for this seems to have been the influence of the New Right in general, and some members of the first TTA Board in particular. The danger is that in the absence of a clear articulation of values through which to ground the Standards,

> ... the default position for many new teachers would be a predominantly middle class, predominantly white and predominantly monocultural set of assumptions which would not of itself challenge, for example, heterosexist and ablebodied assumptions about 'normality'.
>
> (Ainsworth and Johnson 2000 forthcoming)

Although we know that some TTA officers attempted to address this by leaving spaces for progressive interpretation, we cannot presume that everybody comes to the Standards with adequate knowledge and understanding of how oppression or discrimination operate. Even in its own limited terms the Standard that explicitly refers to teachers' 'legal liabilities and responsibilities' in relation to anti-discrimination legislation does not automatically translate into progressive pedagogies. Schools have not yet been taken to court for consistently consigning black boys to lower ability groups (or excluding them from school altogether), nor is there any legal redress for parents who object to their daughters' education being directed at 'civilising' the behaviour of the boys or dominated by the need to negotiate the continuum of sexual harassment (Mahony 1989).

An example of an attempt to redress these absences is provided by Ainsworth and Johnson (2000), who argue that the lack of an explicit value base in the QTS Standards should be remedied by an explicit statement of values around four major elements,

- enabling students to become reflective, creative and critical thinkers;
- the facilitation of an analysis of what constitutes social justice;
- enabling students to understand and identify how discrimination operates and how to develop strategies to counter it;
- enabling students to recognise, accept and work with differences in a positive way.

(Ainsworth and Johnson, 2000)

In this approach, values would be incorporated into the body of the Standards themselves, either as descriptions of the performances through which specific values are realised or grouped into a separate unit of qualification, as in the Care Sector Standards (Mansfield and Mitchell 1996). An alternative approach is to include a preliminary general code of practice or statement of the principles which are intended to inform standards in action. The standards for teaching in Further Education published by the FENTO (1999) adopted this approach, as did the group which developed the Northern Ireland teaching profiles (Whitty 1996). So even within the parameters of a standards framework there are at least two ways of trying to address issues of professional values, neither of which is evident in the QTS Standards. Instead, we are left with a diminished, technicist account of the beginning teacher in which the work s/he does in relation to teaching as a 'moral trade' (Connell 1993) is outside the discourse of the Standards and therefore not officially recognised. Yet this is itself a value-laden position. We are faced with the worst of all possible worlds in the form of Standards that are presented as neutral embodiments of a single version of professional practice whose implied claim to objectivity denies the values implicit in them and precludes dialogues over alternatives.

There are also indications that there are disjunctions between these Standards and the values, aims and purposes of the school curriculum, as they are expressed in the introduction to the revised National Curriculum (DfEE/QCA 1999). If, in this revised environment, the QTS Standards emerge as outdated and ill-suited to the purpose of equipping teachers to 'meet the challenge of change', then they will need to be rewritten and 'teacher training' will need to be 'reformed' (again). This would also have implications for the Standards defining what it means to pass through the threshold, to possess 'advanced skill' and to 'lead' a school effectively. It is at this point that one must ask whether a 'standards-led' initiative is the most sensible way of 'steering' in a fast-changing world where the combination of social diversity and competing ideologies over the purposes of schooling and the roles of teachers make for a highly unstable and uncertain context. As a senior union official said to us – 'some of these Standards are backward-looking for a profession that is about to change'.

We would not want to deny the importance of the policy text, nor underestimate its influence in defining the parameters of what 'counts'. As one headteacher put it,

> I am generally opposed to this development which takes us further down the road of making important what is measurable. We must be unique in spending time on the wrong agendas.

However, it is generally recognised by policy analysts (though perhaps not by policy makers), that 'the pudding eaten is a far cry from the original recipe' (Raab 1994, p. 24). Although a straightforward, technically rational relationship between policy text and 'implementation' is often presumed by policy makers, in reality, interpretation and realisation create different local contexts of use, impact and meaning.

Use and impact of Standards

Our research shows that over one-third of the organisations who were using the Standards had also amended them and that, taken together, the overall framework of Standards was being used for a variety of purposes. These included: planning and provision of professional development; selection and recruitment; appraisal; development of staffing policies; self-assessment; dismissal of staff; preparation of job descriptions; and the award of qualifications. In addition some Standards (e.g. Subject Leader Standards) had been creatively adapted for use with staff for whom they were not originally intended (e.g. pastoral staff). One LEA in particular was very positive about Standards as a resource for developing their own work.

> We're finding the Standards excellent in a whole variety of ways for validating the work that we were already developing ... I think there's an inherent danger in sets of standards that are fit for all and determined for all ... you need to be sensitive to the context within which people operate but we don't operate them like a tight corset ...

So far the evidence seems to show that one positive element in the way that the Standards are being used is that they have provided the seeds from which a thousand (different) flowers have bloomed. Whether all these flowers are equally beautiful is of course another question, and this takes us back to the heart of the conundrum with standards. Whilst on the one hand a needs assessor for the NPQH reported ruling out a candidate described as 'three goose steps to the right of Ghengis Khan', on the other hand, an NPQH trainer suggested that this judgment would not be universally applied.

NPQH TRAINER: The big questions aren't dealt with at all in the Standards – what if the candidate is a Nazi? I've got a woman at the moment and she's not a nice person … she shouldn't be there. I wouldn't want her near my child. She's horrible.

PM: Horrible?

NPQH TRAINER: She can't stand kids … but there's nothing in the NPQH Standards that says you have to like kids or care about them – or other human beings come to that. So even the written reference from the head teacher wouldn't necessarily have addressed it – depends on what that person thinks the Standards mean.

The problem is arguably less significant where the Standards are being used for professional development purposes, for one presumes that debate around interpretation is part of the agenda for discussion. But where qualifications or reward require assessment of individuals then consistency and fairness become crucially important – this was after all one reason for introducing the Standards in the first place. In order to explore whether the Standards are capable of doing this work (of ensuring consistency and fairness) there is no better place to look than the QTS Standards. Unlike the minimalist AST Standards, those for QTS are lengthy and OFSTED regulates their application through regular inspection of ITT providers. If consistency is achievable anywhere one would expect to find it here.

Consistency – whose interpretation?

In terms of our questionnaire responses and at the time of our research, 89 per cent of those involved in the daily provision of ITT courses were using the QTS National Standards either for final assessment or while OFSTED were inspecting their courses or in order to complete the Career Entry Profile. However, in addition to, or occasionally in place of, the QTS National Standards (if they were not being inspected), over 40 per cent were using an amended version and over 25 per cent were using documents they had developed locally with teachers and the local community. Interviews revealed that such variability may be in the process of changing as people begin to feel the pressure of inspection.

> … we're in the process of giving up our own profile which is much better actually – it's been developed over years with teachers and students. But the work in having to map it on to the Standards for OFSTED to prove compliance and the extra paper for schools – we're giving up I think, just resigned and weary.
>
> (HEI Secondary Tutor)

This does not mean that consistency is round the corner. Even those using the National Standards found that 'the "standard" of the Standards is not clear' and that 'the devil is in the interpretation' (Headteacher). The following comment was made by a person working on the GRTP:

> I'll give you an instance under 'other professional requirements'. They ask people to have a knowledge and understanding of the Race Relations Act ... but knowledge of the Race Relations Act could have nothing to do with anti-racist practice in the classroom. So I have interpreted it in the way that I feel would be the most beneficial to those trainees which is to put together some research tasks, action research in the school. And I make it a requirement. ... That's the way that I've interpreted them.

One HEI, however, reported that they had been 'rather conservative' in their interpretations on the grounds that

> ... progressive interpretation may carry risks, there's no time for it and it's dangerous ... not really part of the agenda these days, a sign that you've not moved with the times and you're not really paying attention to the Standards ... it's not what counts as giving value for money.
>
> (Head of ITT)

This would seem to support Clarke and Newman's (1997) suggestion that as 'the calculative frameworks of managerialism' (p. 76) become embedded throughout organisations, their precepts may become internalised in the form of a 'dispersed managerial consciousness'. As we shall see later, this carries the danger that issues of social justice begin to slide off the agenda.

In recognition of the problem of interpretation, a number of exemplification materials have been developed which are intended, as a TTA Board member said, 'to help people navigate their way through these things'. In 1997/98 there were three OFSTED documents relating to the inspection of ITT providers which explained the inspection framework (OFSTED 1997a), provided subject-specific exemplifications of the National Standards (OFSTED 1997b) and defined what would constitute evidence that the training is enabling the Standards to be met (OFSTED 1997c). By 1999 three new initiatives were underway which were described as follows:

> ... there's going to be eventually video and resource materials for early years, Key Stage 1, Key Stage 2, humanities subjects, science subjects ... and they can use that across the partnerships in order to have agreement trials. There's also the ethnic minority exemplification materials. And then the third lot of stuff that's around is in relation to the ICT curriculum which has got twenty-two subjects, specific sets of material that shows what those Standards look like in relation to individual subjects. However, I mean you know, it's a bit like sort of running around, you know, in circles. Because you know, you can exemplify and exemplify and exemplify.
>
> (TTA officer)

This highlights one of the problems with 'standards', namely that they assume that outcome statements or accounts of expertise are self-explanatory. They are not and, as the TTA officer recognises, attempts to be more explanatory can lead to a bottomless pit of potential exemplification or a 'never ending spiral of specification' (Wolf 1995, p. 55). In the end, there is no avoiding the role of professional judgment, as the officer also seems to recognise.

> I mean I prefer to think about it as more of a framework for people's very sound professional judgment. These are people that have been doing this job, you know, for a very long time and are very, very skilled in it.

But if this is the case, we seem to have lost one of the primary purposes for which QTS Standards were developed in the first place, namely, 'consistent and reliable assessment' (TTA 1997b, p. 8). And, if we can now rely on this 'very sound professional judgment' why are ITT providers being subjected to continual inspection? Our evidence suggests that staff working in ITT certainly do not feel that they are trusted to exercise professional judgment, rather that their energies are being redirected into satisfying the hunger of an ever-increasing bureaucracy that defines the constitutive elements of compliance.

> … when people say they're on their knees they mean it. I spend half my life these days on the floor with all these documents – trying to map them on to each other to find out what on earth we're meant to be doing. There are so many and I'm never sure I've got the latest so in a sense you're always kept on the hop.
>
> (HEI tutor)

Judged by one HMI we interviewed as 'a phase of madness', it is this use within the assessment and inspection context that transforms the QTS Standards from a useful tool for professional development within a benign 'framework for people's very sound professional judgment' into a technology of surveillance and control viewed as more serious 'than just a bureaucratic nightmare'.

HEI TUTOR: We're moving more and more towards a position where it almost feels like policing the students. In the past, feedback on their lessons in school was a formative and supportive process; … Whether they were measuring up to the Standards did of course form the backcloth but we didn't kick into summative assessment mode until towards the end of their practice. Now, almost from the beginning of the course, we have to show that we are setting them regular personal targets and monitoring whether they achieve them. This means we are also policing the school mentors. More and more of our meetings which should be professional development for them are being devoted to ensuring that they fill in the necessary forms, pick up fast on any problems and ensure that students address them immediately. So everyone is policing everyone from OFSTED down. … In such a climate, it's a struggle to retain a non-punitive attitude when we know the results of the inspection will have such serious repercussions.

PM: So is this just during your inspection year or …
HEI TUTOR: You're joking, I'm not doing this next year. I'm going to teach properly.

It is as yet very early for the impact of the QTS Standards to be known, if indeed it is ever possible to isolate the effects of one initiative from a range of other variables. What we can do here, however, is to report a range of perceptions and emotions about the ways in which the Standards are being used. These should not be underestimated, since they will influence people's degree of commitment in negotiating what they believe to be the positive and negative features of the initiative. Within our questionnaire we asked HEI tutors how they perceived the impact of the QTS Standards on the quality of their courses and on their own teaching.

Of the HEI tutors who responded, 63 per cent thought that the QTS Standards would help to improve course planning, student assessment and procedures for dismissing failing students; 82 per cent thought that target-setting with students would improve, even though they may have disagreed with the nature of the targets themselves or their potential for creating an 'atomistic' or 'mechanistic' approach to teaching. There was also a high measure of agreement that consistency within partnership had improved, though for some this seemed to reside in increased powers of coercion:

> The only real 'advantage' is that 'dissident' schoolteachers can no longer tell student teachers to ignore what the 'university' says as it is no longer the 'university' saying it, rather the TTA!
>
> (HEI tutor)

However, when we asked whether people felt that the overall quality of their courses had improved, the response was much more negative. Few (8 per cent) were unambiguously positive and predictably concerns tended to highlight issues such as the growing levels of 'bureaucracy … operating on political expediency lines', 'over-regulation', and the loss of opportunity to explore a more 'idealistic view of teaching' than the model represented by the Standards. As one person put it, 'they have "helped" to prescribe that "model" that I should "deliver"'.

Another tutor, in interview, went further by claiming that even outside the context of inspection.

> I know that my teaching has not improved. I think that if … [I] … wound the clock back five years my students got very much more from me because I had more time to think about my teaching. … everything looks nice and neat and tidy on paper now but … where students miss out is that so much energy has travelled into everything else that what suffers is the quality of the teaching. I think that by the time I reach the point where I should be thinking really creatively about what I need to be doing with the students, I'm played out, I've been doing admin. up to here. I'm always looking over my shoulder and preparing documentation.
>
> (HEI tutor)

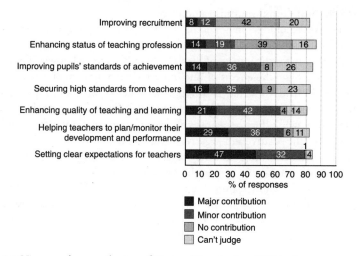

Figure 2.3 Views on the contribution of National Standards to TTA's aims.

Although, as we know, the framework of Standards has changed with the change of government, the general aims of the Standards have survived beyond the TTA's original framework into the Green Paper. Of these, our evidence shows that the only area in which the Standards are predicted to make a major contribution is in helping to set clear expectations for teachers.

In relation to the potential impact of the Standards on individual teachers, again the prognosis was mixed. A common view was that 'for some teachers it could lead to enhancements – for others it could be damaging to creative practice' (Head of ITT). Evident in the majority of the responses was the view that positive impact on individual teachers was dependent on the Standards being used within a context designed to support and develop staff or when their use was underpinned by professional values.

> Well used by professionals who commit their established professional values to the application of the Standards, they have a potential for huge gain. Conversely they are open to somewhat arid, mechanistic application which would do little good.
>
> (NPQH Assessment Centre manager)

A number of respondents drew attention to the crucial role of schools in determining the impact of the Standards. Schools, for their part, were generally underwhelmed by the initiative and tended to suggest that Standards would not address the real problem which they saw as 'demoralisation' and the fact that 'teachers currently feel overwhelmed and undervalued'. One headteacher foresaw a danger that 'the Green Paper may torpedo developments by causing a psychological block about this type of activity'. Overall only 20 per cent of LEAs, no HEIs and 5 per cent of schools agreed that the Standards would enhance the commitment and morale of teachers. Conversely, 57 per cent of LEAs, 90 per cent of HEIs and 63 per cent of schools thought that the

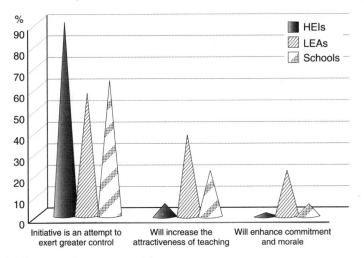

Figure 2.4 Percentage in agreement with statements.

Standards represented an attempt to exert political control over the teaching profession (Figure 2.4).

In addition it may be that the Standards will impact negatively on the micro-environment of the school, as emerged in one primary school where we interviewed a number of staff at various levels of seniority. First, in a context where, according to the Deputy Head, teachers are already 'terrified of failing', the Standards were thought to be contributing to the feeling that 'they've got to be this perfect person'. Second, it was suggested that the Standards may create a heightened sense of surveillance which the Headteacher articulated in these terms:

> There's a difference between planning a lesson in writing, for you to deliver it, and planning a lesson because you're writing it for someone to check up on whether you're doing the job.

Again, this could lead, as was found in Australia when the AST grade was introduced, to teachers diverting their energies away from the business of teaching and into the concern with image management (Smyth, Shacklock and Hattam 1997). Third, framed clearly within a 'value-for-money' framework, the same primary school which OFSTED described as having an excellent record of professional development for NQTs, was in the process of deciding not to employ them because of the costs and risks of the procedures around the Induction Standards.

HEADTEACHER: I'm not being flippant. It used to be that headteachers thought Newly Qualified Teachers were great because they're cheap. ... I can see instead of Newly Qualifieds being a premium, Year 2 teachers are going to be great ... I mean it's getting as though it sounds very cynical.

DEPUTY: ... if you get one who fails ... I mean who is going to want to take that on really?

HEADTEACHER: I would be very reluctant to take a risk. ... you have to now document all that you have done to support that person ... like when you've got an incompetent teacher. ... you've really got that system under another name, being introduced for a Newly Qualified Teacher right from the start. But if you've got to be hard-nosed about finance ... if you look at the salary scale of what you pay a Newly Qualified Teacher and what you pay a Year 2 teacher. A Year 2 teacher is probably cheaper because of all the processes and all the meetings you've got to arrange for NQTs.

The point being made here went beyond the particular policy in question, which the Head and Deputy believed could probably be 'fixed' over time. The wider problems, which they could not fix, were twofold. The first was that the potential of the Standards initiative was being undermined by the way it was becoming used for regulatory purposes with all its associated bureaucratic procedures of assessment and control. The second was that, at the level of practice, insufficient attention had been paid to the problems of managing the policy as responsibility was passed down the line in a context of low trust.

> What I'm saying is ... this school has got a kite mark to say it can deal with teachers properly. ... But basically, this is questioning the whole time whether the school is competent, whether the NQT is competent. You're not trusted to have done it properly. You've got to put the evidence up each time and when you're already pressured ... It's a different mind game – horrendous.
>
> (Headteacher)

So far we have raised questions about the adequacy of the procedures for developing the Standards and explored some major issues about their content and the values underpinning them. We have suggested that in terms of 'fitness for purpose' they are seen as providing helpful guidelines for setting agendas of professional development sensitive to local context. However, they do not resolve issues of consistency and fairness when used for assessment purposes, and rely heavily on interpretation for translation into practice. The proliferation of exemplification materials designed to address the problem of interpretation operates to divert energy away from the job itself and into the paperwork that 'proves' the job is being done 'correctly'. As a cultural device, the danger of 'standards' is that despite their variability and interpretive character, they get treated as 'facts' of quality, and the preoccupation with the technologies associated with them functions to remove from debate all the difficult questions about the purposes of schooling and the role of teachers within it. High levels of compliance with these 'facts' is sapping the creativity, energy and 'fun' of teaching. Even the LEA officer who reported being 'very satisfied' with the Standards went on to say 'except they lack heart and soul'. It would be difficult to think of a greater indictment against what are, after all, Standards for *teaching*, not bean counting.

3   Managing and modernising teaching

> ... there is never a gap. I mean from half-past seven to half-past five I'm working every day without a break plus marking at home if I've had a meeting in the afternoon, which I have at least two afternoons, sometimes three a week. So that's ten hours a day five days a week, plus marking. And that's just to manage what I have to do. That's not anything else. I mean I'm also responsible for record-keeping and assessment in school ...
>
> (Primary school teacher)

> ... there's a big silence in the whole Green Paper ... about contact time – that to me is the real problem with the 'something for something model' – it doesn't account for the fact that most teachers are already giving everything.
>
> (LEA policy officer)

This chapter is set in the context of the proposal by the UK government to introduce a 'performance-management' policy as a basis on which to organise the management and remuneration of teachers in England. The performance-management model envisaged in the Green Paper is firmly embedded within the dominant managerialist ideology which sets the context for restructured levels of the teaching force and redesigned patterns of progression. 'Standards' (as we have seen in Chapter 2) are an essential element of the technology of performance management in specifying skills defined as valuable and supposedly amenable to measurement. No account of performance management would be adequate which did not also clarify the value assumptions which underpin it, or grapple with its implications for patterns of social justice and differentiation. We shall explore both of these dimensions. Furthermore, as has been discovered in other sectors and countries which have endeavoured to introduce such policies, some of the proposals contained in the Green Paper have generated a storm of controversy and opposition. We shall illustrate the contours of this in relation to the reactions of teachers, unions, governing bodies and local education authorities, and others.

The Green Paper establishes quite an explicit marker as to the direction in which the government would like to travel in its project to 'modernise' the teaching profession. In its form it looks both backwards to a whole swathe of initiatives begun under the previous Conservative administrations, and forwards with the particular orientations of Tony Blair's government. In this sense the Green Paper and its attendant technical documents and subsequent circulars and consultations constitute both a reflection on what has gone before and a prefigurative sense of what is to come. While some of the parts may be familiar, the overall assemblage constitutes something new for teachers. A great deal of the 'devilish detail' of the Paper is as yet to be resolved and it will be some time before the outcomes and impacts of the various strands and elements of the policy emerge. To take but two key examples, we do not as yet know how the embryonic GTC will operate, nor how broadly it will define its role as a voice for the profession. We cannot even be sure how tight the proposals for performance management will prove to be and how they will be realised in practice. We do know, however, that experiences elsewhere provide an agenda of legitimate concern which needs to be kept in mind as policy beds down. We shall now move on to explore the broad parameters within which the Green Paper is framed. Sometimes this will lead us into retrospective reflections on the way in which policy initiatives have influenced current proposals. For example, there are clear continuities with policies which the TTA had already put in train; sometimes these connections are acknowledged, sometimes not. Of course, there are also strands which go considerably further back in history and which are being represented as though entirely fresh.

Background to the Green Paper, performativity in practice[1]

The Green Paper which was published in December 1998 (DfEE 1998a) announced the Labour government's firm intention to introduce a thoroughgoing performance-management model to form the basis for the overall restructuring of the teaching profession within schools. In a clear break with the past when 'isolated, unaccountable professionals made curriculum and pedagogical decisions alone' (para 13, p. 14), teachers of the future will need

- to have high expectations of themselves and of all pupils;
- to accept accountability;
- to take personal and collective responsibility for improving their skills and subject knowledge;
- to seek to base decisions on evidence of what works in schools in this country and internationally;
- to work in partnership with other staff in schools;
- to welcome the contribution that parents, business and others outside a school can make to its success; and
- to anticipate change and promote innovation.   (p. 14)

In order to achieve a 'new professionalism', teaching is to undergo a process of 'modernisation'. In a set of measures heralded as giving 'something for something', the proposals include an increase in the number of teaching assistants, and the introduction of a performance-management system in which a restructuring of the profession, the introduction of annual appraisal, professional development and performance-related pay are all underpinned by a framework of standards, namely the NPS framework. A 'fast-track' procedure will be established by means of which identified 'high-fliers' could move more rapidly through the school hierarchy. It is envisaged that movement through the various positions within the structure would be accomplished by evaluation against the relevant Standards, undertaken by headteachers and, in some cases, with the assistance or ratification of nationally trained, external assessors.

Before moving into discussion about the implications of these proposals some pre-liminary points are worth making. First, many of the elements within the Green Paper, most obviously induction and appraisal, have been emerging for some consid-erable time. The proposals as envisaged constitute an editing, condensation and reworking of these elements. Second, what is described here will feel very familiar to some international colleagues, for example, from Australia, the USA and New Zea-land. On the other hand, some of our colleagues from elsewhere in Europe have expressed the view that a great deal of what goes on in England is a form of 'localised dementia' which has little to say to them. As one of our Swedish interviewees recently said to us, 'what is happening in teacher education in England is a story we use to frighten the children'. This brings us back to the question raised in Chapter 1 of whether the movements currently taking place in England are symptomatic of wider, global trends. It is an ongoing question of where, if at all, there may be points of con-vergence now or in the future and the extent to which such difference is merely illusory. We have found it important, in trying to compare the English situation with that of elsewhere, to pay attention to the *basis* on which comparison is being made. It may be, for example, that OFSTED or the TTA and their modes of operation are unique but the functions they are designed to undertake may well be replicated elsewhere.

When the Green Paper proposals were introduced, the government was somewhat shaken by the scale of the responses it received to its consultation, and by the vehe-mence of some of the responses. Many of the details of the original proposals have been the subject of intense negotiation (DfEE 1999b; DfEE 1999c). Early on, the timetable for implementation became disorganised and serious anxieties were expressed from within the system about the financial, regulatory, legal and logistical 'state of readiness'. Even as structures were being established at the DfEE to manage the policy, the STRB was still deliberating on the final proposals forwarded by the DfEE and the mountain of evidence and argument it had received from other sources.[2] The final details of the initiative will of course be very significant for the pay and conditions under which teachers work, but how they will fundamentally affect the core work regime being proposed for teaching is another question.

The roots of performance management

Whilst this is not the context in which to go into detail over the history of perfor-mance management as an ideology and set of operational procedures, it is important to emphasise that its roots lie deep in the private sector and that it was moved into the public sector as a key element in the managerialist restructuring of the public services during the 1980s and 1990s. In England we now find that there are performance-management systems at work in almost all areas of the public service, for example in health, housing, tax collection, employment services, local authority provision, as well as in the private sector (Armstrong and Baron 1998; Rogers 1999). Under the Labour government the White Paper *Modernising Government* (Cabinet Office 1999a) demonstrates a clear will to continue in these directions. It is in this context that the Green Paper is located.

> Pay must be flexible and put service needs first. This means reforming outdated systems by tackling aspects which make insufficient contribution to perfor- mance. It means challenging outdated assumptions, for example, the idea that 'fair pay' means everybody should get the same increase, or that pay and condi- tions must all be set nationally. It involves introducing greater flexibility for local managers to set pay and conditions in accordance with local needs, where appro- priate within national frameworks.
>
> (para. 28, p. 8)

And again,

> The Modernising Government White Paper made clear that a person's pay should reflect their output, results and performance. This means that those who contribute most – whether they are teams or individuals – should be best re- warded, and that systems which give automatic pay increases to poor or inefficient performers should be challenged. This is a continuing theme of pay re- forms proposed by government across the public sector.
>
> (DfEE 1999f, para. 30, p. 8)

Modernising Government also makes it clear that policy decisions should be based on sound evidence.

> This Government's declaration that 'what counts is what works' is the basis for the heightened interest in the part played by evidence in policy making. ... The raw ingredient of evidence is information. Good quality policy making depends on high quality information, derived from a variety of sources – expert knowl- edge; existing domestic and international research; existing statistics; stakeholder consultation; evaluation of previous policies; new research, if appropriate; or sec- ondary sources, including the internet. Evidence can also include analysis of the outcomes of consultation, costings of policy options and the results of economic or statistical modelling. To be as effective as possible, evidence needs to be provided by, and/or be interpreted by, experts in the field working closely with policy makers.
>
> (Cabinet Office 1999b, para. 7.1, p. 31)

These claims concerning evidence sit somewhat uncomfortably with the determina- tion of the government to drive ahead with 'performance management' despite the weight of evidence which points to its negative potential. Commenting specifically on the performance-related pay element of the proposals, Richardson says

> In an earlier report I concluded that the attempts to employ a whole variety of individual performance-related pay schemes in the UK public sector had not been a notable success. About a dozen different studies of their impact all conclude that only small minorities of public-sector employees report any sense of enhanced motivation from performance-related pay, while much larger numbers perceive that it leads to jealousies among employees and to a reduction in trust between employees and management.
>
> These outcomes are not accidental. Rather, they reflect either the intrinsic unsuitability of individual performance-related pay for many parts of the public sector, or design faults in the ... schemes actually adopted, or problems in the way that potentially successful schemes are actually implemented.
>
> (Richardson 1999, p. 1)

In addition, a Swedish colleague told us of his experiences over the preceding two years.

> We introduced this system of merit pay a couple of years ago in Sweden at the Universities. Now when these were introduced, they were all tied to saying that this would raise efficiency. ... as far as I know there exists no single study that proves or that can even produce the slightest hint of evidence that merit pay has increased production in schools or in Universities. Now I'm talking about another source of knowledge, ... from my position in the University where I have to deal with this, I can say that I have seen no positive evidence whatsoever but I have seen a lot of negative evidence which I can point to very precisely.

He went on to catalogue these as

> ... merit pay creates the culture of silence – I'm not going to share my ideas with you because you might go off and do something. It creates a lot of idiotic discussions of – did you recognise what I have done there – why didn't you take it in – why does he get £5 more than me, 10 crowns, 100 crowns or whatever. Totally meaningless discussion which all show mistrust and envy. Second, merit pay tends to promote the salary aspects of your work, namely it craves visibility. This has two consequences. It changes the nature of work itself so that it is recognised by someone, so it creates boot-licking. This leads to promoting everything that is conformist and the person, the unmarried white male who is seen after school hours, leaving traces of his sweat. Is that what we want to promote? And it strengthens the administrators' power who are suddenly those whose boots it's most necessary to lick. It's an administrative decision which in its essence gives more power to the administrators. That's all it does, gives more power to the administrators.

Also, in terms of the emphasis laid on 'leadership' in the Green Paper, research evidence suggests that

> ... lack of systematic evaluation means that many top managers' views are not based on sound evidence. ... effects are quite complex, and the points at which problems emerge may be far removed from where the basic problems lie.
>
> (Marsden and French 1998, p. 2)

Despite such reservations, performance management constitutes a key element of a managerially driven version of Human Resource Management in which

> [F]or some managers in local government, and indeed for some politicians in central as well as local government, 'performance' appears to have achieved an almost magical significance, and has led to the creation not just of Performance Management but also performance reviews, performance audits, performance plans and performance appraisals.
>
> (Rogers 1999, p. 1)

One of its strongest legitimating devices lies in the presumption that you can move systems of personnel management across from context to context, and that the basic principles and working assumptions remain the same. It is depicted in a technicist form as a 'free-floating technology' capable of being applied in diverse contexts and where the nature of context-specificity is deemed of less relevance than techno-universality. In this sense it works within a universalistic paradigm which accords well with certain deterministic versions of globalisation. A corollary of this universalistic presupposition is the presumption that problems encountered within performance management are issues of presentation, logistics and technique. This was evident in the response which the government made to the consultation resistance it encountered, when it defined most of the problems as issues to be resolved through further adaptation and negotiation. Managerialist ideologies are fundamentally grounded in the notion that there exist sets of principles and procedures which can be applied to bring about 'effective, efficient and economic' modes of operation. Of course, these have to be applied in specific contextual circumstances that have to be taken into account in devising effective operational procedures, but the working presumption is that the general principles are pre-eminent and circumstances subsidiary. This is a highly contentious and value-laden point, since to most people 'on the ground' it is precisely 'context' which gives meaning and flavour to their actions and lives. Consequently, the 'context' within which schools are placed is crucial as providing the starting point within which one works. We find this referred to again and again in the public policy literature and people's experiences, and it is emphasised in terms of local government by Rogers (1999), writing as a 'critical friend' of the performance-management movement.

> While performance management aims to increase the capacity of councillors and managers to determine and manage the performance of their own affairs it is

being applied in an environment where both the definition of performance and the operational processes for achieving that performance are being increasingly determined not just by central government but by wholly or partly autonomous audit and inspection agencies. Rather than encouraging an approach of self-reliance, responsibility and creativity they are likely to produce a culture of compliance and conformity – with worrying consequences. Performing becomes mere conforming. (p. 24)

As an extension to this, little recognition is accorded to issues of structure, power and conflict which are ever-present in social contexts such as schools but are wished away, or rendered invisible in managerialist accounts (Angus 1994; Mahony and Hextall 1997c).

As an approach, performance management also has deeply totalising characteristics. For example, workers (teachers in our case) are presented as units of labour to be distributed and managed. The characteristics of these labour units are deemed largely irrelevant provided that they comply with certain specifications and working criteria. This renders the structural characteristics of groups of teachers (or other workers) – such as ethnicity, gender, sexuality, and class – marginal and discrimination invisible. Thus, for example, the Green Paper makes no mention of, say, gender or ethnicity in its proposals. Placing this point more generally within management theory, Hartley (1997) writes

People are thereby regarded as a resource, to be managed, efficiently. (On this, note how personnel *officers* are currently being redefined as human resource *managers*. They must therefore 'record' people as information which can be managed, as a resource.) All this is to say that the performativity, efficiency-seeking principle is thereby rendered almost as commonsense. The effect of this would be the 'suppression' of difference. (p. 128, emphasis in original)

Rather, it speaks the language of 'all' teachers, which, given the mal-distribution of equal opportunities available to teachers, renders this apparent language of inclusivity potentially socially excluding. This ignores Connell's reminder that

... Teachers collectively form a workforce, and the character of that workforce bears on issues of social justice. We need to consider, for instance, how socially representative the teaching workforce is; how it is selected and trained; what are its paths of promotion ... (pp. 63–4)

It is also totalising in its reliance on fundamentally individualistic notions of motivation, achievement, performance and progression.[3] Once again its basic operating unit is that of individuals, ambitious for their futures, jealous of their achievements and personally motivated in their orientation to teaching. There have, of course, always been teachers (and academics, and even, perhaps, politicians) like this. But what these proposals do is to elevate this version of being a teacher above a version that stresses team-work, collaborative practice and a communitarian, non-competitive orientation. In doing this it takes it as axiomatic that the individualistic model will prove to be more 'efficient, effective and economical' in relation to its outcomes. Time and again the teachers we interviewed drew us back to this issue.

> ... I think teaching is a sort of collegial profession where you give of yourself and you share with your colleagues and that's what you're actually imparting to children as well, that you learn together.
>
> (Primary school teacher)

> ... it is very difficult to be positive about it because we come from a situation where people in the primary school, particularly in the primary school, I think, work very closely together in order to make the job work ...
>
> (Primary school teacher)

> I would say, very competitive, very ambitious people will perhaps use the situation if it's presented to them.
>
> (Primary school teacher)

These comments suggest that either the restructuring envisaged for the profession will flounder because it goes against the grain of what it means to teach successfully, or that it will succeed by dint of creating 'changes in the way public servants approach their work, and think about the use of the resources at their disposal' (Marsden and French 1998, p. 1).

Once again the teachers we interviewed voiced an awareness of these transformative demands.

> I think there's a tension between a school of thinking that's very much to do with youngsters and learning and teaching, and managerial systems that's to do with demonstrating efficiency and productivity and so on. I don't think they always sit terribly happily together.
>
> (Secondary school teacher)

And again:

> ... being measured, performance indicators ... are to do with being a good bureaucrat, being able to show how you've matched targets. That's not matching the target, it's *showing* how you've matched the target and I think that's in one sense the real difficulty with the bureaucratic system we're under. And also, that we're being very narrowed in our teaching, ... You're in a very tight scenario about how it's being prescribed that you should teach these things. That's incredibly frustrating, demotivating and also I would have thought demoralising for quite a percentage of teachers.
>
> (Headteacher)

One of the major teaching unions in its response to the Green Paper was quite clear about the hierarchical and divisive presumptions it sees underpinning the performance-related pay element of the government's proposals.

> ... [Performance management] attracts the Government because the premise of payment and reward for excellence and improvement is predicated on it being discriminatory. By definition, not all will fulfil the predetermined criteria. There will be gateways, hurdles and thresholds. A minority will be paid more – perhaps a great deal more – others, a majority, will not.
>
> (NUT 1999, para. 59)

Parenthetically, the individualising orientation also drives directly to the heart of collective models of organising and protecting teachers, their rights, conditions of service and rewards. Insofar as unions are left with a role within such a model it is to patrol the boundaries of the system to ensure that the practices are conducted in accordance with the established procedures. They are by default themselves painted into an individualistic rather than collectivist purpose vis-à-vis their members.

Nature and definitions of performance management

A clear definition of performance management can prove elusive. What many people provide is a description of the various elements which go to make up an overall account of the technology involved in operating a performance-management model or regime. As Ironside and Seifert (1995) say,

> ... unitarist management ... treats neither the subject nor the process [of performance management] as problematic. All that is left, perhaps, therefore is to describe the functions and activities and skills and then provide some anecdotal examples.
>
> (pp. 137–8)

From an avowedly managerialist perspective Helen Murlis (1992) at least places some of the major elements which ground performance management clearly within its HRM home.

> One of the major lessons emerging ... is the need for effective performance management to underpin the pay system. A good working definition of performance management is that it is 'the process which links people and jobs to the strategy and objectives of the organisation'. Good performance management is about operating a process which increases the likelihood of achieving performance improvements. Current thinking in this area indicates that management needs to be practised by the integrated operation of four processes ... planning for performance, managing performance, appraising performance and rewarding performance.
>
> (p. 65)

Following very much the same orientation, Armstrong and Baron (1998) cite the

Institute of Personnel Management as having produced the following definition of performance management as a result of a major research project in 1992:

> A strategy which relates to every activity of the organisation set in the context of its human resources policies, culture, style and communications systems. The nature of the strategy depends on the organisational context and can vary from organisation to organisation.
>
> It was suggested that what was described as a 'performance management system' complied with the textbook definition when the following characteristics were met by the organisation:
>
> - It communicates a vision of its objectives to all its employees;
> - It sets departmental and individual performance targets that are related to wider objectives;
> - It conducts a formal review of progress towards these targets;
> - It uses the review process to identify training, development and reward outcomes;
> - It evaluates the whole process in order to improve effectiveness;
>
> In addition, 'performance management organisations';
>
> - express performance targets in terms of measurable outputs, accountabilities and training/learning targets;
> - use formal appraisal procedures as ways of communicating performance requirements that are set on a regular basis;
> - link performance requirements to pay, especially for senior managers.
>
> (Armstrong and Baron, 1998, pp. 44–5)

In his comprehensive review of the field, Rogers illustrates the dominant parameters with instances drawn from private and public sectors, and from varied contexts within these sectors. He concludes his definitional excursion in the following way:

> Perhaps the major weakness of the many attempts to implement Performance Management has been that it has been perceived only as a set of individual and often poorly related techniques.   (p. 10)

Addressing the same issue of definition, Ironside and Seifert once again bring a markedly more critical orientation to their interpretation of the management of human resources. As they say:

> One general view of the emergence of HRM as an important part of the management of British enterprises in the 1990's suggests that it, in all its forms, simply represents a modern version of managing resources in a recession. ... The dominant slogan for managers in the private sector is 'more for less', that is productivity and/or efficiency gains at all costs. If this is the case, in crude terms, then an important issue for the management of recession in public services

becomes the implementation of the necessary changes with the minimum of opposition. The main features of the changes based on this model include work intensification, deskilling and lower unit labour costs through reductions in staffing levels and/or lower relative rates of total remuneration. One possible way to minimise opposition to these changes is to try to convince staff of the benefit and/or inevitability of the changes, and this is achieved through isolating staff as individuals and seeking to convince them of the correctness of this new model management.

(p. 136)

What becomes apparent from such a reading of the theory and practice of performance management is that it has implications at a number of different levels: the personal, the institutional, the systemic and the societal. However, the boundaries and interconnections between these are all too often smudged and presumptions are smuggled in that there is no tension or dissension in moving across analytical boundaries. Perhaps the classic illustration of this lies in the implicitly invoked presupposition that what is good for the system is good for the individual – 'what's good for General Motors is good for the USA!' as the old saying goes. Also, any thoroughgoing analysis of performance management would need to take account of a variety of different lenses and standpoints which, in relation to education, would include

- learning, teaching and pedagogic perspectives;
- professional/union perspectives;
- managerial/economistic perspectives;
- technical/logistical perspectives;
- equity/social justice perspectives;
- social/political perspectives.

The official discourse of performance management, as exemplified for instance in the Green Paper, slides across these perspectives without any break of stride. Differentiating between perspectives in this way may serve an important analytical function: by revealing ways in which only certain kinds of perspectives are pulled into play in official discourse whilst others are sidelined or completely ignored; by providing a basis for distinguishing between and/or pulling together critical features which are derived from different levels or perspectives and which are held in separation.

The following quotation from Marsden and French, themselves quite critical of the principles and practice of performance management, reveal the subtlety of the controversies accompanying this managerial strategy and stress the need for secure analytical critique.

From the mid-1980s, the British public services have led the world in pioneering new performance management systems. Major changes in management information systems have been introduced with a view to clarifying management's goals, and to analysing the efficiency with which resources are used in achieving them. ... Although in public debate much has been made of the 'ideological' motivation of Mrs. Thatcher's and John Major's governments, the high cost of public services in the national budgets of all countries, and the increasingly complex demands placed on them by their citizens, have been at least as important a driving force behind the reforms. It is almost certainly the latter which explain the world-wide interest in the success or otherwise of Britain's public service reforms.

(p. 1)

Clearly there are no 'innocent readings' in this area. We would argue that for our purposes the following elements are of importance in grasping the significance of performance management. First, it is presented as a way of delivering the purposes and outcomes of the organisation in a way which is transparent and explicitly communicated. Second, from the viewpoint of the management as stakeholders, it enables them to identify and differentiate between participants in terms of the contribution they make to the achievement of these purposes and outcomes. In doing this it enables a more 'effective' distribution of the reward, training and progression resources of the organisation to enhance its capacity to meet established objectives and respond to the demands of change. Profitability, productivity, efficiency, value-addedness, and value-for-money or best-value are clearly key concepts in this respect. Third, for the employee, performance management is claimed to provide a clear specification as to what is expected, the targets/standards/criteria to be met and the rewards and other benefits which will result from meeting those criteria. It should also enable an employee to see where their contribution fits within the overall vision or scheme of the organisation. Further to this, an effective performance-management system should articulate with training or professional development provision and this in turn should mesh with the organisational models of progression and promotion (see also Lawn 1995). Taken together, all of these are founded on an organisational 'map' which locates people in various positions within the structure, clarifies the expectations attached to these positions, charts the dynamics of the relationships between the positions and specifies the potential lines of progression which exist between them. Fourth, in relation to the public sector, the situation is patently different from that within the private sector: we shall return to some of the detail later. However, for the government in its role as 'super-purchaser' of public services, the great promise offered by performance management lies in reductions in public-sector expenditure, and hence taxation levels, and the greater visibility of precisely how public resources are being distributed and to what effect. In short, it provides a proxy bottom-line accountability comparable to the private sector, and also conveys the image of the government operating as a responsible and rational 'consumer' on *our* behalf. All of this is centrally driven whilst being presented within a culture of decentralisation, delegation and disaggregation of 'institutional decision-making autonomy' to smaller units of delivery. But as Paul Hoggett (1996) has said,

... the British experience indicates that steering by use of incentives and sanctions and the setting of meta-level rules (what DiMaggio and Powell (1983) call 'the power to set premises') can be an extremely effective form of 'hands-off' control, indeed probably much more powerful than 'hands-on' regulation and direction.

(pp. 25–6)

Further concerns surrounding performance management

There are many different sources to which one could turn for analysis of 'performance management' both as an ideology and as a set of working practices. For example, we could delve into the world of management and personnel theory, we could explore the economics of labour and profitability, we could consider some of the historical and contemporary analyses which have been provided within the social policy literature, and, of course, we could look at the educational management literature. In our research we have found that much of the comment and analysis being presented in the 'academic' literature has been echoed in the responses to the current proposals coming from teachers, professional associations and unions.

We have already alluded to some of the important analytical comments which are made about performance management. Illuminating though they are, we cannot hope to rehearse here all the detailed questions about procedures, logistics, resourcing, timing, duties, responsibilities, training procedures, appraisal mechanisms and so on, around which so many practitioners, unions and professional associations have expressed deep gloom.[4] As the Professional Association of Teachers concluded its response to the Green Paper, quoting one of its members,

> The overly complicated and bureaucratic procedures proposed will make the headteachers' and senior managers' lives a nightmare. The proposals are, quite simply, unworkable!
>
> (PAT 1999, para. 59)

Marsden and French introduce a rather sanguine view of the relationship between pay and performance which sits uneasily with the speed and lack of forward planning with which the government are currently proceeding.

> ... although at first sight tying pay to performance may appear a simple and logical process, in practice there is a large number of problems that management has to overcome. ... The complexity of the linkages between pay and performance are such that only well-thought out schemes have any chance of success.
>
> (p. 4)

The NAHT make a comparable point when they say

> The Government is proposing to introduce the world's biggest performance management system without a proper structure to support it. The Green Paper gives the clear impression that it has not grasped the enormity of the exercise or the preconditions, including full costs, which must be met for its success.
>
> (NAHT 1999, p. 21)

Even a very supportive LEA officer said to us

> I mean there's a lot of good about it but it is trying to do so much isn't it? It is try-
> ing to re-structure the pay system at the same time as introduce performance-
> related pay, at the same time as introduce a performance management system
> and those three things are, need not be connected and in many ways shouldn't be
> connected either, you know. ... the pay issue so colours and dominates in the
> people's thinking about the validity of it. Whereas you need an agreed basis and
> acceptance of its validity, of its accuracy, of the methods that you use, you know,
> the sources of evidence you're going to draw on, of how you monitor, those
> things [need] to be accepted without money flowing ...

In the light of such comments we are led to question whether performance management is anything but a 'sophisticated' device for restructuring the pay element within
the education budget. By claiming to operate a rational and transparent system of pay
for performance which is founded on the notion of 'something for something', does
it in effect achieve the purpose of getting 'more for less'? The SHA makes it quite
clear how it interprets these questions.

> [the] SHA questions whether a system of performance related pay, such as that
> proposed for teachers, exists in any other profession. Such schemes have been
> seen to demotivate employees in other fields, especially where the scheme rests
> upon an inadequate general salary level or is cash-limited, and many schemes in
> the private sector have been abandoned.
>
> (SHA 1999, para. 5)

One of our interviewees showed concern about the impact of cash-limitations, or
what in the general literature is often described as the quota system.

> ... the teacher lets the head know that he or she wants to be considered for assess-
> ment and thereafter builds up the record for the portfolio of evidence ... the head
> teacher would say, that's splendid and you're really doing well but actually we
> haven't got any more money so you can build up your portfolio if you like but it
> might be a waste of time. But you also need, of course, the external assessor in-
> volved to moderate or to validate the head's judgment even if the go-ahead is
> given. I think that's a main issue, where this billion pounds over two years, an ab-
> solutely splendid sum of money to make available, but what happens after the
> two-year period is still a bit unclear.
>
> (LEA officer)

An officer whom we interviewed from a non-education sector union with long experience in the performance-management field summarised the quandary as follows:

> ... the current system isn't working because you've almost got the situation
> where the performance appraisal system is being driven by the pay system rather

than the other way round which was never the intention. Their sort of broad view is that performance pay should support the performance appraisal system. We're arguing that in reality it's turned out to be the other way round and that by linking it to pay it's actually discredited performance management and it's actually obscured or hindered the objectives of the performance management system because of the link to pay it's led to you know, people aren't confident that it's being operated in a fair manner because of the actual links with pay. … If we look at appraisal, which is a key element within the performance management system, that appraisal process could connect to a number of different subsidiary things. It could connect to staff development. It could connect to identifying training needs. It could connect to meeting certain specified targets or standards or levels of competence. It could connect to models of promotion and progression. And it could connect to pay. … driving by pay does a disservice or deflects from the value or the contribution that the other elements could make to the appraisal process.

There are also criticisms directed at assumptions being made about what motivates teachers and enables them to improve. There are fears that the demotivating effect for the majority of teachers will far outweigh the rewards for the few unless significantly more money is made available on a long-term basis to enable the majority to achieve the higher scales. Related to this are concerns that what motivates teachers is not simply money (though no-one has yet claimed that teachers could do with less of it). Even if individual self-interest were the overriding motivator (rather than a professional commitment to doing the best job possible), it has been pointed out that the proposals may turn out to be self-defeating in respect of the system as a whole. In reporting its members' responses, the SHA underlines the general point being made, namely that

> … there has been a clear and widespread view that the Government's proposals for performance related pay will not achieve the stated objectives. It is widely believed that the proposals will create divisiveness and jealousies amongst colleagues, threatening the collegiality which has been built up in schools over many years.
>
> (SHA 1999, para. 10)

The concern is that good educational practice or innovative teaching, far from becoming shared amongst a school staff, will be seen as a personal commodity to be sold in the internal market of the school. A teacher in a very positive school depicted it as follows:

> I just think it is going to be incredibly divisive, … people come into school and instead of sharing all your ideas and sharing everything that you do, I think it is just going to end up with people keeping everything for themselves and feeling, well if I'm going to get good results then I'm going to get it for me.

On the other hand this teacher felt that the majority of teachers are not motivated in the ways presupposed by policy-makers.

> I mean how many teachers are going to sit there, gosh I'm super, I'm going to go for that? Most teachers are in it for the job. They are not there to blow their own trumpet. And I don't know that those that should be recognised will ever get recognised.
>
> (Primary school teacher)

In addition, the term 'insulting' recurred in our interviews with teachers.

PRIMARY SCHOOL TEACHER: I mean if OFSTED had been in and looked at you and whatever – I've been inspected three times now and always got high ratings. Why should I set myself up for going through another hoop? It's just yet another hoop that you have to go through and you feel well, you know it's insulting, why should I have to keep proving myself?

IH: Does this mean you won't be applying to go through the performance threshold?

TEACHER: Absolutely not – just pay us a decent wage, we all work hard here.

The potential implications of this for relations between staff within schools and between schools and their constituent communities are well summarised by these comments from the NUT.

> The Government's proposals ... would profoundly damage the professional culture of co-operation and teamwork that is at the heart of successfully managed schools. The pressures caused by the performance management structure and the tensions between assessors and assessed would generate distrust and counter-productive competition between colleagues. In particular, serious divisions would develop between teachers separated by their success or failure in 'passing' the threshold.
>
> These differences would be exacerbated by their inevitable visibility to pupils – and to parents. Parental pressure would build for pupils to be taught by teachers who had passed. Anxiety and objections would build where pupils were taught by teachers who had not reached, had decided not to apply or, worse, had been failed in their applications.
>
> (NUT 1999, paras. 14/15)

One of our teacher interviewees expressed these concerns in almost identical terms.

> I think it makes a two-tier system. I think people who don't move through the threshold are going to feel that they are being looked at and thought, why not, why haven't you applied? Do you think you wouldn't be able to achieve it? And so people who are in that position are going to feel like a second-class citizen. ...

And there's no point in saying people don't know because there are parents on the Governing Bodies and things do get out, you know.

(Primary school teacher)

Since we cannot hope to engage with the full range of these issues we are limiting ourselves to some major general controversies which have powerful resonance for us and to which we have found ourselves returning.

Defining values, principles and criteria: issues of quality and quantity

These are key issues because it is on these that all of the other issues depend. Almost all contemporary analysts are keen to point out the vital significance of creating an agreed value framework within which to operate. Echoing the developmental/regulatory distinction we drew in the previous chapter, Rogers depicts performance management as potentially an element of a reflexive or learning process for institutions and individuals. He also points to the democratic implications of such an orientation.

> Performance Management is not just a process for ensuring that public service organisations and their employees are well placed to produce the performance which society requires of them, it is also part of the process by which performance itself is defined, by which criteria of performance are established and by which societal, political and managerial judgments are made of those who are performing. Performance Management creates the performance required of local authorities – it does not just ensure that local authorities are well enough managed to produce the required performance. (p. 3)

If performance management is to have a significance beyond the narrow question of performance-related pay, then the overall value system within which the whole framework is to be located needs to be negotiated. This also has to be something to which employees feel that they can express a commitment, otherwise it will not succeed in motivating and encouraging their commitment. Within the private sector this value framework can (arguably) be limited to material factors, for example, profitability, turnover or productivity and the criteria used within the performance-management framework can reflect this value structure. This is clearly not the case in the public sector generally, where

> determining the relevant dimensions of performance has been a major area of controversy across the public services as staff and their representatives have often argued that quantity is being stressed at the expense of quality ... deciding on valid criteria for performance measurement management is ... much more than a simple technical issue, but one which relates to people's beliefs about the goals of the service they work for. ... a great many staff are strongly committed to a certain idea of public service, and there is much disagreement about the suitability of the targets chosen by management.

(Marsden and French 1998, pp. 5–6)

There are echoes here of Australian experience where Smyth and Shacklock (1998) describe how professional discourses of teachers were often felt to clash with the managerially oriented manner in which the standards for ASTs were couched. They illustrate how the construction of the evidence base for application took so much time that it actually diverted teachers' time and attention away from the very thing that they were good at. They argue that such an approach can hence become counter-productive as an initiative because of its transference of energies. One of the primary school teachers we interviewed expressed this dilemma very cogently. Originally this teacher had worked in the financial sector and had been attracted to teaching

> ... because I wanted to give of myself. I wanted to be fulfilled. I mean at the end of the day, [finance management] is how much profit can you make on a packet of soap and that wasn't fulfilling me. So while I'm with the children, I really enjoy teaching.

But the changes that are now in train mean that as far as this teacher is concerned

> I'm giving less of myself to the children and giving more of it to pieces of paper.

This is posing a real dilemma.

> I don't want to give up teaching because I love the ... gleam in their eyes and that sort of thing. And yet you sort of think, well why am I doing this? Because you're working on Sundays. You're working in the evenings. I'm in at seven o'clock you know, and you think, this is lunacy. ... am I going to be doing this – I can't see myself doing this for the next twenty years. I really can't. And if I'm going to be pushing paper and doing lots of paperwork, I might as well get paid for it, you know.

One of our interviews was with a headteacher who regularly advised or inspected in other schools nationally. This very experienced and dynamic head of a stable, successful school said that one of the things which caused staff concern was

> ... the extent to which teachers feel they no longer control their own working lives. Increasingly, there are sets of regulations and requirements and expectations built around those teachers who are at the peak of their professional expertise and yet who don't have the autonomy to define how they work.

In their response to the Green Paper ATL made the following trenchant point under the heading of 'shared professional criteria':

> ATL has previously warned against the damaging effect of alterations to appraisal which would make it seem to teachers as little more than an assessment of them by others over which they have little control as to its direction or outcomes.
>
> (ATL 1999, p. 6)

In the Green Paper, the NPS framework is intended to stand as a set of proxy performance indicators. However, defining what is to count as an appropriate outcome in education is difficult enough; finding indices which adequately capture these outcomes is yet more difficult, and developing devices with which to appraise achievement of these outcomes is of yet another order. Certainly this cannot be adequately accomplished by imposing a preordained template and then claiming to have resolved the problem. As we shall see later there is a *genuine* problem as regards attempting to identify the particular contribution, say to a pupil's performance, which is contributed by any given teacher rather than by a whole history of teachers. There are also *real* issues about the significance of external factors which are quite literally beyond any school's or teacher's control. Further than this, there are *legitimate* questions to resolve about the extent to which certain key educational values are amenable in principle to conventional appraisal procedures and necessitate quite differently formulated procedures, for example collective appraisal, peer appraisal and community involvement. To take such a critical stance is not a flight from rigour but a redesignation of its constituent properties.

Standards and working the system

In order to sharpen this critique we need to consider directly the role of 'Standards' within the proposed process of restructuring and modernisation. The NPS provide the foundation criteria for the evaluation of the various forms of evidence which the teacher is meant to present and it is against these that the individual teacher's performance will be appraised. As one of our LEA interviewees said, ' ... appraisal is the glue that holds it together'. In order to 'meet the Standards' you have to be the kind of person that the Standards have in mind, capable of accomplishing the activities that the Standards entail, of living within and conducting the relationships presumed at different levels, and of working within the assumptions which form the Standard boundaries. As the previous chapter has indicated, the generation, form and content of the NPS have been and continue to be the subject of intense debate. This is likely to remain an issue of considerable uncertainty and anxiety, not least because it is unclear exactly how the regime of Standards will eventually become established. To add to the confusion, in a recent consultation document on performance management (DfEE 1999) standards for teachers receive virtually no mention. They are only alluded to in relation to the threshold and even here there is yet more uncertainty. In a recent explanatory note on 'how we expect the performance threshold to operate in 2000–2001' the DfEE said

> *What will the standards be?*
> Work is underway by the Hay Group to identify the characteristics of effective teaching which will underpin the standards. ... They are working – with schools – to ensure that the threshold arrangements are clearly and demonstrably rooted in recognised models of good teaching.
>
> (DfEE 1999f, p. 2)

The relationship between this and the work on the NPS framework which has already been put in place by the TTA and the DfEE, remains uncertain. As we shall see later, such initiatives also raise troubling questions about the government's perceived view of the role of the GTC in the establishment and negotiation of professional standards.

Equity issues

Later we shall be focusing our attention directly on issues of social justice. However, it would be inappropriate to leave this discussion without hinting at some of the important issues raised by the performance-management proposals. The procedures and practices of, for instance, appraisal, constitute the dynamics through which the *positions* designated within the performance-management structure get populated. In doing this they accomplish both a *distributional and relational* function at one and the same time (see Gewirtz 1998). A range of concerns have been expressed that the implementation of the system will be inconsistent and unfair. Although at a common-sense level it seems legitimate that people who work harder should receive greater rewards, in practice there are a host of logistical problems. For example, despite the apparent transparency of appraising staff against National Standards, in practice interpretation of the Standards means that judgment is always going to be a subjective process, grounded partly in the needs of the school as well as on the perceived talents of the individual teacher concerned. Australian evidence (Down *et al.* 1997; Smyth and Shacklock 1998) has indicated that those who 'succeed' are likely to be those in possession of 'valuable' (policy-enhanced) skills: for example, ICT capability. Leaving aside questions of favouritism or the tendency of managers to over-rate their own staff in an effort to retain them, those who have experienced the enhanced pay element of performance management seem less than sanguine about its supposed transparency. A recent letter to the *Times Educational Supplement* (23 July 1999) read

> As someone who has worked under a performance pay system for the whole of the 1990s, I would reassure teachers that performance-related pay will be nothing as simple as a crude relationship between results and payments.
>
> Payments there will be, for some, but such is the complexity of PRP, no one will know why they did or did not get the money.
>
> (Keith Flett, p. 16)

Related to this is the concern that those groups who have traditionally suffered discrimination within the labour market will experience even greater difficulty in negotiating the hoops and hurdles integral to the system being proposed. In a recent article commenting on the Green Paper, Ian Menter (1999) says

> One would expect a government which is committed to equality of opportunity to be signalling the importance of monitoring procedures designed to ascertain whether the achievement of promotion and increased remuneration is spread

evenly by gender, ethnicity and able-bodiedness. Nowhere is there any reference to the possibility of unfair outcomes of such new practices. ... After all it is not just important to increase recruitment from minority ethnic communities, it is crucial that career development opportunities are fully accessible to such recruits.

(pp. 48–50)

In Chapter 5 we shall explore in greater depth the social justice implications of the 'new regime' of performance management for teachers, for the teaching profession as a whole and for the social and political contextualisation of education. For the moment we simply signal that this issue has been a major concern of the teaching unions.

> ... The increase in discretion on pay decisions at the school level and the concentration of power over such decisions in the hands of the headteacher are not likely to promote fair and equitable pay decisions based on equal opportunities considerations.
>
> (NUT 1999, para. 94, p. 10)

As we have indicated, there is no explicit reference to a recognition of equity distribution, e.g. by ethnicity or gender, as significant in patterns of progression and promotion. Nor, in the technical documents accompanying the Green Paper is there, as yet, any reference to the skills required to monitor or deliver an equal-opportunities element within the performance-management model. This is despite the fact that, as the NUT argues, evidence in other occupational areas

> ... suggests that those points in the PRP system where management bias and subjectivity can enter – the appraisal, and the subsequent translation of the performance rating into a pay award – are the areas where discrimination can and will occur.
>
> (NUT 1999, para. 157, p. 18)

Indeed the NASUWT are even more helpful in their tutoring of the government – devoting a whole section of their consultation response to an analysis of the 'Proposals vulnerable to discriminatory impact'.

> It is highly regrettable that equality issues are not addressed, particularly when within the teaching profession there are recognised, significant imbalances in gender, race and disability. Consequently, as this factor is not acknowledged within the proposals, no system is set out to ensure discrimination does not occur in their application or to prevent the current imbalances being perpetuated or aggravated.
>
> (NASUWT 1999, para. 6.2, p. 24)

It is worthy of note that at no point in its detailed submission to the pay review body (STRB) does the DfEE deem it worthwhile making any reference to the issue of equal opportunities. One is forced to wonder whether such questions are seen as unimportant or somehow outside their zone of responsibility, or perhaps they have simply 'overlooked' them (Gillborn 1999).

Public-sector employees are increasingly working within regimes of performance management. This raises significant contemporary questions about the forms of regulation and control which are embedded within such transformations of occupational relations and their broader consequences for social relations in general. Brian Hoggett expresses some of the dilemmas in the following quotation.

> The paradox of Britain in the 1990's therefore is the co-existence of an unregulated economy with an excessively regulated public sphere. … unlike the Utopia of high trust, high skill, participatory firm commitment to quality drawn by some variants of the flexible-specialization thesis, what we seem to be heading towards in both the private and public sectors in the UK is the development of a high output, low commitment work culture in which trust has become a value of the past and where quality counts far less than quantity. …
>
> (Hoggett, p. 28)

Questions of the most enormous democratic significance are being raised by the increasingly porous nature of the relationships between what we used to call the public and private sectors. The discourse of 'professionalism' is being used in England to accomplish the task of redefining both the activity of teaching and the structural relationships between teachers. The boundary lines between these sectors, which have never been watertight, are becoming increasingly blurred under the impact of privatisation, market relations, deregulation, various forms of devolution and delegation of powers and responsibilities, and the emergence of what is sometimes described as the contract state. Into this catalogue we would now add the performance-management system being proposed by the Labour government as yet another example of this osmosis. Such considerations take us well beyond the confines of education policy, let alone the even more specific terrain of teacher education and professional development, but addressing them is critical if there is to be a sustained and informed public debate about 'effective' schooling. Questions about the direction of governance and decision-making in education policy are powerfully germane to any discussion on the future shaping of teaching and the teaching 'profession'. This is especially so since one of the significant features of the debate around the Green Paper has been the boundaries which have been drawn around the consultations. These have been conducted almost entirely within the confines of the educational establishment, with scarcely any recognition that the issues raised have significance and relevance for wider public constituencies. It is becoming ever more urgent that robust and representative governance structures are put in place which are capable of rethinking the nature and form of teaching, for, as Terri Seddon has put it,

> What is brought into view is not just schools and teachers, nor education and the state. Rather one can consider the changes in education in the light of large-scale

social and historical processes that are challenging traditional articulations of knowledge, power and social groups both in and beyond nation states.

(1997, p. 243)

Reformulation of teaching, teacher education and professional development is something which has a long history and which intermittently (as now) achieves a very high profile in the policy politics of education. From the background of the Green Paper proposals it is to these wider-ranging debates that we now turn.

4 Teachers' work and the language of professionalism

Commentators have long endeavoured to explain and account for the changing form and character of teachers' working lives. The work which teachers do occupies an intersection of many, often paradoxical, influences. Teaching falls within a web of social, economic, cultural, political and, in some cases, religious expectations, demands and cross-currents. At one moment teachers will be seen as curators in 'museums of social virtue' (Waller 1961), whilst in the next breath being exhorted to be tour guides on the information superhighway. None of this is in any sense new. Teachers have always had to negotiate, reconcile and struggle with competing priorities – it goes with the territory. Of course the territory is different in different schools and different contexts. Working with seven-year-olds is not the same as working with teenagers, the rural is not the urban, culturally diverse contexts are different from the 'white highlands'. It is developing the capacities and insights to work productively within such varied currents and situations which makes teaching such potentially creative and exciting work. So what is it that so many people seem to be identifying as different in the current context of teaching?

Teaching as an activity now comes with a much stronger official frame around it. We have argued that this takes the form of firmer definitions as to the purposes of teaching, clearer specifications of the what and how of teaching, more rigorous and assertive vetting and regulating procedures, and a 'fixing' of positions and functions within the structure of the occupation. In short, teaching as an activity has become much more tightly bounded, and this tighter bounding is externally defined and imposed. Having spent the previous chapters exploring the ways in which the NPS framework has been established and the performance-management model envisaged in the Green Paper, we shall, in this chapter, consider the assumptions about the nature of teaching that are entailed and its implications for teachers' work, sense of identity and 'professionalism'. For the moment we will rehearse the way in which teaching is construed in the effective schools movement, and then return to the issue of 'modernisation' and its implications for the structure of teaching.

Effective teachers for effective schools

The literature on 'effective' schooling and school improvement affords a prominent place to the development of effective teaching and school leadership in its accounts of the various factors which combine to make up an effective school. This drive for effectiveness and higher standards is directly tied into the National Curriculum, since the 'effectivity' of schools is predominantly judged in accordance with criteria derived from it, mediated through examination results, assessment gradings and the performance indicators of OFSTED inspection reports. This process has been described as one facet of a developing 'audit society, obsessed with constant checking and verification' (House of Commons Select Committee 1999, p. x). The resulting league tables have subsequently been linked to the fostering of competition and a market orientation which is part of the drive for quality. A variety of alternative types of schools has been, and continues to be, introduced to 'enhance' the choice and diversity available to parents as proxy consumers. In the light of such pressures, schools and other educational institutions have been increasingly driven to market themselves and their qualities. Concomitantly, teacher education, professional development and quality teaching are to be interpreted through the lens of such 'effectivity'. Thus in her initial announcement concerning the NCITT, Gillian Shephard (then Secretary of State for Education) said that it would be

> Based on the National Curriculum for pupils, [and] will specify the essentials of what must be taught to trainee teachers in each core subject . ...
>
> (DfEE 1996, Annex p. 1)

In short, the definition and specification of what it means to be and become an 'effective' teacher became indissolubly tied to the definition of knowledge and knowing as designated within the National Curriculum and as evaluated in 'practice' via OFSTED inspections. Subsequent developments and extensions of these NCITT requirements (for example, in the form of the literacy and numeracy programmes) have been framed in accordance with centrally driven prescriptions concerning what and how children should be taught. Also, given that the Standards identified within the Green Paper are intended to build upon the foundation of the QTS Standards, we have seen how this model of effectiveness underpins teachers' progression throughout their careers.

In many ways all of this makes eminent 'common sense'. Who could possibly question such a coherent and strategic vision? It surely makes no sense to have established an overall policy regarding school education without at the same time ensuring that the teaching force is capable of delivering that policy. In order for this to be accomplished, trained leaders need to be equipped with the managerial skills to ensure that the policies will be translated into effective practice. Similarly, it is necessary to know who within schools is responsible for which aspects of the policy, what their responsibilities entail, and, so the argument goes, be able to reward those who show the greatest capacity to undertake such responsibilities. In order for stasis in the system to be avoided, a tailored training and development programme needs to ensure a supply of fresh, appropriately skilled staff to step into levels of responsibility when needs and opportunities arise. This is broadly the training and development model within which the TTA and DfEE have been working. It is a model which appears to be superficially plausible and precisely tailored to deliver the necessary enhancement in school standards and effectiveness.

Why then might we want to raise questions about such an approach? Certainly not because we are not committed to improving pupils', students' or teachers' educational experiences. Certainly not because we are already well satisfied with the quality of learning experiences currently provided in schools. And certainly not because we are unconcerned about how current teaching and learning will best enable us to educate 'the citizens of the future'. Our concerns stem from disagreements with the value position upon which this work is grounded. They stem from differences as to the adequacy of the policies being proposed to achieve their stated outcomes, even taken on their own terms. They stem from alternative perspectives on the effectiveness debate and from concern about the procedures through which the model has been established and is being put into place. Finally, the very conceptions of schooling, education, society and the future upon which the model is founded seem to us highly questionable.

One of our most basic concerns about current definitions of school effectiveness is that they contain no sense that any relevance is accorded to where students come from, the nature of their life experiences, or their prospective destinations. An Australian commentator, Laurie Angus (1993) has neatly identified the assumptions underpinning such an approach and their implications for the model of the teacher and teaching within which they operate.

> ... educational practice is conceived of in a particularly mechanical way. ... In keeping with economistic definitions of effectiveness, it is the bit that comes between 'input' and 'outputs'. It is seen largely as a set of techniques, the 'core technology', for managing 'throughput' rather than a complex and always unpredictable process of ongoing construction of educational practice. Practice is imposed rather than constructed, negotiated or asserted; it is a set of techniques to be employed by teacher technicians on malleable pupils.   (p. 337)

There are a number of ways in which our concerns return us to developments in NPM and managerialism. For example, school effectiveness arguments are firmly anchored in the broader issues of competitiveness which frame and contextualise much current public policy and practice, both nationally and globally. If the quality of teaching is crucial in making some schools more effective than others, so the argument goes, then we need to produce more effective teachers. Joel Spring (1998) quotes Blair as an exemplar of that internationally dominant set of assumptions which claim that

> In today's world there is no more valuable asset than knowledge. The more you learn, the more you earn. It's as simple as that. Education is an economic imperative.
>
> (Blair 1997)

Within the domestic public policy arena, as we have seen, the concept of 'effectivity' has come to occupy a central position in the justifications for transformations in the wider field of public management. Any ambiguity and dispute surrounding the definition of 'effectivity' are officially camouflaged by the mantra-like incantation of 'economy, efficiency and effectiveness' but even the most cursory glance at the literature on public policy reveals intense discussion about the content and meaning of these concepts which fully mirror debates that have been taking place in education. Similarly, if it is only possible to speak sensibly about the effectiveness of schools in the light of clearly specified criteria, it is also obvious that the regulatory apparatus, performance indicators and accountability mechanisms, as well as the procedures established for recording and reporting, all become critical. It is precisely the translation of such seemingly neutral, technical requirements into practice that reveals problems in the measures of effectiveness and improvement. And, of course, it is these which provide the frame within which teaching is to be conducted and its 'effectivity' calculated.

Leadership

Like much of the more general 'managerial' literature, many authorities in the school effectiveness field have identified 'leadership' as occupying a critical position. It was therefore no coincidence that of all the many places in which the TTA could have begun its work, one of its very first initiatives was directed towards headteachers, nor that this constituency has remained centre-stage throughout. The DfEE has underlined this significance recently by according heads a central role within the new performance management proposals and, following the Quinquennial Review of the TTA, bringing responsibility for headship back beneath the Department's aegis and proposing the establishment of the National Leadership College. But the question of how the role of the head is conceived within different conceptions of what constitutes an effective school is a matter of considerable debate. Unfortunately the model represented by the TTA-initiated NPQH training presented a dominantly hierarchical, 'hands-on' management model which placed other participants in the school community in a largely responsive relationship to the head's vision. For example, in the *National Standards for Headteachers* (TTA 1998c), heads 'embody for the pupils, staff, governors and parents, the vision, purpose and leadership of the school' and they 'provide educational vision and direction which secure effective teaching' (p. 9). Under such a model, to quote Angus (1994) again,

> Other organisational participants, such as teachers, parents and students, ... are generally viewed as essentially passive recipients of the leader's vision. ... on the basis of this account of leadership, the main skill required of most participants is for them merely to adopt the leader's vision and slot into the leader's definition of school culture. ... The elitist implication of this view is that leaders are more visionary and trustworthy than anyone else.   (p. 86)

However, we know from our experience of working with headteachers and from the growing literature on the subject that there are *other* models of leadership (Leithwood *et al.* 1999) that would emphasise more democratically oriented capacities. Writing about 'school cultures' in the Danish context, where policy is less centrally driven, Lejf Moos (1996), says

> The Folkeskole is not the embodiment of the headteacher's beliefs or values. The vision or mission of the school is not disseminated from the top down. ... where a discussion of goals and values takes place, it is a shared dialogue between teachers and 'management'.
>
> (p. 23)

This is an ideal which would be echoed and even extended to include other stakeholding members of the community. To that extent, Glatter's (1996) comments would resonate with many.

> ... we in 'mainstream' educational management have become too preoccupied with what might be called the institutional side of leadership and management to the extent of disregarding or at least underemphasising policy and contextual factors. In doing so we may be playing into the hands of those who accuse educational management of being too technocratic and mechanistic and of paying insufficient regard to values.
>
> (p. 3)

Paying regard to values is no easy matter, as those developing the Scottish Professional Qualification for Headship discovered (Reeves and Casteel 2000). We become inexorably drawn into questions about the social and political presumptions which underpin what it is that 'leaders' are expected to achieve (Grace 1995). Lurking within the detail of current leadership and management proposals are two general issues, one of which is education-specific; the other locates these education-related developments within a wider social frame.

The first issue is that schools are already quite differentiated organisations: headteachers, deputy headteachers, senior teachers, curriculum coordinators, team leaders, heads of departments, posts of responsibility and heads of year form just the beginning of a list which could be continued. Current proposals both reconstitute the organisational and managerial scheme within a finely grained, hierarchical model and provide much closer and more detailed specification of the positions within that scheme. By providing training within this specification, it also defines how occupants of these positions relate to others within the scheme and ascribes 'line-management' responsibilities and accountabilities to the people privileged to have received training. This, in turn, unproblematically locates individuals as 'leaders' or 'led' – binaries that become internalised as 'the natural order of things'. These orientations have deep implications for the nature and texture of social relationships within schools and their constituencies and are predicated upon a particular version of 'leadership' which delimits the negotiating space accessible for other, competing styles of leadership.

Comparable transformations in social relationships have been widely discussed in other sectors of the public service. These have often been highlighted by references to the professional/managerial split. In the health, criminal justice, housing and other social welfare sectors, it is being claimed that there is a growing divide between the orientations of those who see themselves as occupying client-related professional positions and the managers who administer the service as a whole. As a corollary to this the power of these areas is also being judged as shifting towards managerial 'leaders'. At times the managers in this context have been imported from outside the service, often from outside the public sector altogether, but in addition, 'professional' positions have been redefined as 'managerial' with attendant retraining and job-respecification. As we were writing this book a school in the North of England appointed a Chief Executive rather than a headteacher, and that appointee came from outside the schooling system. We also know that the embryonic National Leadership College is intended to be heavily influenced by inputs from outside education. Clearly it would be blinkered not to make best use of skills, competences and aptitudes which reside outside education, but there is a debate yet to be had about the 'fitness for purpose' of importing practices from elsewhere because they are presumed to be more effective. Janet Newman (1994) amongst others has argued that such a reformulation of management and leadership has important implications in gender terms. It remains to be seen over time whether the redefinition of leadership within schools will constitute an erosion of the limited opportunities available to minority ethnic teachers and women within middle and senior management structures. We shall return to these questions later but clearly they have wide implications for the redefinition of 'professionalism', for the social/occupational control of the teaching force, and for the social distribution of occupational patterns of social justice.

Defining the effective teacher and 'modernising' the structure of teaching

Leaving on one side for the moment the highly contentious concept of 'professionalism', it is now becoming clear from the Green Paper and subsequent elaborations that the government feels that it is close to establishing an overall shape for teaching which will take us through into the new century.

The major elements of the structure are laid in position. Even before career entry and then through all stages of professional development, procedures have been put in place for coordinating and regulating the occupational lives of teachers. The lines of progression are set out. The Standards which are to pertain to various structural positions have been established. The formal progression and appraisal mechanisms which will locate persons to positions are in place. The resource allocations and reward structures have been outlined. Regulatory, monitoring and surveillance procedures and agencies are up and running. Those bodies with responsibilities for these activities, whether schools, LEAs or HEIs, will increasingly find themselves operating in accordance with priorities, regulations, criteria and indicators established at a distance, with limited scope for adaptability or autonomous action at a local level. Taken together, this constellation constitutes a powerful intervention which both reshapes the nature of teaching and presages fundamental restructuring of lines of power, responsibility and accountability within the teaching profession. The various strands of activity interconnect and constitute a much more assertive and systematic control of the education and development of teachers.

Underpinning these moves are mechanistic and technicist assumptions which reshape what may or may not be construed as 'professional'. In terms of content and approach, teachers' work is being calibrated to the extent that whole areas of their occupational lives are being pre-defined in accordance with requirements which circumscribe the degrees of choice and decision-making within which they operate. In constituting the indicators on the basis of which teachers' performance will be evaluated and rewarded, such specifications represent the very antithesis of what is normally associated with the notion of 'professional'. Yet on an everyday basis teachers will continue to have to make decisions, selected from the available range of practices, tailored to specific circumstances, within the realisation that consequences will need to be sensitively evaluated and reflected upon. It is this which begins to meet the criteria for critical practice and to move us beyond the perception of teaching as 'technicist delivery'. Yet insofar as such activities move outside the 'sight-line' of the established performance indicators they become literally lost from view and hence are overlooked in the evaluation of schools' or teachers' work. A friend of ours (not a teacher) who has been working in secondary schools trying to overcome young people's reluctance to register as voters, complained that she was having great difficulty negotiating with schools which were 'being OFSTEDed'. She grasped that they were under pressure but was mystified that it was felt that OFSTED would not find such work worthy of note if they went into a school where it was happening.

Recently it has also become apparent that there are moves further into the heart of teaching by making 'pedagogy' central to issues of improvement/effectiveness. Having claimed that there exists 'a vow of silence on pedagogy' (which seems as extraordinary as accusing the Catholic church of refusing to pay attention to the soul), Anthea Millett (1996b), laying down a marker for this move, proposed a pedagogic model composed of

> four soundly-based elements: the need for a secure command of the material to be taught; the need actively to teach; the need to have high expectations of pupils, and ensure appropriate pace and challenge; the need to have effective working relations with pupils. (p. 6)

Apart from rendering invisible the labours of all those people who have spent the greater part of their professional lives working with beginning teachers to recognise and develop precisely these elements of expertise, the real issue around pedagogy is its relevance for a changing world. An OECD (1994) report, for example, states that

> Increasingly, teachers are diversifying their pedagogical strategies to incorporate pupil-centred and small group techniques, which are more consistent with contemporary theories of human learning and also more appealing to students who prefer more interactive learning. ... The complex interactions of personalities and pedagogies make classroom dynamics increasingly unpredictable, and teachers must be adept at improvisation. As there is more to think about, reflection becomes an expected part of teachers' work, ... Collaboration among teachers is also increasingly being required, ... (p. 70)

In contrast to this, the model of tight regulation and surveillance being established in the English context represents a move in the opposite direction where teachers are expected to know and follow guidelines for 'delivering' content through procedures established from above. Similar trends have been widely and critically discussed in other spheres of public policy. For example, an article on social work 'competences' by Lena Dominelli (1996) provides a chilling comparison with the experiences of those working in education. Paradoxically, this restrictive formulation is presumed to provide a sense of purpose, value and progression for practising teachers, and a motivational inducement for people considering entry to the occupation. Thus what many would see as symptomatic of the *de*-professionalisation of teaching – namely, the increasingly dominant machinery of regulation – becomes redefined within the language of 'professional standards' as the very foundation of 'professionalism'.

It may be claimed that we have caricatured both the TTA's position and subsequent policy developments and that there is no intention of introducing such a mechanistic model of teaching. However, for a debate on this question to be possible there would need to be a context within which it could be conducted. As we argue below, it is just such contexts which are being progressively removed and undercut in schools, in HEIs and in training and development partnerships. A major concern is that, apart from the 'thin democracy' of consultations, definitions of 'good' teaching, 'relevant' professional development and career enhancement have all been placed beyond debate. For example, we have already seen that criteria for 'effectiveness' have increasingly been tied to central prescription and what can be measured. The implications of such issues go well beyond a concern with teaching. Since teaching and learning are symbiotically linked, such a reconfiguration of teaching also marks a major claim to define what it is going to mean to become an educated, or at least 'schooled', person. Tight boundaries are being placed around the nature of the 'thinkable'. Built directly into these developments are silences which convey deep messages as to the models of teaching and learning within which the policy is working. These are not simply models of how teachers should teach, although these are certainly present, but also implicit models of how the policy-makers see teachers learning and the theories of commitment and motivation with which they operate. It is implications of this order which move the issue away from the allegedly particularistic concerns of a group of 'self-interested professionals', closeted in their 'ivory towers' far from the 'realities of everyday-life', and transform it into a contest about the nature of the social and what it means to be a citizen, equipped with educational resources in the broadest sense. If teachers become so tightly controlled, where is the space for difference of viewpoint within the system? The Advisory Group on Citizenship (QCA 1998) made the points with great clarity when they said

> It is vital that teachers have the knowledge, understanding, skills and confidence needed to be successful in the interactive teaching approaches which underpin effective learning in citizenship education. (p. 30)

> For teachers to confine their endeavours to the inculcation of knowledge and the transmission of skills, no matter how useful they may be, is to restrict the

enterprise of schooling to just a scheme of training. Education, as opposed to mere training, requires an encounter with other experiences, such as active participation in group decision-making, and the development of further qualities of mind beyond retentive memory. (p. 57)

Our concern is that there is a debate which demands attention but which appears to figure little on the agenda within which a 'quality' teaching force is being prepared for the coming years. For example, why are we not asking what questions or problems this new form and structure of teaching are intended to address/resolve? Where are the contexts in which the principles, values, assumptions, presuppositions and ideologies which underpin these new developments are being rendered explicit and open to debate? Given all that is known about the problematic nature of the concept of 'standards', endlessly repeating that the purpose of the policies is to 'raise standards' becomes a contentless assertion, not a statement of principle or strategy. Similarly, although it is claimed that '[T]ackling teacher supply and recruitment should be the TTA's top priority in the next phase of its work' (DfEE 1999a, p. 1), there seems to be little understanding of what might motivate or even inspire teachers to enter or remain in teaching. Few currently labouring with the difficulties of supply and recruitment would dispute the urgency of the TTA's task, but many are questioning the wisdom with which the issues are being confronted and the style and strategy being adopted to address them. As one of our major teacher associations (ATL 1996) has said,

> Why, when other employers are valuing autonomy, talent, creativity, intrinsic motivation towards quality and improvement, active participation, high employee self-esteem, and investment in continuing professional development, would one enter the low-trust, tight control, centrally and seemingly ideologically defined environment of teaching? (p. 4)

Modernising teaching

Our earlier discussion of the Green Paper mapped the broad contours of the way in which the occupation of teaching is being structurally 'modernised'. This makes it possible to envisage a fairly coherent account of the possible shape of a teacher's career from the point of entry through the different stages of their working life if they wished to pursue progression. The dynamics involved in the process of moving from one stage to another have also been 'formally' outlined though the precise details have yet to emerge of the kinds of things teachers would need to do, the nature of the training they would be expected to follow, how they would know how to make these moves, who would be responsible for ensuring that they knew about these processes, how they would be sponsored and by whom, and who would judge them to have done what was necessary to make the transitions. In relation to each of these various stages and levels the consequences for the contractual obligations, pay and conditions under which teachers would be working have also been established, though it will be some time before the interplay emerges between the DfEE, the GTC, the STRB, schools themselves and professional associations or unions in terms of responsibility for establishing final working conditions and levels of remuneration. It is also an open question as to what differences (and of what kind) will result for teachers working in different types of school. The consequences for individual teachers who decide not to enter into this model of career progression are not known, nor whether this is even a choice that individuals will be able to make. It may be that obligations on teachers to undertake such moves become formally or informally established with direct or indirect sanctions for those opting out of the model of progression. In terms of policy outcomes, it also remains to be seen to what extent the proposed changes constitute a genuinely radical transformation of the existing situation within which teachers spend their working lives and organise their careers. For example, given this pattern of restructuring it remains to be seen what proportion of the profession is envisaged as occupying the new positions and how these compare with the structural characteristics of teaching which already exist. In marketeers' terms, are we in the presence of a massive (and costly) exercise in re-badging or a genuine exercise in cultural and structural re-engineering? If the latter, it is important to consider who might be the winners and losers in this new shape of teaching. This moves the argument from general considerations of the working conditions under which all teachers operate, through to more specific reviews of the likely impact on particular categories or cohorts of actual or prospective teachers. We shall return to this issue of opportunity structure and social justice in some detail in the next chapter.

Clearly such questions are of enormous significance and material relevance for all of those who will find themselves working in education. It is not yet possible to do more than present them as an agenda of concerns which it is to be hoped will be rigorously monitored, analysed and evaluated. We cannot afford to allow the motivation and morale of teachers to decline even further, with the concomitant disastrous consequences for recruitment and retention and, perhaps even more damagingly, for the educational experiences made available to future cohorts of learners. Demoralised and demotivated teachers are unlikely to make effective teachers, nor attractive and inspiring role models.

For the moment we shall 'park' these highly specific concerns and try to step behind the policy to address its broad context and what C. Wright Mills once called its 'vocabulary of motives'. In common with others, we have already made reference to the fact that what is currently happening in education and public policy can best be read through an appreciation of the 'big picture'. This itself is a complex canvas with globalisation, managerialism and newly emerging patterns of cultural and social diversities at play across its surface. Since we are in this chapter focusing on the occupational refashioning of teaching, we shall add to the complexity by considering contemporary changes in the labour process.

Once we think of teaching as a large body of employed people then it becomes relevant to articulate the changes which are being put in place with contemporary analyses of the restructuring of work. How, if at all, does what is happening in teaching link to other areas of public-sector employment and to other 'professionalised' occupations where it is being claimed that a process of hierarchical restructuring of working conditions and control procedures is occurring? This is leading to the segmentalisation of workers into primary, secondary and peripheral elements of the labour force, with all its consequences for social justice. If there are such links, then what are the implications for the control and regulation of teaching and for the nature of what this means teachers can and cannot do in their everyday work? Why are these changes happening now and why are they taking these forms?

So far we have talked about the bigger picture in terms of NPM or managerialism. In reality these are broad terms within which are a welter of debates and controversies concerning different ways of understanding and explaining the changes, including, during the past decade, a significant body of scholarship around analyses of teachers' work. Terms such as 'fragmentation', 'empowerment', 'intensification', 'flexibility', 'segmentalisation', 'individualisation', 'multi-skilling', 'teamwork', 'hierarchy', 'resistance', 'surveillance', 'performativity', 'power and regulation', and numerous others, have gained currency as descriptors of the changing material circumstances and regimes within which teachers in various national and regional contexts have experienced their working lives. Such accounts have their parallels in narratives of work in other public and non-public sectors. A bewildering array of explanatory frameworks orbit these lexicons, ranging from 'corporate managerialism', 'the contract state', 'post-industrialism', 'post-Fordism', 'neo-liberalism' all the way through to the ubiquitous 'post-modernism'. As others have found before us, teaching, and we are sure other occupations, resolutely fails to fall comfortably into these empires of the mind. None of this is intended to belittle the significance of attempts to make sense of these chaotic changes. What it does, however, is highlight the contradictory and paradoxical nature of teaching. It can be at one and the same time an activity within which there can be a sense of 'empowerment', albeit experienced within a regime of surveillance and regulation. Ambition in an individualistic sense may gain its sustenance within a school atmosphere of sustained teamwork. Ethnographic accounts of teachers have revealed time and again the ways in which apparently clear-cut differentiations smudge into one another. Perhaps the reason why trying to make sense of these tensions is so confusing is that we are collectively asking the wrong questions. Perhaps we are searching for resolutions of our dilemmas in the wrong places, namely, in precisely those official discourses which are intended to play a game which is not of our choice.

The work of teaching

In drawing attention to the common features which exist between the ways that teaching and other forms of work are being depicted both within and outside the public sector, we can quickly identify comparable languages being used and referred to. For example, when Christopher Pollitt (1993) wrote

> Managers now work to create the right 'climate', to encourage identification with corporate goals, high motivation, internalisation of 'constructive attitudes' …

> (p. 24)

he could have been writing about teaching, but equally about other areas of public provision, or a whole raft of commercial organisations in the manufacturing or service sectors. He could also have been referring to work in widely dispersed geographical locations, nationally and internationally. Certain themes insistently recur in discussions about the changing nature and shape of work, although contextual variations are significant for detailed analysis. Of course it makes a difference whether one is working as a teacher, or an ambulance driver, or on the line for a new technology firm. But the language and procedures which frame and define the nature of the activities are beginning to bear striking similarities to each other – as indeed are statements of principles and values and techniques of monitoring, evaluation and control. So the language of 'vision', 'mission', 'standards', 'leadership', 'quality', 'value-for-money', 'choice', 'transparency', 'flexibility', 'commitment', and so on can be traced snaking their way across corporate plans, mission statements and institutional charters.

In this respect, we have been very taken by the apposite nature of the arguments put forward by Gee, Hull and Lankshear (1996). Although at various points they directly address issues of education, predominantly they direct their attention to a consideration of the impact of 'new capitalism' on the definition and structure of work and working relationships. The illustrations upon which they focus are drawn from a high-tech electronics firm in Silicon Valley, USA and a rural village in Nicaragua. However, their argument sharply illuminates education in its beam. In order to follow the thread of their argument we shall need to introduce the term 'Discourse' which they use to describe a 'set of related social practices'.

> A Discourse is composed of ways of talking, listening, reading, writing, acting, interacting, believing, valuing, and using tools and objects, in particular settings and at specific times, so as to display or to recognise a particular social identity. ... The Discourse creates social positions (or perspectives) from which people are 'invited' ('summoned') to speak, listen, act, read and write, think, feel, believe, and value in certain characteristic, historically recognisable ways, in combination with their own individual style and creativity. ... Discourses create, produce, and reproduce opportunities for people to be and recognise certain *kinds of people*.
>
> (p. 10)

Expressed in these terms it is apparent that the Green Paper and its attendant policy implication constitutes a Discourse. Its presentation, structure and detailed proposals amount to an attempt to reconfigure the ways in which teachers talk about, think and act in relation to their teaching. Within its proposals it further presents a technological apparatus (what Gee *et al.* call 'tools and objects') such as standards, appraisal, performance thresholds, inspection frameworks, and so on with which teachers are expected to operate and through which their activities are perceived. The Green Paper also lays out a preferred structure of positions within teaching and provides a guide as to what it would need for someone to make themselves available for such opportunities as may exist. Some might say that there is nothing much new in all of this, that this is the way in which persuasion and commitment have always been built and sustained. What Gee *et al.* help us to grasp, however, is the complexity and range of the procedures which are currently being put in place across so many diverse fields, the interactions that are at play between cultural, structural, institutional and personal levels of impact, and the intentionally obscured dominance of certain values and goals underpinning the policies. So, for example, in relation to the Green Paper there are embedded within the proposals, assumptions about hierarchies, about what counts as evidence for progression, about theories of motivation, about models of teaching/learning and personal relationships, about the balance between individual and collective systems, about compliance and contestation, about visions of and for the future, and so on. They themselves are very clear about the obscured yet core tensions inherent in such 'visions' when they say

> ... the very language that objectifies the ends, goals, and vision of the organization, and which thus underlies the culture of the organization, is *insulting* if spoken directly to the workers/partners ... The problem can be put another way: real commitment and belief, as well as real learning, require that learners be able to engage in genuine dialogue and contestation with viewpoints, but such genuine contestation is ultimately problematic in a business setting where in the end, profit is the goal and the competition is at one's heels. ...   (pp. xiii–xiv)

This returns us to the culture of 'competitiveness' to which we have previously referred, but additionally it raises two other issues which have figured in our interviews with education workers. First, there is this term 'insulting', which may seem to be somewhat overdrawn. However, in interviews with teachers we did find that this was an idea which they themselves frequently used in describing how they felt about their exclusion from genuine debate and decision-making. The sense we gained was that they felt they had views about the values, principles and practices which should underpin education which they would have liked an opportunity to air. And, as an extension of this, that things were being done *to them* over which they had little say and less control. This was demeaning to their 'professional' knowledge and experience and also left them feeling 'off-message' in every sense.

> This year was crunch time for me. I actually didn't want to come back after the holiday because I was thinking, well here we go, numeracy hour now and just when you think you've got a year to consolidate, there's something else new comes in and that has gone home much more this year than any other year I think. And it's made me quite depressed, you know. It's the methodology that's at the root of my problems. It's telling me that you do it this way. But the pace is too great for the children we've got. And you're thinking, well hang on a minute, they haven't had like four years' head start. They've just arrived in the country and they're are coming into this cold. I mean I've even found an Inset day has made me feel quite depressed, I can't get on top of it.
>
> (Primary school teacher)

Issues of compliance and commitment were given a further twist in the following interview where a very experienced teacher reported an attempt by staff to debate with a head why a particular policy was being adopted and were unambiguously reminded of the 'ultimately problematic' nature of contestation in the competitive inter-school environment.

> ... the new head came in with a very, very different style entirely. Very much a business manager. ... she's always appointed people, I don't think that are necessarily compliant but that will go along with her vision ... there was a lot of anti-feeling in the school about a proposal that staff thought might adversely affect other schools in our area – just a lot of questioning really which she couldn't understand – why people would question it. Why were staff wanting to disadvantage the school, it was almost disloyalty really. The school isn't an active union school – there was only one meeting but that caused tremendous bad feeling and you know, staff that were fronting that meeting were just thought of as totally disloyal and then it became quite unpleasant. ... The person who spoke on behalf of the staff, the head took it as a personal attack ... that person eventually left ... I think it was made clear that there wasn't much of a future there in the promotion stakes.
>
> (Secondary school teacher)

As Gee *et al.* argue, the evasions and tensions embedded in the new work regimes create real problems of commitment and loyalty in and for organisations which are increasingly being driven by external and internal competitive demands and ideologies. In the face of what they describe as the 'danger of widespread cynicism', they see contemporary management texts as proposing two solutions:

> ... One solution is 'visionary leadership' ... the second proffered solution to gaining 'over the top' commitment: not visionary leaders but the creation and maintenance in the organization of 'core values' and a culture that induces (socializes) everyone into such values: ... Fast capitalist texts are not simply attempts to describe a reality already in place; they are what we might call 'projective' or 'enactive' texts ...   (pp. 31–3)

We have already seen both of these strategies at play in the Discourse around the effective schooling movement and the standards industry. Nonetheless it is salutary and educative to witness precisely the same devices at play in widely diverse sectors. It is also powerful to view a policy document, such as the Green Paper, as a 'projective or enactive' text, namely, as something which is intended to call into being the very institutions, beliefs, and persons which it depicts. As Gee *et al.* see it, this is what is truly at stake: 'new kinds of people engaged in new social practices' (p. xiv).

In giving an account of their work it is important to recognise that Gee *et al.* do not fall into the trap of mechanistic determinism. Debates do go on, Discourses clash and individuals will insist on having their say and mounting challenges. At all levels of our experiences of working on this research we have found individuals and institutions putting forward quite different visions and interpretations to counter 'official models'. Modifications take place which represent the interventions of quite contradictory value positions, and, on the ground, things are enacted which bear only a tangential connection to the initial intentions. Clark and Newman (1997) capture the politics of this well in their general comments on the discourse of HRM.

> ... it is also important not to assume that new subjects can simply be read off from new discourses. There are dangers in assuming that the disciplinary and surveillance processes which subject individuals to new forms of power and control are effective. We would want to emphasise that subjects are caught up in the interplay of different, and sometimes conflicting, discourses. ... When we explore how managerialism is enacted in practice ... what we find is a picture of uneven development, variability and complex articulations of old and new regimes. ... issues of consent, compromise and contradiction are important in theorising the process of change. (pp. 94–5)

All of this we entirely agree with. And yet it is equally important not to romanticise the possibilities of inevitable resistance. The issues of 'consent, compromise and contradiction' will not take care of themselves and the debate has often been so constructed that it becomes extremely difficult to find a basis on which to engage. This has been a very common experience for those wishing to engage critically with educational debates over 'standards and effectiveness' or who have wished to swim against dominant policy tides, for example, over the reintroduction of selective procedures in schooling, or the imposition of formal literacy and numeracy demands on very young children. Again we can do no better in setting up the democratic and personal tensions involved than by referring to Gee *et al.*'s work.

> ... This indeed is the great dilemma in regard to Discourses: it is difficult to criticize and change them from *within* (they will simply dis-member us) or from *without* (why should they listen to an outsider?). ... A Discourse perspective simply argues that historic sociocultural struggles are enacted by and on people's bodies and minds, often with much pain and injustice. (pp. 13–14)

Having reached this point, we shall now return to some of the more general arguments about the nature of contemporary work. It may be that they will help us to understand what has been happening to teaching and also enable us to move our argument forwards. It is self-evident that changes are taking place in the nature of the job market, the character of the labour process within that market and the control procedures which are being implemented within that process. At the most general level there are hesitant discussions about the prospective impact of the 'information revolution' on the overall levels of employment, changes in the patterns of segmentation and responsibility within work, and the stability or impermanence of employment once acquired. Much of the debate in official circles is informed by the implicit realisation that there exists a decreasing interrelationship between the 'health' or 'competitiveness' of economies (global, regional, national or local) and high levels of employment within those economies. 'Lean, mean and flexible' and 'downsized' are descriptive terms which are now applied to economies judged to be competitive, efficient and hence, worthy. This is a moral calculus which, whilst not entirely new, has begun to shift to a new consensus. Expressed most directly it means that capital no longer 'needs' as much labour as it has done during previous periods of industrialisation. Further to this, such labour as it continues to require is 'needed' in a different form, for different periods of employment and under changed social relations of control, production and consciousness. Of course all of these general comments and conditions must be hedged around with a recognition that they will take variant forms in different areas, different industries and, for example, between public and private sectors of employment.

Whilst our research projects have not been directly focused on the detail of such issues, we have nonetheless encountered their reverberations in every aspect of teaching. Teachers form a significant fraction of the labour force within most national economies. In Australia commentators have more readily accepted this 're-ality' by openly talking about the education 'industry', a form of language which still rings discordantly in English and European ears. Financing the employment of teachers also absorbs a large proportion of the education budget, which itself constitutes a high proportion of the GNP. Additionally, teaching is also at the heart of the process of producing and reproducing the complex technical and social relations which characterise this newly emergent, embryonic world. Teachers are being required to equip generations of learners with the skills they need in order to be useful for employment when it offers itself. They also need to play their part in the tangled acquisition of the behavioural, cultural and social characteristics which will make learners 'ready' for employment, and attuned, in as general a way as possible, to the forms and 'disciplines' of the employment opportunities which present themselves. Since these new forms and relations of work are going to pose new demands and impose fresh anxieties and discomforts, then there are also new patterns of accommodation and assimilation to be accomplished. Teachers (along with others) have their part to play in preparing the ground and instilling these. But, of course, this needs to be a form of reflexive analysis. Whilst exploring what teachers have to do in preparing learners for work, it must also examine what is happening to teachers in being prepared for that work themselves. It is this which melds together changes in the patterns and forms of training and development of teachers, with the literacy and numeracy hours and with the frenetic concentration on the 'technological fix' of ICT. But it is also this which, as we shall argue, grounds the differentiation between 'classes' of teachers, their institutions of training and preparation, with structural groups of pupils in their redifferentiated schools. There is nothing novel in this recognition, but the conditions within which it is located and the nature of the possible engagement with those circumstances is what generates the 'shock of the new'. The cultural and social expectations with which teachers approach their work, and which become part and parcel of the consciousness through which they reflect on and feel about their working lives, have an impact (albeit not deterministic) on the learners with whom they spend those working hours. To quote a question raised by Woods, Jeffrey, Troman and Boyle (1997),

> What are the children learning about society when they see teachers engaged in
> some of the 'compliance games' reported here?   (p. 85)

Such ideas on the remaking of consciousness and personal identities through and
within changing forms and patterns of work is a refrain which is being picked up
within contemporary literature. For example, Catherine Casey (1995), once again
making use of a high-technology engineering company to ground her analysis,
explicitly examines the ways in which there are linkages between the changing institutional practices which take place at work and the ways in which people think about
themselves and conduct their relationships. Although her work is located in a private
sector company operating in the USA, she argues that the training packages, language, approaches to staff development and performance models are becoming
increasingly common globally and across occupational sectors. Indeed many of her
insights connect closely with experiences we and others have been picking up on
within education. For example, she says

> What is happening here is more than an assumption of a corporate organizational
> role; it is the internalization of the values and practices of the new culture and
> identification with the company over and above previous occupational identifi-
> cations as those older forms of identification are displaced. The new culture pro-
> duces 'designer employees'.   (p. 143)

This possesses more than a passing resemblance to John Smyth and Geoffrey
Shacklock's concept of the 'preferred teacher' as an emerging category within schools
and education policy. In Catherine Casey's work we also find arguments being established which resonate with the ethnographic literature on the reformulation of teaching and its impact on the sense of identity through which people make sense of their
lives and attribute value and worth to them. Thus we find Casey saying, on the basis
of her detailed ethnographic researches,

> The most obvious and pervasive effect of working in the new culture is a condi-
> tion of ambivalence. Ambivalence is a manifestation of an incomplete
> internalization of the new cultural values and behaviour. ... Most [interview-
> ees] express ambivalence in the same breath as they express devotion and
> commitment ...
>
>   (p. 154)

Working on the basis of equally intensive ethnographies, Woods *et al.* (1997) express
comparable insights on the feelings with which teachers operate.

> In fact, teachers may experience feelings of enhanced professionalism and stress at
> the same time. What pushes them in one direction or the other, one might argue,
> is the particular conjuncture of other factors that apply, and the balance between
> intensification and professionalization, as mediated perhaps through national
> policy.   (p. 165)

As we can detect in this last quotation, for teachers, as for those in many other occupations, the concept of 'professionalism' has occupied a key, symbolic place in the attribution of worth and esteem. Clearly the transformations which are currently occurring in the nature of teachers' work will have an impact on this perception of 'professionalism' and its significance. Susan Robertson (1996), writing from the perspective of educational restructuring in New Zealand, makes the following observation which links to many of the issues we have been exploring in this chapter:

> The outcome of the reorganisation of teachers' work is increased segmentation for the purposes of organisational flexibility, pedagogical deskilling, a new conception of professionalism linked to managerial activity, the reconstruction of teachers as learner-manager, an expansion of tasks to include management activity, and tighter external controls. ... There is little scope in the promise of professionalism to wrest a degree of autonomy because the crucial margin for determination – that is ideological control – has been unceremoniously split from teachers' work ... (pp. 50–1)

In invoking the idea of 'ideological control', she is here using a distinction between ideological and technical controls as sources of autonomy which had been developed by Derber (1982).

> The former involves teachers losing control over the goals, objectives and policy directions of their work. The latter refers to a lack of control over the skills, content, rhythm and pace of their work, ...
> (Robertson, p. 44)

As we have seen, policy changes over the last decade or more have been increasingly divesting teachers of autonomy in both these respects and as such have been redrawing the boundaries around the connotations of teacher professionalism.

A changing configuration of professionalism

Within recent policy texts there has been an abundance of language and concepts relating to 'professional' and 'professionalism'. As Eric Hoyle and Peter John (1995) have said, 'profession', despite the theoretical and conceptual debates which surround it, remains a powerful 'concept-in-use', and as such it persists as an 'object of attention and a component of educational discourse' (pp. 1–2). In the same vein Jenny Ozga (1995) emphasises the point that in order to understand the 'use' of professionalism it cannot be treated as a static or neutral category but must be grasped

> ... in its historical and political context, to appreciate its function as a form of occupational control and to consider its capacity for the concealment of differentiation in and stratification of the workforce. (p. 21)

There is currently much debate and an enormous literature about both the reconstruction of professionalism within teaching and the reconstruction of teachers as individual professionals. These debates reflect three main themes: tensions involved in concepts of professionalism; contemporary transformations in the social and economic contexts within which teachers are located; and specific changes in the nature, control and definition of teaching as an occupational category. As Geoff Whitty (1996) has put it,

> ... there has been something of a move away from the notion that the teaching profession should have a professional mandate to act on behalf of the state in the best interests of its citizens to a view that teachers (and indeed other professions) need to be subjected to the rigours of the market and/or greater control and surveillance on the part of the re-formed state. ... [this] is partly concerned with the reconstitution of teacher subjectivities to accord more closely with the demands of education in a society where the prevailing mode of regulation is changing ...
>
> (p. 12)

The literature echoes the divergence between empowered, up-skilled, flexible images of teaching on the one hand and occupational intensification, fragmentation and differentiation on the other. Teachers may experience both the positive and negative aspects of these features at the same time. Opportunities for professional development and a structured qualification system may be locked into increasing occupational demands and a requirement that one moves into a supervisory or regulatory role vis-à-vis one's colleagues. Comparable redefinitions of what it means to be a professional and of the nature of professionalism in the context of high surveillance/low trust are currently receiving much attention throughout the public sector. As with teaching, managerial transformations are raising tensions and contradictions in the very nature of what it means to be a professional within the public sector. Under the impact of changes in the health service, social services and probation services, for instance, there has been considerable discussion of the relationship between professional and managerial orientations. Clarke and Newman (1997), for example, provide a detailed account of the processes through which managerialism has reshaped the bureau-professional regimes which characterised the public services during the era of the welfare-state settlement. They identify what they call the processes of *displacement, subordination* and *co-option* as having been crucial in this transformation. We quote them at length below because whilst they offer a generalised, theoretical account of an important shift in the patterns of power and control in the public sector, their account also captures what it has felt like to be on the receiving end of this struggle.

> *Displacement* refers to the process by which management has superseded bureau-professionalism in the way public services are organised as regimes. Here organisations are reshaped around a command structure which privileges the calculative framework of managerialism: how to improve efficiency and organisational performance. Complete displacement is relatively rare: the dominant relationship

between bureau-professionalism and management has been one of *subordination*. This takes the form of framing the exercise of professional judgment by the requirement that it takes account of the "realities and responsibilities" of budgetary management. ... Where "need" was once the product of the intersection of bureaucratic categorisation and professional judgment, it is now increasingly articulated with and *disciplined* by a managerial calculus of resources and priorities.

But many areas of professional service are characterised by a rather different strategy: that of *co-option*. This refers to managerial attempts to colonise the terrain of professional discourse, constructing articulations between professional concerns and languages and those of management. ... These are strategies in the struggle between regimes. They produce new focal points of resistance, compromise and accommodation ...

(pp. 75–6, emphasis in original)

In a way which echoes some of our earlier comments about ambivalence, they note that many public-sector institutions constitute a 'hybrid' form with people being pulled in contradictory directions.

Such positions are often an uncomfortable place to be because they are subject to conflicting demands and expectations in a field of tensions between service and corporate concerns. Such hybrid formations are also the focal point for "devolved stress" as significant organisational tensions and conflicts come to be embodied in single individuals.   (p. 77)

These arguments fit broadly into the general discussion currently underway about issues of *deprofessionalism* and *reprofessionalism*. Very broadly, the deprofessionalism thesis claims that the professional status of teachers (and other professionals) is being eroded and that the occupational status of teaching is increasingly becoming indistinguishable from that of other workers. Sometimes this is linked to the removal of teachers' bargaining rights, sometimes to changes in teachers' working conditions, sometimes to the increasing regimes of control and surveillance which teachers experience, sometimes to the decline in the respect and trust accorded to teachers, and sometimes to a combination of all of these factors (and more) (Grace 1991).

The *reprofessionalism* argument claims that the changes in the social, economic and political contexts within which teaching is taking place are leading to a *redefinition* of the nature of contemporary professionalism (again it is important to stress that this does not only apply to teaching). At least two levels of transformation can be identified. First, the changing nature of institutional structures and the internal reshaping of those structures alter both the definition and status of all of those who work within organisations, including 'professionals'. The second, interconnected, level concerns the way in which the definition and application of the term 'professional' are being reworked by the impact of state activities. Following Larson (1990), Terri Seddon sees the process of 'reprofessionalization' as a response to changes in the 'structural linkage between scarce resources of knowledge and expertise and scarce resources of status and reward that is endorsed by the state' (Seddon 1997, p. 234). For public employees this involves an endless negotiation between what professionals can claim to know and be able to do, which in our case has direct relevance in terms of standards and pedagogy, and the positions and reward structures being set in place via the proposed performance-management systems. In particular, the reworking of the public sector is repositioning the working conditions and locations of many public-sector employees who have come to see themselves as occupying professional positions and identities. The central argument underpinning this is that it has always been impossible to separate the notion of professional from the legitimating and regulative activities of the state. In Roger Dale's terms (1982), professionals have always worked in positions of 'regulated autonomy' vis-à-vis the state. In consequence what is currently occurring is a contemporary redesignation of the boundaries and form of that relationship. In short, 'professional' continues to be a powerful and evocative 'concept-in-use', but one which is variably 'pulled into play' or 'sidelined' depending upon context and purpose. We can see these shifts operating at the same time within current policy strategies and statements. Thus within the Green Paper and its subsequent documents one gets a gradual dilution, almost to the point of disappearance, as we progress from general statements to 'technical' documents of implementation which could be referring to any worker, in almost any context, in almost any occupational sector. Thus even the front cover of the Green Paper proclaims that

> We all need good teachers, whose skills and dedication are recognised and respected. That means a first class profession, well led and well supported. It means backing high standards with high rewards, which recognise the talents of those who teach our children.

As we have seen in the previous chapter, once you move inside the document, the case is established for 'modernising the teaching profession' through

> ... a new vision of the teaching profession – with good leadership, incentives for excellence, a strong culture of professional development, and better support for teachers to focus on teaching – to improve the image and status of teaching.
>
> (p. 6)

Throughout the Green Paper 'the imperative of modernisation' is expanded and becomes the justificatory framework for the development of a 'new professionalism', with a clear set of requirements and 'objectives' underpinning the modernisation process. Their repetition emphasises the government's intention 'to develop an education system which achieves consistently high standards ... seeks constant improvement and takes change in its stride'; 'to recognise the key role of teachers in raising standards; 'to ensure we have excellent leadership in every school ...'; 'to provide rewards for success and incentives for excellence and to improve the esteem in which the profession holds itself and is held by the community (para 34, p. 19). Bartlett, Knight and Lingard (1992) remind us of the ways in which political discourse uses such unproblematised repetition to generate a version of 'common-sense'.

... each section of the text traverses the same terrain, but in increasing detail, so that by the end ... we are so familiar with its features that it assumes a necessary and material presence. (p. 24)

In the next paragraph the inspirational discourse style of the policy is made explicit in an avowedly invitational manner.

> We will be accused of being visionary and excessively ambitious. We plead guilty. After the years of drift, vision and ambition are surely what is needed. Creating a world-class education service was never going to be easy but that is what the economy and society of the future require. A modern teaching profession is central to this process. If teachers rise to the challenge of modernisation in the next few months they themselves, along with pupils and parents, will undoubtedly be major beneficiaries. We urge all those with an interest in the future of our education system to give this Green Paper the most careful consideration and to grasp the historic opportunity that now presents itself. (para 35, p. 19)

This very powerful language is doing a job that reminds us of the points which Gee *et al.* make about the reculturation process adopted by 'new capitalist' enterprises.

> ... the new capitalism puts a great deal of faith in creating goals, core values, a vision, a 'culture' – whatever one wishes to call it (*we* would call it creating a Discourse) – and communicating it to workers (partners). ... [it] is now quite open about the need to *socialize* people into 'communities of practice' that position people to be certain kinds of people. They now realize that they are in the business of creating and sustaining Discourses, though they don't use this term. (pp. 19–21, emphasis in original)

In a later chapter we shall be considering the important new space created by the establishment of a General Teaching Council. Without moving into this debate prematurely it is worth noting that such a Council is manifestly sanctioned and sponsored by the state. The language in which the government has announced its birth and proposed its purposes bears close comparison with the celebratory style of the Green Paper. Thus in his preface to the original consultation (DfEE 1997b), Stephen Byers, then Minister for School Standards, wrote

> We intend to set up a General Teaching Council (GTC) by the year 2000. It will play an important role in raising the status and standing of the teaching profession, and will contribute to our drive to raise standards.

> There has long been agreement that a GTC is desirable. It will enhance the standing of teachers by giving them a clear professional voice, independent of government but working with us to raise standards. It will help restore the morale of teachers, who for too long have had too little say in determining the shape and future of their profession. It will celebrate the best of teaching, by drawing on the

dedication and experience of those who have made teaching their vocation. It will be able to promote a positive image of teaching both within the profession and outside.   (p. 3)

Clearly such positive modes of formulation are a genuine and welcome attempt to speak positively and persuasively to teachers and to address them with respect through the language of professionality. But at the same time this very notion of the profession is being reshaped in terms which are being defined by the government and which predominantly require 'response' from the professionals within those terms of engagement. For example, it is indicative to note the language being used within the substance of the 'objectives' statements above. These are literally formulated as statements rather than invitations to debate or discuss or reflect. Kevin Harris (1994 – quoted in Robertson 1996) draws out the implications of this subtle move when he says

> ... within this larger process of adopting forms and processes of corporate managerialism, professionals such as teachers are being redefined as straight-out contracted workers subject to direct management and becoming positioned in such a way that their expertise and professional knowledge is decreasingly called upon with regard to decision-making in areas central to the needs and requirements of those whom they teach and serve.   (p. 42)

This is an interesting perspective on the notion of a modernised professional, as someone who is both being addressed as a 'professional' but whose responsibilities, powers and rights are designated as lying well outside realms of policy reflection or deliberation. This shift of positioning and status becomes even more evident in the Technical Documents which are intended to translate the visionary image of the Green Paper into the harsh reality of working lives and the performance-management system within which they will be experienced. In the *Performance Management Framework for Teachers* (DfEE 1999e), which is intended for heads, LEAs and other governors and employers, a striking feature is the way in which the language of professionalism has almost entirely disappeared. In these documents its usage is so circumscribed that it is almost solely used in conjunction with the phrase 'professional development'. In the light of his own reminder that 'Teacher professionalism is not a fixed idea, it is situational and relational, it has contradictory aspects (progressive and conservative) and it is not homogeneous' (1994, p. 187), Martin Lawn comments that in contemporary terms

> Professionalism as an employer discourse has almost entirely disappeared; this is a sign of its lack of significance to the new time. The overtones of a responsible group, working with the State, are no longer necessary or even valid. Teacher professionalism is now being redefined as a form of competent labour, flexible and multi-skilled; it operates within a regulated curriculum and internal assessment system in a decentralized external school market. The dominant version is now a notion of individual responsibility and incentive reward legitimated by the

Citizen's Charter idea of efficient service and performance incentive. (Yet curriculum and professional autonomy were once linked closely together so that a reduction of control over the former was seen as inevitably weakening the latter.)

(Lawn 1996, pp. 112–13)

As we have already argued, the apparent 'professional' enhancement and flexibility promised within the performance-management system also open up avenues of sponsorship and discrimination, whilst enabling increasing exploitation and patterns of differentiation within the occupation. We have thus far been referring to the 'profession' or occupation of teaching as though it were an undifferentiated whole. Clearly it is anything but.

5 Social justice in teaching

Our arguments in this chapter are placed within a wider context of social justice issues in education generally. Thus although we have concentrated our attention on gender and 'race', we recognise that issues of social justice and social exclusion have considerably wider ramifications. Also, we are predominantly focusing on teaching even though it is clear that what is happening in teaching both reflects and impacts upon wider questions about the form and shape of education in general. As the concluding chapter of Showunmi and Constantine-Simms (1996) says,

> ... any attempts to attract Black and ethnic minority students [into teaching] must be underpinned by an effective, established commitment to equal opportunities. An Equal Opportunities policy must be in place, clearly stated and widely publicised. Moreover, policy implementation should be monitored by management staff and students and the policy reviewed at regular intervals.   (p. 165)

From its inception, the TTA was given a brief for ensuring 'equal opportunity for access to the profession, in particular for students from ethnic minorities and for students with disabilities' (DfE 1994, para. 35). Within a year, this remit concerning the composition of the teaching force had broadened to include male teachers, particularly for the primary sector. These priorities, framed within a clear statement of the need to 'ensure that the teaching profession is fully representative of the society in which our children live' (TTA 1998b, p. 8), have been maintained under the Labour government and were incorporated into the TTA's continued responsibilities for teacher supply and recruitment and initial teacher training following the Quinquennial Review (see TTA 1999a, pp. 6–7). Issues of recruitment are, self-evidently, of vital importance in any attempt to secure full representation. Yet it is not enough to simply take account of the composition of the teaching workforce as a whole. Opportunities for progression and promotion within the occupation have as much bearing on issues of social justice as concerns about access. Therefore we shall pay attention to the use of the NPS framework in the placement or positioning of persons within the occupational structure of teaching as well as concerns about recruitment. Our focus will be on ethnicity and gender, since we have found little written evidence of activity in relation to people with disabilities, save for an 'audit for trainees with disabilities' mentioned in the 1998–2000 *Corporate Plan* (TTA 1998b, p. 8).

Even at the fundamental level of recruitment, it is crucial to at least acknowledge that the categories under which target-setting and monitoring procedures are to be established for minority ethnic teachers need to be very carefully addressed. These are not easy issues: categories of ethnicity and 'race' come with weighty histories of oppression and colonial identifications and resistances. Recruitment initiatives which are intended to speak to minority ethnic individuals and communities will, at the very least, need to demonstrate an awareness of subtleties of identity and diversity if they are to overcome an impression of being out of touch or insensitive. As Bruce Carrington *et al.* (1999) conclude from their recent research project,

> With more than one in eight of all teacher trainees failing to provide details of their ethnic origins when applying for PGCE places, a review of the present system of ethnic monitoring is now needed. The official categories used for this purpose are problematic in that they tend to be at variance with subjective definitions of ethnic identity. For example, they take no account of people who regard themselves as having 'hyphenated' identities (e.g. 'British-Pakistani' or 'British-Caribbean'), or those of mixed parentage. (p. 5)

Minimally this means proper consultation with and listening to organisations and constituencies who can best communicate the range of perspectives that need to be incorporated. For instance, a senior teacher in a thriving inner-city school told us that 'they would very much like to recruit more teachers from the Turkish, Vietnamese and Chinese populations' but that current TTA recruitment policies in relation to ITT were 'not particularly sensitive to such issues'. This was echoed by the head of an ITT provider institution who made the point that the ethnic classifications used by the TTA do not match the self-designations used by students. For this reason, this institution did not send the TTA a target figure for minority ethnic recruitment, because it did not accept the categories under which it was being expected to set targets.

Initiatives targeted at minority ethnic individuals and communities also need to be sensitive to the ways in which

> ... racism and discrimination, although endemic or even routine, are not often highly visible or apparent. They are embedded in the day-to-day social practices which constitute organisations as social settings.
> (Jenkins 1986, p. 238)

The coupling of 'diversity' with 'quality', evident in an early speech by the Chief Executive of the TTA, was but one example of the routine set of racialised assumptions built into recent recruitment initiatives.

> Our Corporate Strategy contains a range of further measures, including plans to

increase the diversity of entrants to teaching and teacher training, consistent with maintaining quality.

(Millett 1996a, p. 7)

This thorny issue recurred persistently whenever our interviewees discussed the TTA's recruitment initiatives. There are, of course, many candidates for whom the question of 'quality' is deeply insulting given the character of their formal qualifications. For others, however, the crux of the issue appears to be that given the discriminatory and racist ways in which many minority ethnic pupils experience schooling, their formal educational achievements fail to articulate with their capacities and abilities. If they later wish to move into Higher Education, including teacher education, they may well need to avail themselves of 'non-traditional' modes of entry, for example, via Access courses, or by invoking APL or APE entry procedures. However, these may collide with the criteria of 'entrant quality' by which training institutions find themselves judged. This creates a dissonance at the very heart of the policy, which is founded on a political and cultural schizophrenia which at some point will need to be confronted and addressed. As Bruce Gill (1998), amongst others, has repeatedly said, there has to come a recognition that issues of quality and equality are not separate but indissolubly bound together in any model of social justice and inclusive society. The significance of this was underlined by the personal experience of one of our interviewees at a job interview.

> You know, when that was said at my interview, 'How do you recruit more black students without affecting quality?', the rest of the board didn't gasp in horror, … they didn't think it was a provocative question to try and provoke me or get me to show my stamina or my mettle in academic argument. It was a normal thing to say … I really wanted to say to her, think it through, how would you feel … , we can't recruit enough men so let's recruit women but will that reduce quality. Wouldn't you feel that as an insult?
>
> (HEI tutor)

Connected to recruitment and categorisation is the issue of 'monitoring'. Recent national data on the numbers and positioning of minority ethnic teachers is not available, thus making it impossible to discover whether opportunities for promotion are being fairly distributed or not. A member of staff at the CRE told us that the DfEE stopped collecting monitoring data in the early 1990s because they considered that the returns they were receiving from LEAs were too unreliable to form a secure basis for generalisation. This was confirmed by a DfEE staff member who further informed us that an attempt in 1998 to find out whether it would be possible to collect such data from LEAs met with a 'patchy' response, 'unsurprisingly as it's not mandatory and some people aren't very happy about it'. Given this context it is no surprise to discover that data on minority ethnic achievement in relation to, for example, NPQH was not recorded by the TTA because of its 'unreliability'. However, this is a chicken-and-egg situation since the unreliability of the data is a direct consequence of the fact that candidates are merely *invited* to complete the detachable sheet for 'Equal Opportunities Monitoring' at the end of the application form. This is despite the fact that one of the firm commitments that was made following the joint regional conferences held by the TTA and CRE was that the Agency would 'monitor ethnicity of those receiving headship training' (TTA/CRE 1998, p. 6). We have tried to obtain such monitored returns from the TTA but, having been passed from section to section, we were finally told that they do not exist because they are too 'unreliable'. In the case of ASTs we could find no evidence of monitoring at all, neither by the DfEE nor by the Westminster Education Consultants who are administering the scheme. In the words of a DfEE official, 'it was not something we thought about, we didn't think it was particularly important'. In the end, unreliability of the data can only be seen as reflecting a deeper problem, namely lack of concern for the career opportunities available to minority ethnic teachers.

That these are not new issues is illustrated by the following quotation from Jenkins, referring to a major ESRC project on racism and recruitment in 1986.

> Ethnic record-keeping is the exception rather than the rule, and *monitored* ethnic record-keeping appears to be very unusual. ... This lack of accountability is perhaps one of the most important preconditions for the flourishing of racism and discrimination within organisations.
>
> (p. 237, emphasis in original)

It is significant that in discussions about minority ethnic teachers, official arguments have remained centred on recruitment of beginning teachers, framed within a concern to achieve a numerical 'match' between teachers and pupils.

> At present, ethnic minorities account for about 6% of recruits to ITT. We aim to help ensure that, by the earliest possible date, this figure matches the proportion of ethnic minorities in the school population – currently about 9 per cent.
>
> (TTA 1999, p. 6)

This reveals a crude lumping of 'ethnic minorities', underpinned by the presumption that minority ethnic teachers *per se* 'match' minority ethnic students. Also, as an interviewee pointed out ' ... we want black teachers but you don't hear the TTA saying we want black headteachers'. In the opening press statement of the CRE's high-profile Leadership Challenge Campaign (CRE 1997), the Chief Executive of the TTA was one of an enormous range of signatories drawn from the ranks of 'the great and the good' in the public and private sectors. This appears to have signified little in terms of the TTA's own 'leadership strategy' and it remains to be seen whether the new National College for School Leadership will take up the 'challenge' as energetically as other public and private sector bodies appear to have done (CRE 1999). To do so will hardly constitute a revolutionary move. In her role as Secretary of State for Health under the former Conservative government, Virginia Bottomley (1993) said

> I want to stress that taking action to promote equality in employment is not just a

matter of moral justice or of fairness to people from minority ethnic backgrounds. It is good, sound common sense, and it makes business sense too.

(p. 1)

Similarly, Tony Blair has underlined the 'efficiency' of fully harnessing 'the talents of all sections of our community' (CRE 1999, p. 3), and even the armed forces have managed to reposition themselves as 'fighting a war on racism', grounded in 'commonsense not political correctness' (CRE 1999, pp.64–5).

In broadening the discussion to take account of 'progression and promotion', evidence suggests that minority ethnic teachers fare disproportionately badly in terms of career progression (Osler 1997; Siraj-Blatchford 1993). There are also claims within the public and private sectors that minority ethnic managers, for example, experience 'adverse selection' that results in a 'cement roof' (Stewart and Bapat 1996). The processes implicated in this are often complex and subtle. They require sophisticated understanding, from those who do not experience it, of how discrimination operates. The following comments, made by two of our interviewees, about the likely impact of current policy on issues of career progression possibilities for minority ethnic teachers, are cases in point.

> ... if progression through the threshold is going to be determined by the headteacher ... with external validation – black teachers are going to say, well ... I know the head, very nice person she is but she does not understand the issues, alright. Well, dealing with that blockage is absolutely fundamental before you even decide whether a colleague might know the issues and might be acting on prejudice.
>
> (LEA officer)

And again, reporting on the experience of a colleague, another interviewee said

> When she's been assessed, the people assessing her haven't been aware of her experience in an inner city school, of the equality issues that she's facing, or even thought they were credible ... she's really felt that the people who were making judgments about her aren't really aware of the realities of schooling let alone the realities of race equality. ... this is a particularly aware teacher ... going along and feeling that the people who are supposed to be training her for NPQH haven't really got a clue.
>
> (HEI tutor)

Yet both progression and promotion provide the very rationale for the performance management model outlined in the Green Paper. Speaking of the experience of performance management within the Civil Service, one of our interviewees spoke about the equity issues that had come to light and the ways in which unions had responded.

> [We] said, 'look we've got – statistical evidence ... there is a strong case there is discrimination happening here, ... can you explain why this is actually

happening?' And they got some management consultants in – did this report and they identified, 'yes, there is a problem, it's statistically significant but we don't think this was due to discrimination in the system'. So we said, 'well what is it due to?' 'Well we don't know.' So it was like, they've identified there is a problem, they don't think it's caused by discrimination but they can't explain what it is. From my point of view that's completely unacceptable. There obviously is a problem and from our perspective the only factor that can account for it is the fact that you know, to do with gender and 'race'. And that implies there is something in the system that is discriminating on those grounds. ... it all depends on the criteria that you use, how you measure performance but it is a real minefield.

(Union officer)

In our interviews the 'something in the system' was partly seen as emanating from the specific contexts in which minority ethnic teachers were employed.

... in terms of career progression, ... if you were in a school ... it's quite a tiny community and ... your reputation is made within that small community and ... if they [senior managers] are coming with limited ideas about what a black teacher is there for or can achieve or whatever, then it can be a very stifling environment – one where they are under-estimated, where their skills are specified or where their skills are kind of seen as only fit for certain types of jobs. ... [black women and men] were saying again and again and again that schools were using them to discipline black children, to keep black children in check, to deal with parents, black ethnic minority parents, all those kinds of things. So that whether or not they were skilled in a wider sphere that was one difficulty.

(HEI tutor)

This issue of school context was also referred to in relation to issues of sponsorship and support as important elements in making progress through the system.

... in terms of people's career structure ... the school was the confining thing ... Then – it's at school level that most big decisions are going to be made. It seems to me that – it is not a question of being formally selected it's a question of being supported and encouraged to apply in the first place. ... Now with black people that seems to be magnified in some way and ... as Standards are put forward there are more hoops to jump through, or hurdles to jump over

(School governor)

The NPS framework was not seen by these interviewees as enhancing opportunities by making the criteria for progression explicit. On the contrary, the tension between the role that minority ethnic teachers were expected to fulfil and the view of teachers' work implicit in the NPS was regarded as yet one more barrier to progression. As one interviewee put it,

> ... racism isn't like a concrete ceiling. It's like one of those fences that are held together with wire, you know, you give it a good push and it goes down in one place and pulls up in another until you can find ways round.
>
> (HEI tutor)

These contextual factors become even more pressing in the light of the restructuring of CPD, and the funding-driven closure of a range of LEA and HEI courses which formerly provided networking contexts. Increasingly teachers will be dependent on school sponsorship with fewer and fewer legitimate or recognised avenues through which they can informally network and gain educational qualifications. Another of our interviewees stressed the critical importance of these informal networks and the support to be gained from being invited to

> ... network with us, come and meet with us, we will show you how to fill in the application form. We know what they're looking for. We know where you'll fall down even if you have all the criteria and it's the only way that you'll get by.
>
> (School governor)

Issues of selection and sponsorship, which play a crucial role in career advancement, raise real questions about the extent to which patterns of promotion will be fairly distributed, given the tendency of dominant networks to promote 'people like us' (Collinson and Hearn; 1996 Kanter 1993). How LEAs, schools and other sponsoring bodies will undertake their activities, how sensitive they will be to the need to guard against their own preconceptions and assumptions in relation to who gets selected, on what basis, by what criteria, through what procedures and with what protection in terms of appeals and grievance, all remain to be seen. These are issues which organisations such as NAME and ARTEN have been raising consistently over many years. In its response to the Labour government's document *Excellence in Schools* (DfEE 1997a), NAME made the following comment about the section which dealt with minority ethnic teachers:

> We are dismayed to find no mention in this chapter of the disproportionately small number of teachers from minority ethnic communities, especially in senior posts and as Head teachers. ... We look for urgent action to attract more minority ethnic recruits into teaching, and to ensure that minority ethnic teachers are fairly represented at all levels of professional advancement, including Head teachers, and among Advanced Skills Teachers.
>
> (NAME 1998, p. 6)

Continuing with this theme in their lengthy response to the Green Paper consultation, ARTEN emphasised that

> Both headteachers and Governing bodies must be provided with race equality training in order to ensure that the recruitment, retention and promotion of

minority ethnic teachers is fairly carried out. Any selection process must be monitored by ethnicity.

(ARTEN 1998, p. 2)

If the future behaves like the past, some of those with responsibility for promotion and progression will undoubtedly retreat into the old refrain of 'the best person for the job', but while this has a common-sense plausibility, it can merely obscure issues of context, value orientation and structural discrimination.

> Living in a predominantly white society, it is easy to think that the only way of surviving is to act like most people. As most people are white, this means acting like white people. So if you want a good graduate job then one sure fire way of getting it is to look like and behave like those that employers are used to recruiting – generally white middle class men. Unfortunately, this doesn't always work.
>
> (Kohli 1996, p. 4)

There has been this same appeal to 'common sense' in current attempts to recruit more male teachers.

> If present trends continue, there will be very few male class teachers in primary schools by 2010. Secondary teaching too is now attracting fewer men than women. There is a general consensus that this is not desirable. All else apart, a profession where one sex or the other predominates to such an extent is simply not a true reflection of society today. And, if we are to continue to attract large numbers of high quality candidates for teaching, we cannot afford to write off half the human race.
>
> (Millett 1996a, p. 6)

This theme continues right through to Anthea Millett's valedictory speech in December 1999.

> ... the percentage of males entering training in 1997 was 13% onto primary courses and 40% onto secondary. These figures represent a steady decline over the last 10 years and more up to date figures reveal that this decline is continuing. That means a chronic under representation in teaching of about half the population. ... The challenges that these statistics pose are obvious. The feminisation of the profession leads to an absence of male role models for many of our pupils, particularly those from the majority of one parent families.
>
> (Millett 1999, p. 2)

However, behind the preoccupation with representation, other highly stereotyped assumptions have occasionally peeped through.

In an article that reveals the disparities between policy-makers' expectations of male teachers and those of the teachers themselves, Pepperell and Smedley (1998) provide details of comments from policy-makers which exemplify the kinds of assumptions being made in relation to the recruitment of men, namely that they provide 'role models', 'make better advocates' and help to address the under-achievement of boys by exposing them 'to some of the values that men may show, a competitive edge'. (pp. 347–51) Such assumptions present a very narrow, traditional conception of masculinity which seems out of touch with a growing volume of research that argues that masculinities are socially constructed and organised in a variety of ways to produce a gender regime characterised by internal hierarchies of power and creating a 'patriarchal dividend' for men in relation to women (Connell 1995; Lingard and Douglas 1999; Salisbury and Jackson 1996). They also suggest that we can best locate the concern with the recruitment of men into teaching firmly within the international preoccupation with the 'underachievement of boys' (Mahony and Smedley 1998). In this debate, it has been additionally suggested that more men teachers are needed to exert firmer control on boys, to compensate boys for paternal absence (often framed as the problem of single mothers) and to counteract the exposure of boys to too much girl-orientated teaching, material and pedagogy that threatens their maturation into 'real men' (Elwood *et al.* 1998).

As Sandra Acker (1995) amongst others argues, such assertions about what boys need if they are to grow into 'real men' are not new. Both in the past and now they hinge on particular conceptions of the culture and modes of masculinity into which boys have to be inducted as well as assumptions about what women signify and represent. What is unacknowledged in the 'more men into teaching' drive is any sense that we may need to address the question of what sort of men we are talking about (Mahony and Smedley 1998).

Much of the current debate has been conducted within a construction of the 'problem' as one of the 'feminisation' of teaching (Millett 1999; TTA 1996c). This is misleading in a number of ways. It is an empirical fact that there are currently more women employed in school teaching than men, but once one begins to explore the nature of women's employment then a number of issues emerge about positioning, hierarchy, promotion and progression, and patterns of power and responsibility (Blackmore 1999; Collinson and Hearn 1996). There has been little official acknowledgement of the low proportion of women appointed to headship until recently, when it was said that

> ... large numbers of teachers, especially female primary teachers, are not coming forward for headship, or even for training to become headteachers, despite having the potential to succeed. The figures are stark. Women make up 83% of primary school teachers yet only 53% of primary heads are women. ... The issues are similar in secondary schools. 52% of secondary teachers are women yet only 24% of headteachers are female. ... The candidates are out there; what we need to do is convince them that headship is for them.
>
> (Millett 1998, p. 14)

Whilst this is a welcome acknowledgement, it is accompanied by no recognition of the material circumstances which stand in the way of women's progression through teaching hierarchies. In this sense there is a clear danger that the performance-management framework will privilege the male 'career' orientated teacher

> ... who is single mindedly purposeful in the pursuit of career goals, following a linear progression through carefully planned steps. This model ignores the competing pressures of home and family circumstances on career.
>
> (Hall 1996, p. 34)

One senior LEA officer expressed concern that current policies would further serve to differentiate the teaching force across already differentiated schools.

> I think it is a male model ... When we actually interview NQTs, the percentage of men is very low, and they want to go into Church Schools. ... The class sizes are small, it's very structured and if you're a male in a Church School and you do well, you'll get airborne fast.

Our evidence from schools also indicates that it may also privilege those in possession of 'valuable' skills. These are palpably being defined in terms that may marginalise the contributions traditionally expected of those groups of teachers who are subject to racialised and gendered assumptions about their roles.

> I think it tends to be the women staff that the students want to talk to about very personal things and of course you don't get any brownie points for that ... a lot of it is invisible. I may be wrong but I don't get a sense that the same demands are made on the men.
>
> (Secondary school teacher)

Furthermore, within contemporary analysis of movements in the occupational structure we find a good deal of discussion about the 'feminisation' of work occurring alongside the masculinist nature of the managerial regimes and technologies developed to control such work (Blackmore 1999; Gee, Hull and Lankshear 1996; Mahony 1999). However, this is frequently used not in a crudely empiricist way but to describe the transformations in work which are confronting both men and women. 'Feminisation' of work in this sense focuses on the changing status and nature of the work process and the relationships and control mechanisms under which work now takes place.

> In both developing and developed regions, the stable, organised and mostly male labour force has become increasingly 'flexible' and 'feminised'. ... Standing (1989) has hypothesised that the increasing globalisation of production and the pursuit of flexible forms of labour to retain or increase competitiveness, as well as changing job structures in industrial enterprises, favour the feminisation of employment in the dual sense of an increase in the numbers of women in the labour force and a deterioration of work conditions (labour standards, income, and employment status). Women have been gaining an increasing share of many kinds

of jobs, but in the context of a decline in the social power of labour and growing unemployment, their labour market participation has not been accompanied by a redistribution of domestic, household, and child-care responsibilities. More-over, women are still disadvantaged in the new labour markets in terms of wages, training, and occupational segregation.

(Moghadam 1999, pp. 134–5)

In relation to the professional occupational sector Moghadam goes on to say

The process of the feminisation of labour continued throughout the recessionary 1980s, not only in the manufacturing sector, but also in public services, where throughout the world women's share has grown from 30 to 50 percent – at a time when public sector wages, like industrial wages, have been declining.

(pp. 136–7)

It is unlikely that it is in this sense that the 'feminisation' of teaching is being seen as problematic, although ironically many features of this changing character of work would, as we argued in the previous chapter, also be true of teaching.

A further consideration is that discourses of leadership and management tend to be masculinist in character. Modern management theory derives mostly from the private sector and even the most cursory inspection of popular texts reveals a great deal about the kind of 'person' represented by the modern manager or leader. Ostensibly pre-sented as gender neutral, these texts privilege competitive masculinities, either by providing examples of individual, 'successful' leaders and managers who are nearly always men, or by promoting images of action-orientated, risk-taking 'people' in total control both of their vision and the place of others within it. Collinson and Hearn (1996), in arguing that there has always been a strong connection between men and management say that in the 1980s

Managers and senior executives were frequently depicted and portrayed them-selves as 'hard men', virile, swashbuckling and flamboyant entrepreneurs who were reasserting a 'macho' management style that insisted on the 'divine right of managers to manage'.   (pp. 2–3)

The 1990s, they argue, brought an increased evaluation of managers and their per-formance, one criterion of which is 'the masculinist concern with personal power and the ability to control others and self' (p. 3). They show how conventional managerial discourse has become redolent with highly sexualised talk and argue that a consider-able amount of business is conducted between male managers through networks established in sports and clubs.

Much of the current literature on the gendered nature of leadership has suggested that the restructuring of the public sector in line with 'best commercial practice' has brought its own version of masculinist management. Throughout our own research the point was repeatedly made that the highly sexualised and militaristic language prevalent amongst some university senior management teams of 'biting the bullet (or the cherry)', 'screwing the opposition', 'shafting uneconomic departments', 'developing the strategy and the game plan', 'hitting the targets', 'upsetting the troops' and 'punching through new initiatives', generates a hostile environment within which to argue that resources are needed to enable teachers to be properly educated.

The National Standards for Headship (TTA 1998c) come nowhere near to reproducing the excesses described above. However, they do represent a hierarchical, individualistic and somewhat heroic management model in which responsibility for and control of others' work are central features of the head's role. In this model, headteachers 'lead by example', 'provide inspiration and motivation', 'create an ethos and provide educational vision', 'create and implement a strategic plan', 'ensure that all those involved in the school are committed to its aims' (p. 9) and they 'monitor and evaluate the quality of teaching' (p. 10). Attributes include 'personal impact and presence', 'resilience', 'energy, vigour and perseverance', 'self-confidence and intellectual ability' (p. 8). Although, in our research, these Standards were variously criticised for 'puffing up headteachers with power' (Headteacher), or demanding the impossible, 'where does it say "walks on water"?' (LEA officer), the gender-biased nature of the language also elicited considerable comment.

> I would say it's very male-orientated language. Maybe it's my understanding of what a male manager looks like but that's – I'm not comfortable with a lot of the language in here – 'command credibility', 'discharging' – sounds like … a battlefield.
>
> (EOC officer)

How control will be exercised will undoubtedly vary between individuals. However, such individuals, whatever their personal politics, do not exist independently of the presumptions and expectations underpinning the context in which they work.

In claiming that there is a considerable fit between conceptions of 'the manager' (or in more recent parlance 'the leader') and particular modes of masculinity, we are not here advancing an essentialist thesis in relation to women and men, quite the opposite and with far more potentially negative consequences. If masculinities and femininities are socially constructed, ordered and practised differently in different contexts, the problem goes far beyond the presence or absence of women and even beyond the relative positioning of women to men. What is at stake are the values, ways of understanding the world and ways of relating to others which are traditionally polarised around the binaries of 'femininity' and 'masculinity'. If success in management is defined in masculinist terms then women (and men) will be pressured to conform to its dictates in ways which may create tensions between their values and their power to act in collaborative ways. Much of the recent feminist literature on women in management (Deem and Ozga 2000; Shakeshaft 1995; Weiner 1995) has been optimistic about the impact of women in educational management. On the other hand,

> … a number of studies have shown that as women move up the organizational hierarchy, their identification with the masculine model of managerial success

becomes so important that they end up rejecting even the few valued feminine managerial traits they may have endorsed.

(Kanter 1993, p. 72)

There is now a highly developed international literature on the impact of the new managerialist movements in relation to work cultures (Itzin and Newman 1995; Limerick and Lingard 1995; Mahony 1997; Walby and Greenwell 1994). As Janet Newman (1995) has argued,

> ... organizational cultures have been highlighted as a significant barrier to change. Even in organizations where equal opportunity initiatives are well developed, their cultures may be resistant and intractable. ... [also] experience has shown that a focus on 'numbers' alone is not enough to bring about organizational change. ... Where women face hostile cultures, the pressures are great and an undue amount of energy has to be expended in developing strategies for survival.
>
> (p. 11)

It remains to be seen whether or not the Green Paper will create cultures that are hostile to women. Some of our interviewees pointed to the individualistic, competitive performance-management model and others to the gender-biased nature of the various sets of Standards as indicating changing cultures of teaching that failed to reflect the contributions of women teachers.

> ... some of the Standards are OK, the language of others ... there are connotations of male ways of teaching ... authority, discipline and control rather than the more subtle strategies you see the women developing.
>
> (Deputy Head)

All of this suggests that even at the most superficial level, calls for more men in teaching are not of the same order as demands for more women headteachers or more minority ethnic teachers or more teachers with disabilities, since the issues involved are not simply reducible to numerical 'under-representation' but relate to the distribution of institutional power. From the discussion above, one might conclude that the real problem is not the 'feminisation' of teaching, but the comprehensive 'masculinisation' of the profession and a repositioning of its values within the calculative and performative frameworks of the new managerialism.

The issues we have raised concerning minority ethnic teachers and gender are not problems specific to education. A common theme within a growing volume of social policy literature during the 1980s and 1990s centred around questioning the extent to which 'equal opportunities' were becoming marginalised. It appeared that ensuring equity for its citizens and workers was no longer being defined as a 'core business' of the managerial state. Within managerialist discourses the 'delivery' of 'products' in 'cost-effective' ways became a major preoccupation, and 'bottom-line' models of management drove off the agenda issues which did not fall into a neat material calculus. 'Diversity' became a fashionable term to replace inequality, carrying with it the clear danger of rendering invisible the structuring of social divisions and transforming them into individualised needs.

On the other hand, regarding the contradictory ways in which the centralisation/decentralisation nexus may operate on the establishment and implementation of equal-opportunities strategies, some analysts argued that the relative freedom of managers to manage was opening up the opportunity for more responsive and locally negotiable patterns to emerge. Research conducted by the Wainwright Trust neatly summarised the contradictory tendencies involved when it asked

- Has devolution, by placing more authority in the hands of managers who take everyday employment decisions, had the effect of improving implementation of equality principles?
  Or,
- Because of the pressures on managers to meet operational and business objectives, have equal opportunities been sidelined?

(Foreman, Bedingfield and Coussey 1997, p. 6)

These questions are made more difficult in relation to teaching, for although headteachers carry a high a degree of accountability and responsibility for performance (including responsibility for staff compliance), their freedom to manage is tightly circumscribed by the highly centralised context in which they operate. There are real tensions to be resolved over the extent to which it is legitimate, sensible or practical for the centre to provide tight specifications of 'standards' to be applied in different localities and regions. Conditions and circumstances may be so diverse as to warrant quite different skills. Different local 'constituencies' may also have views about their 'needs' which do not correspond, and may even conflict, with central definitions (Dashpande and Rashid 1993). It is also in this context of central control that the generalised language of managerialism becomes particularly problematic. In education, the use of such categories as 'headteachers', 'teachers' or 'pupils', renders invisible all the 'messy stuff' which goes with taking account of social context or structural differentiation. By working as though it is dealing with units of (teaching) labour, the current approach falls into a form of economic rationalism which denies the social effects or implications of education policy. Referring to the use of the phrase 'all children' in the Green Paper, Ian Menter (1999) writes

> It is all very well talking about all children, but unless there is explicit acknowledgement of existing inequalities, whether by ethnicity, gender, special needs, or whatever, a phrase such as this remains vacuous. It becomes the rhetoric of 'social inclusion' which we know is one of the key themes of government policy, without action to follow.   (p. 48)

If, as this indicates, the place of social differentiation is neither specified nor recognised, then policy will continue to be framed by and for those who experience no dissonance with concepts which invoke the 'normal', 'natural' order of things residing in 'common sense'. However, as we shall argue, what it might mean to take social justice seriously involves a little more than common sense, not least because, as Griffiths (1998) argues, there has been a recognition that changing circumstances within social policy create

> ... new conditions [which] bring with them new formations of control and sur-veillance, provoking new modes of struggle for justice.   (p. 11)

People who work in schools, be they staff or students, confront contextual circum-stances such as: dilemmas over levels and distribution of resources; acts of violence and aggression; complex patterns of interpersonal and group relationships; struggles for control and dominance; contests over who is and who is not responsible for what happens in schools; disputes over achievement and its definitions; and issues about appropriate ways of educating in the present and for the future. In some cases such issues take demanding and dramatic forms, in others they are woven into the daily routines of school life. In all cases they constitute the experiences within which par-ents, teachers, students, ancillary staff, governors and others inhabit schools. To be a teacher is to be located within these politics and to have certain consequent responsibilities.

To talk in a decontextualised manner about 'pupils', as many of the current policy texts do, can make the activity of teaching appear deceptively simple. As one of our interviewees said, commenting on the NPS,

> When you read this it sounds as if all pupils are the same basically. I mean there is no differentiation in it at all. It's all about – it just gives the impression that we're dealing with a sort of homogeneous group.
>
> (EOC officer)

Teaching involves relationships between people whose personal, social, economic, cultural and political identities and positionings are complex. It seems staggeringly obvious that teaching Anne-Marie, a mother by the time she was fifteen years old, is not the same as teaching Catherine, 'a middle-class boffin' in a working-class school. Working with children recently arrived from war-torn countries and traumatised by their experiences is not the same as dealing with those whose social networks have remained stable since birth. We were forcibly reminded of this point in an interview with a senior LEA officer who had recently moved from a rural context to one located on the edge of a major conurbation. Speaking of the QTS Standards he said

> ... some of them seem almost to have been plucked out of the air and I think that sometimes they don't always reflect the situation in which schools are working. I mean within our LEA you know, there is a high degree of pupil mobility. There are a lot of travellers. There is a high degree of pupils with English as an Addi-tional Language. We have a high percentage of special needs and we have a high percentage of children who are on Social Services registers ... how do you learn to deal with parents who are very irascible and can be quite volatile, you know, how do you deal with that? So they could come in with all these wonderful

competences and Standards but the reality of the situation is something totally different. I found a real culture shock coming from rural ... where the population was static, you know, the kids started in the nursery and 99.9 per cent of them went all the way through to Year 6. Staff rarely changed. If it did it was just for promotion, you didn't have twenty-three supply teachers in thirty-two days. None of that. So we are constantly trying to pick up those issues which aren't really picked up by the Standards because they are plucked out of the air. Some of them are very bland, some of them are very sweeping and they don't – they're not particularly helpful in challenging contexts ... we have something like a three-year burnout, you know, I mean there are some schools this year where 50 per cent of their staff are newly qualified teachers.

(LEA officer)

We have quoted this extract at length in order to set it against the current focus on teachers' subject knowledge and pupil performance, both of which are treated as de-situated and both of which deny that contextual circumstances require sophisticated repertoires of skills which teachers constantly need to develop.

Any social, cultural and economic disadvantage which pupils experience can be compounded if, with well-intentioned but misguided motives, teachers are unwilling to add further pressure in the shape of academic demands.

(Millett 1996b, p. 6)

Schools are also political institutions. They both reflect and reconstitute (or challenge) social inequalities organised around the axes of 'race', gender, class, sexuality and disability. What Connell (1993) has called the 'political order' of the school is mediated through: patterns of teaching and non-teaching staff employment; the messages conveyed in curriculum materials; the organisation of option choices; the basis on which students are grouped; teaching and assessment practices; the assumptions embedded in school discipline; the organisation of the pastoral system; the kinds of language used and the ways interpersonal relations are handled. People in schools, as well as

... people in factories, offices and unemployment lines are all making class and gender as well as race and sexuality. ... Human beings are always and everywhere making not just things, but people and social relationships.

(Brush 1999, p. 182)

Issues of social justice are inextricably bound up in the daily educational decisions about who gets what and how relationships are conducted. The range of social and political identities which young people inhabit are not fixed but neither do they develop irrespectively of the context in which they are formed.

Taking racism seriously, for example, necessarily involves radical scrutiny of everyday practices in schools. Following the racist murder of Stephen Lawrence, the Macpherson Report (1999) makes clear that

... racism exists within all organisations and institutions, ... it infiltrates the community and starts among the very young. Recent research in Cardiff showed that 50% of the racist incidents considered by the Race Equality Council involved young people under 16 years old, and 25% of these incidents involved children between the ages of six and 10 years. The problem is thus deeply ingrained. Radical thinking and sustained action are needed in order to tackle it head on, ... in all organisations and in particular in the fields of education and family life.

(para. 2.19, p. 5)

Schools may decide either to reinforce or to challenge social divisions, more or less superficially. What they cannot do is remain neutral. Yet for more than a decade, policy on teacher education has failed to address the fact that schools exist within, are structured by, or have a role in maintaining inequitable social relationships. Although the Standards for Headship (TTA 1998c) now include the requirement that heads 'create and promote positive strategies for developing good race relations and dealing with racial harassment' (p. 10), the long silence on equal opportunities has not gone unchallenged.

The Government's chief race adviser has accused the Teacher Training Agency of 'sticking two fingers up' at anti-racism. In a blistering attack Sir Herman Ouseley, head of the Commission for Racial Equality, called the agency 'negligent' and ministers 'impotent' in their failure to put equal opportunities firmly on the teacher-training curriculum.

(Ghouri 1998)

In response, a senior TTA officer said that the agency was 'not prepared to prescribe' anti-racist work. This was unconvincing in a context where the NCITT prescribes very tightly the training curriculum for primary and secondary English, mathematics and science. In passing it is also worth noting the speed with which 'exemplification' materials were produced for subject-specific and ICT aspects of the NCITT, as compared with the publication of materials to support work in relation to raising the achievement of minority ethnic pupils. It was promised that this work would have been completed by the Summer of 1999 (TTA 1999b, para. SO3c, p. 6) but the materials were not circulated for consultation until summer 2000.

A similar situation exists around gender issues confronting schools. If teachers are to move beyond current definitions of the 'problem', defined as the underachievement of boys, then they would need to look at the total gender regime of the school for the ways in which particular modes of masculinity and femininity are being encouraged or suppressed. These are not raw, biological 'facts' but social constructions framed within parameters made available to children within the sites they inhabit (including the school). Masculinities and femininities are fluid (Thorne 1993) and internally diverse, mediated through social class, sexuality, region, age, ability and ethnicity. Schools do young people no favours by failing to consider the implications and significance of this, especially as some modes of gender identity are ill-suited to the demands made by the new work order. In a project undertaken with one hundred and thirty fourteen-year-olds about their attitudes to school subjects and their ambitions for the future (Mahony and Frith 1995), it emerged that the ambitions of many white working-class boys clustered simultaneously round two poles of the male labour market. On the one hand they aspired to enter the middle-class professions, even though few of them were ever likely to gain the formal qualifications which would provide a basis for entry into their chosen 'career'. Furthermore, given what is known about the widening social-class divisions in access to Higher Education and the social-class backgrounds and exclusionary networking practices of members of the legal and medical professions, it is highly unlikely that the opportunity really existed for these boys to become barristers, solicitors, doctors or architects. Perhaps knowing this, they nearly always proposed alternatives to their preferred futures in 'masculine' industries which had ceased to flourish. Where local employment opportunities existed at all, these were mostly in the service industries which require high levels of expertise in the expressive aspects of customer service. Qualities such as 'warmth, empathy, sensitivity to unspoken needs and high levels of interpersonal skills to build an effective relationship with customers' (Devereux 1996, p. 13) were patently at odds with the masculinities encouraged in and adopted by some of these adolescent boys (Mahony 1998). In addition, the drab utilitarian view of schooling for which teachers are currently being trained removes key questions concerning the wider role of schools in the social construction of gender. No recognition is given to even the most dramatic example, namely the continuum of sexual harassment occurring in schools, even though research findings have clearly documented both its prevalence (Kelly, Regan and Burton 1991) and its impact (Gilbert and Gilbert 1998). This means that its devastating effects on individuals, its functioning in the social control of women and its role in establishing the internal hierarchy of masculinities, are placed at the periphery of teachers' 'core business'. Thus, while teachers' work is inextricably bound up with re-making social relations, their own education neither pays attention to preparing them to undertake it, nor does it provide them with opportunities to critically reflect on the implications of their own positioning within the complex matrix of power relations. Were it to do so then there would be wider recognition that

> Power relations are tied to the most mundane of everyday performances ... discourses of the everyday are the realms in which subordination is exercised and legitimated.
>
> (Keith 1991, p. 189, quoted in Jones *et al.* 1997, p. 135)

And the daily experiences of class prejudice, racism, sexual harassment and homophobia to which some groups of teachers are exposed and through which many are excluded and marginalised by colleagues would become part of the problem with which policy had to deal (Daley 1999; Epstein 1995; Jones *et al.* 1997; Maguire 1999).

This takes us on to a consideration of the ways that a social justice agenda needs to be revitalised after what Kate Myers (2000) has called the period of 'equiphobia' of successive Conservative administrations. Clay and George (1993) argue that the evacuation of issues of social justice from the agenda of teacher education has been developing since the 1980s. Thus, when John Major dismissed the politics of 'gender, race and class' as diverting schools from their true purposes, he was merely repeating an already well-rehearsed refrain. The Thatcher and Major years were notable for erasing from the collective memory of teacher education many of the insights gained from earlier work which sought to explore the ways in which educational structures and processes are both constituted by wider social divisions, and in turn are reconstitutive of them (unless contested and interrupted by teachers). Such work cannot be simply transported across time, however, for political identities have become complex and unstable as a consequence of globalised economies, developments in technology and communications and widespread movements of people (Zmroczek and Mahony 1999). However, in our rediscovery that racism, for example, is deeply embedded in schools, we should not forget the enormous body of work already undertaken. One 'inefficiency' in current policy-making is that almost no reference is made to anything that has been learned before. This carries the clear danger that, as the poet Santayana has said, 'people who forget their own history may be forced to relive it'.

In December 1997 the Social Exclusion Unit was launched by Tony Blair with a call to 'make it our national purpose to tackle social division and inequality' (quoted in Whitty 1998, p. 5). In a clear break with the past, the ideological repositioning of the Labour Party within 'Third Way politics' has meant that

> ... the old ideologies that have dominated the last century do not provide the answers. ... But there is a big ideal left in politics. It goes under a variety of different names – stakeholding, one nation, inclusion, community – but it is quite simple. It is that no society can prosper economically or socially unless all its people prosper, unless we use the talents and energies of all the people rather than just the few, unless we live up to the ambition to create a society where the community works for the good of every individual, and every individual works for the good of the community.
>
> (Tony Blair, quoted in Hatcher 1997, p. 4)

While the 'Third Way' has been subject to considerable criticism and counter-criticism from a variety of standpoints on the political spectrum, a particular source of disenchantment has been the way that 'inequality' has been redefined as 'social exclusion'. Ruth Levitas (1998) charts the emergence of this term and identifies

> ... three competing discourses within which the concept may be deployed. The first ... is a redistributionist discourse in which social exclusion is intertwined with poverty. The second deploys cultural rather than material explanations of poverty ... The third sees inclusion primarily in terms of labour market attachment.
>
> (p. 2)

She argues that to varying degrees, each one of the three inadequately defines the solution to inequality in terms of moving excluded groups across the boundary to join those who are included.

The term social exclusion is intrinsically problematic. It represents the primary significant division in society as one between an included majority and an excluded minority ... Attention is drawn away from the inequalities and differences among the included. Notably, the very rich are discursively absorbed into the included majority, their power and privilege slipping out of focus if not wholly out of sight. At the same time the poverty and disadvantage of the so-called excluded are discursively placed outside society. (p. 7)

Others, in arguing that a conception of social justice is inadequate if it only focuses on distribution and access, have pointed out the centrality of relational justice which is

... about the *nature* and *ordering* of social relations, the formal and informal rules which govern how members of society treat each other on both a macro level and at a micro interpersonal level. Thus it refers to the practices and procedures which govern the organization of political systems, economic and social institutions, families and one-to-one social relationships.

(Fraser 1997, p. 15, emphasis in original)

In a careful review of Labour Party policy in its early stages, Sharon Gewirtz (1998) conducted a 'social justice audit' under Iris Marion Young's (1990) 'five faces of oppression', namely, exploitation, marginalisation, powerlessness, cultural imperialism and violence. Gewirtz concluded

New Labourism comprises a complex amalgam of apparently contradictory strategies. ... I cannot conclude that subversion or circumvention on any significant scale is likely. The more likely outcome is that the retention of markets, managerialism and pedagogic traditionalism will perpetuate the injustices and oppressions of post-welfarism identified above – namely, a socially regressive redistribution of educational resources, the exploitation of teachers and students, the marginalization of particular social groups and the circumscription of opportunities to challenge cultural imperialism in schools. (p. 63)

An audit that included the impact of recent policy on teacher education, including the Green Paper, would surely be forced to reach similar conclusions. On the one hand, new anti-discrimination legislation to be introduced in 2000 will mean the renovation of school buildings and amendment of curriculum materials in order to ensure access for disabled students (Thornton 1999). On the other hand, the education of teachers pays scant attention to what it might mean to meet the needs of this group (Lloyd 2000). Again, the repeal of the notoriously confused and damaging Section 28 of the Local Government Act 1988 that prohibits LEAs from promoting 'the teaching in any maintained school of the acceptability of homosexuality as a pretended family relationship' (sic), is a progressive move which may help to end some of the misery currently experienced by lesbian and gay school students, teachers, carers and parents (Mason and Palmer 1996). But there is nothing in the education of teachers which specifically deals with what it means to develop non-discriminatory practice (Jones and Mahony 1989). If anything, current definitions of 'preferred' skills and the model of progression that is envisaged are likely to continue the trend of rendering considerations of social justice beyond the core business of schools. This may be the unintended consequence of policy collision, resulting from failures inherent in fragmented government, or it may be that the modes of governance and accountability appropriate for diverse and complex democracies which would enable such issues to be raised have yet to be adequately developed (Hextall and Mahony 1999).

6 Governance and accountability

In the course of this book we have raised questions about how policy gets made and unmade, the processes and structures which through their interplay 'produce' policy, who is playing what part in these procedures and what are the mechanics and technologies which are being brought into play. We have also found ourselves debating boundary issues concerning who gets included in the policy-deliberating frame and whose voices are consciously or by default excluded. Our arguments have been grounded in the assumption that, as Carr and Hartnett (1996) have said,

> In a society which takes democracy seriously, issues about the ways in which teachers are themselves educated will always be central to the public educational debate. (p. 195)

Democratic engagement with such issues is vital if there is to be a robust and sustainable public debate about 'effective' schooling.

As we indicated in Chapter 1, our work on teacher-education policy has connected outwards to broader debates on changing patterns of 'governance' in both the public and private sectors and forwards into considerations of the health of democratic processes generally and what, in Anthony Gidden's terms, it is going to mean to 'democratise democracy'. We do not claim to have exhaustively addressed the issues, even within our own chosen substantive area, but we hope to stimulate a foray into the 'undergrowth' of policy which will spark some debate on contemporary interpretations of accountability, representation and transparency.

Our argument in this chapter will be organised in three broad sections. We begin by drawing together some of the issues that emerge from the working structures and procedures of the TTA and we highlight questions of transparency and accountability that these raise. Then, by examining the documentation and debate which have accompanied the formative stages of the establishment of the GTC, we shall try to discern its significance as a 'democratic' development. Finally, extending these explorations, we shall address the question of what principles and practices could underpin the relationship between democracy and processes of policy formation in teacher education.

We saw earlier how establishing the dynamics of policy becomes very problematic in the context of the complex structures and working procedures characteristic of 'reinvented government'. Tracing the parentage and trajectories of particular policy lines was not made easier by the 'steers and bends' provided by individuals working formally and informally within the TTA. Whilst the Secretary of State retains ultimate ministerial responsibility for the TTA, it is the Board which is formally responsible for internal policy development within the Agency. However, in the context of assertive management, fast policy, fragmented staffing structures, kaleidoscopic working groups and external contracting of key activities, formal structures of policy accountability become highly attenuated. A clear example of this was provided by the trajectory of the consultation the TTA undertook for the DfEE on induction. The outcomes of this consultation were never even considered by the TTA Board but went direct to the Department. As we have indicated above in our illustration of the 'career' of the QTS Standards consultation, a mist obscures the processes of reconciliation which come into play when there are differences of opinion between the Board, Committees, and Working Groups. The following transcripts provide a brief sense of the complexities and multi-tracking involved in chasing policy.

> We were told the Board wouldn't like what we were proposing, they wanted something else. We didn't agree with what the Board wanted and people became very irritated. One person suggested that in that case it would be better if the Board did the work they wanted done and saved everybody's time and effort ... Nothing much happened in response to that, there was one more meeting with too much to do and what was produced ... a lot of us didn't agree with. I seem to remember that the final thing implied that a group of experts had produced it.
> (Working Group Member on Standards)

Relations and reconciliations between the Minister, Chair, Chief Executive, senior Civil Servants and TTA officers can prove equally opaque.

TTA BOARD MEMBER: There is an issue of conflicting loyalty. When a Minister rings up and tells an officer of the TTA to go do something, they tend to go do it, whether or not it's the Board's priority. So ... there's been some comments at Board Meetings about [an officer] having to go off and contribute really to policy, to DfEE policy when it is not the Board's policy ... So [the officer] was in quite a difficult position over that.

PM: Where does policy steer actually come from then, where ... should it come from?

TTA BOARD MEMBER: Oh! As there's a QUANGO, it's the Board's policy.

IH: Others might say, what you've been asked to do is to implement the Government's policy.

TTA BOARD MEMBER: No, the Government didn't give us a policy and if it was Government policy, why would we be there? I mean in a sense there's Government policy. ... we would like to have better quality teachers . ... there is a DfEE observer on the Board ... s/he will tell us what DfEE policy is in these various areas but s/he doesn't tell us what our policy ought to be with respect to teacher training. I mean we could all get sacked ... if we were stupid and quite right too ...

there isn't much point in having a QUANGO with the objective of improving teacher training if you don't let it get on with the job, is there?

One very experienced TTA officer who possessed wide political, negotiating and administrative experience provided us with a graphic account of the operation of what Whitehall insiders like to call 'the usual channels'.

> [It] … has always been the case that there has been a very close relationship be-tween QUANGOs of various kinds or for that matter HMI and the Department so that there is a lot of subterranean to-ing and fro-ing so that you know what will work and what won't and where you're going to have to push, to get a Minister to change his or her mind. And if you don't do that you're just not competent. I mean it's not a question of morals, it's a question of competence. If you want something to happen you've got to know whether it will happen and if it won't happen you've got to go around creating the climate where it will happen and you've got to do that in Ministerial Aides' and in Ministerial minds and what …
> [X officer] just described is the last bit of that before you know that if the Board sends it across, broadly speaking it will be acceptable.
>
> (TTA officer)

However, for another TTA officer the matter was not without its tensions.

> TTA OFFICER: Now the Board may say, oh we don't like this, we don't like option a) and b), we ought to say option c) but it would be for us to say and what are you going to do if the Secretary of State doesn't like option c).

The intervention of individual TTA officers further complicates the problem of tracing policy origin.

> WORKING GROUP MEMBER: Because of the fragmentation it's much more possible for an individual officer to stamp their own particular version. … We've ended up, because we as a group were never allowed to think through the fundamental issues, with a really rigid model which is basically the view of that one person. Who that officer speaks for God only knows!

Matters become even more complicated once consideration is given to the network of external relationships through which the Agency operates. These are not new concerns.

> In describing the tendency for boundaries between government and groups to become less distinct through a whole range of pragmatic developments, we see policies being made and administered between a myriad of interconnecting, interpenetrating organisations. It is the relationships involved in committees, the policy community of departments and groups, the practices of co-option and the

consensual style that perhaps better account for policy outcomes than do examinations of party stances, of manifestos or of parliamentary influence.

(Richardson and Jordan 1979, pp. 73–4)

However, the problem is exacerbated by the supposed separation between policy and
administration, one key feature of the 'arm's length' relationship which Agencies are
meant to have with their sponsoring departments. The result, it seems, is that only
some of the people are on the 'inside of the game' some of the time, and that, as has
been discovered in the recent relationship between Ministers and Agencies, concepts
of accountability and responsibility can prove very difficult to tie down. One of our
interviewees who had long experience of working in Whitehall illustrated these complexities very clearly.

> [As an Agency] … it is supposed to be executive functions but in actual fact they
> are making policy and so you were getting further and further away from any
> kind of political accountability or seemingly any kind of accountability and you
> get this strange focus on personalities … Now it seems that so much of govern-
> ment has been devolved out to the Agencies that we don't actually know who is
> doing anything any more or who is responsible for it.
>
> (NPQH trainer)

As the following quotation indicates, this becomes even more complex once external
bodies, perhaps contract-based, are built into the system.

> When the politicians were nominally to blame for any problem arising from out-
> side relationships, at least someone was. There may be gaps in the accountability
> system with the changes described here, in that accountability may be evaded al-
> together. If a problem arises from the bureaucracy's relationship with the outside
> both the public servant and the politician can claim it is not their fault.
>
> (Hughes 1994, p. 232)

The issues we have been addressing in this section move us well beyond our particular
concerns with and concentration upon the TTA. The public policy literature, from
which we have quoted, speaks volumes about the general nature of the 'deficit' we are
confronting. Increasingly the power of policy-setting is becoming firmly centralised
whilst 'responsibility' and a delimited version of accountability are being passed
down the line. Such slippery patterns of political accountability and representation
make questions of policy determination and steering extraordinarily complex to tie
down. These are the real, public costs which lie behind the concept of the 'democratic deficit'. In the recent House of Commons Select Committee Report (1999) on
the work of OFSTED, the following comment was made which we feel could be
applied equally to the TTA:

> The political commentator and author Peter Riddell has recently argued that
> changes to the structure of government, particularly those which led to the

creation of a large number of executive agencies and non-departmental public bodies, have 'challenged traditional ideas of accountability, and Parliament has so far failed adequately to adjust'. He argues that in many cases parliamentary procedures and constitutional theory 'have not kept up with changes in the management and organisation' of the public sector.

(para. 196, p. lvii)

Whilst we do not have space here to explore the academic debate on policy formation/administration/implementation and trajectory, our own experiences lead us to echo Daws' observation that

> At each point, policy is a response to complex and diverse elements, including a range of constraints imposed by other levels of public and educational policy, different administrative contexts, varying ideologies and the personal idiosyncrasies of the people involved.
>
> (Daws, cited in Taylor, Rizvi, Lingard and Henry 1997, p. 154)

And, of course, transparency is not helped by the fact that those in power may well be 'economical with the truth', be guilty of sins of omission or commission, 'spin' in a misleading manner, or be intentionally evasive for political ends. An overt instance of this was found in the interview which Kenneth Baker (Secretary of State for Education under Margaret Thatcher) gave on 16 September 1999 to the *Guardian* newspaper.

> But did he realise that the introduction of 'parental choice' would polarise the system and effectively kill off the comprehensives? 'Oh, yes, that was deliberate. In order to make changes you have to come from several points.' ... Stealth was essential. 'I was not going to take on the comprehensive system head-on. ... So I believed that if I set in train certain changes, they would have, er, a cumulative beneficial effect.'

And later,

> Lord Baker may laugh, but it is striking how many of his reforms were rooted in whim. Mrs Thatcher had told him to go away for a month or two and come up with something. So he did. (p. 4)

The articulation of the specifics of the TTA with the wider structure of changes in social policy and administration raises serious issues when we come to consider questions of information access, accountability and attribution of responsibility. For anyone not already in the know, it becomes extremely problematic to discover how you can find out what you want to know, let alone discovering what you ought to want to know. In trying to trace 'responsibility' it is easy to get lost in an organisational net(work). There are numerous ways in which the democratic process of accountability can become confused and subverted in the routines of bodies like the

TTA. Anxiety in this respect was reflected in both our interviews and questionnaire returns. When we asked respondents to make judgments about the TTA, 'accountability' received the highest number of negative responses and the lowest number of positive responses of all the criteria on which we asked people to rate the activities of the Agency.

Margaret Simey has made some telling points about the principles underpinning the concept of accountability which highlight the increasing 'democratic deficit' in the UK.

> ... accountability is not a mechanism or a routine but a principle. More than that, it is a principle which serves a specific purpose. In a democracy, that purpose is to provide the basis for the relationship between the society and its members, between those who govern and those who consent to be governed. The word consent provides the significant clue.
>
> (Simey 1985, p. 17)

Maintaining a distinction between political and managerial accountability is vitally important. Not only do these two notions of accountability not necessarily map onto one another, they may indeed exist in tension or conflict and the criteria by which they are to be judged or evaluated are not identical. As Ferlie *et al.* say,

> A contest between alternative notions of accountability is evident, and is a key aspect of the current debate around the rise and nature of the new public management.
>
> (1996, p. 195)

In short, transparency (political accountability) and 'value for money' (managerial accountability) are not the same thing and tensions between them need to be reconciled. Decisive decision-making and enforcement (managerial accountability) need to be held in balance with questions of responsibility and representation (political accountability). As Hughes (1994) writes,

> Accountability relationships in the private sector are increasingly seen as a *model* – the best available practice for the public sector. ... [this] will mean greater effort in developing performance indicators as surrogate measures analogous to those measures such as profit which exist in the private sector. ... The private sector has no real equivalent of political accountability, for which precise measures are never likely to be found. ... But, as long as the private sector remains the *model* of accountability, the public sector will be vulnerable to arguments that it is not accountable, and to reductions in its size and scope, made on accountability grounds.
>
> (p. 238–9, emphasis in original)

Once political accountability becomes subsumed within a managerialist model, its effects and those of its legitimating rhetorics become all-pervasive as the stress on commercial styles of management replaces the former public-service ethic. Where once we worked, in teacher education, with beginning or experienced teachers, we have during the course of our research heard them variously described as 'customers', 'units of resource' or, more cynically, as 'money on legs'. 'Providers' search for 'niche markets', wonder whether they are projecting their 'visions' effectively and whether they are 'delivering' their 'products' in 'cost-effective' ways. The competitive language of sex and war has also become pervasive as opposition is 'shafted', 'game plans' developed and 'targets' hit or overshot. Whether such approaches enable us to adequately equip and support teachers who are endeavouring to enable young people to be able to act responsibly and critically as citizens, in an increasingly complex world, is a question notable for its absence. Extremely demanding issues arise when we try to interpret what is meant by terms such as 'efficiency' or 'standards' and to establish democratic and equitable procedures for the representation, reconciliation and operational implications of differing viewpoints and value positions about the role of teachers and what counts as 'effective teaching'.

Such issues are of direct, strategic importance in any consideration of (teacher-) education policy. When we asked people about the prospective future of the TTA, our questionnaires revealed that, even amongst those respondents who were most favourably disposed towards the TTA, it was felt that changes needed to be made in the procedures through which policies were initiated, legitimated and implemented. The majority of respondents also wished to see structural changes to render the governance of teacher education more representative, and this was often connected to support for a General Teaching Council.

The English GTC

Background

Shortly after its election in May 1997, the Labour government announced its intention to establish a General Teaching Council for England (and Wales).[1] This intention was formalised within the *Teaching and Higher Education Act* which became law in July 1998. Prior to the introduction of the legislation, the DfEE undertook a consultation that dealt with general issues surrounding the proposal (DfEE 1997b). During the passage of the Bill through Parliament, a further consultation was conducted that focused directly on the issue of the composition of the GTC (DfEE 1998c). Elections for the Council took place in Spring 2000 and the GTC began operating in September of the same year.

In his foreword to the 1997 Consultation, Stephen Byers (then Minister for School Standards) laid out the basic thinking which underpinned the government's initiative.

> [The GTC] will bring together and reflect the interests of all those with a stake in ensuring high standards in teaching – parents, employers, higher education and the wider public as well as teachers. The GTC will take its place in our new national partnership to raise standards in schools.
> Our aim is to set up a professional body which will encourage all teachers to

play their part in the challenging programme of reform … The GTC must represent the highest professional standards and speak out where standards are not what they should be. We are not interested in a talking shop for teachers or a body to defend the way things are.

(DfEE 1997b, p. 3)

In an introductory letter to teachers and headteachers (September 1999), Carol Adams (Chief Executive Designate) said that the Council will

1 raise the status and public standing of teachers by acting as a self-regulating body to represent the professional interests of teachers and supporting teachers through its activities.
2 provide a strong, independent and united voice for teachers to shape change and influence policy on major educational issues, by advising the Secretary of State on, for example, standards of teaching and professional development.
3 maintain and guarantee high professional standards through the Register of Teachers, Code of Conduct and Practice and its advisory role on entry to the profession.

Decades of conflict and indecision, accompanied by vigorous campaigning by teacher unions and a whole variety of educational and professional pressure groups, preceded the introduction of the GTC in England and Wales (Sayer 1999; Tomlinson 1995). Previous endeavours foundered on the twin rocks of resistance from governments unwilling to relinquish power and authority over such a significant occupational group, and competitive struggles between teacher unions and professional associations over questions of status and weight of representation. Echoes of both quandaries can be found in the current legislation. Nonetheless, in stating its commitment to found a GTC the new Labour government was at one with the general orientation of the educational world. In both of our research projects we had asked questions about our cohorts' positive or negative responses to the idea of a GTC. Across the cohorts there was a preponderant desire for such a professional council to be established. In the second project we specifically asked whether people felt that 'responsibility for standards in teaching ought to rest with a GTC'. Virtually 80 per cent of our total respondents expressed agreement with this statement, and there was no cohort for whom a positive response fell below 67 per cent.

GTC and TTA

This, then, constituted the general support for an embryonic GTC. However, it has to be remembered that the GTC is being established alongside the TTA. Both the legislation and official documents leave much of the interface between the two bodies (perhaps intentionally) hazy. Whilst in the past the TTA appeared to possess a wide remit for policy development and implementation in the field of teacher education and professional development, within the regulations now in place the GTC is accorded largely *advisory* functions (see, for example, paras. 2 and 3 of Carol Adams' letter above). A large number of the responses to the GTC Consultation drew attention to the unresolved tensions within the proposals between the intended remit of the Council and work currently falling within the ambit of the TTA. This ambiguity persisted through to the Quinquennial Review (DfEE 1999a) which reported that

> ... a significant number [of respondents] are unclear about the GTC's remit ... They see potential for confusion in the apparent overlap between the current functions of the TTA, and the potential future functions of the GTC.
>
> (p. 19)

At the completion of the Review the situation seems no clearer, since the Executive Summary merely restates the problem.

> Following the formation of the GTCs and the leadership college, there will be a need for the DfEE to provide a coherent and strategic view across teaching issues. A clear division of roles and responsibilities is also needed between the TTA and the GTCs.
>
> (p. 1)

For its part, the Agency echoed the open-ended language of partnership which figures so largely in contemporary official discourse. In her address at the launch of the 1998 Corporate Plan, Anthea Millett spoke as follows:

> ... we shall forge a close relationship with a brand new partner whose arrival is imminent – the General Teaching Council. I very much welcome the creation of the GTC. I know I am not the only one here who recognises that it has great potential to add value. In order to realise that potential it will be vital for the Council to maintain a clear focus on supporting high standards for the teaching profession. And, at a time when there is increasing debate inside and outside schools about what should be the structure of the teaching profession in the next century, the GTC has the potential to provide an important leadership role.
>
> (Millett 1998b, p. 10)

Similarly in an interview a TTA Board member said

> ... it's not going to be fundamentally different from the relationship between the TTA and other, you know, existing players. I mean this is just a new body and we've got lots of issues of partnership that occur, when you're talking about QCA or OFSTED or other agencies, ... It's impossible to be absolutely firm but I would apply exactly the same principles to looking at the relationship between the TTA and GTC as I would to the TTA's relationship with other bodies.

One important element of the tensions between the GTC and the TTA is that whilst the majority of the membership of the Council represents and is elected/nominated by the teaching profession, the TTA Board members are appointed directly by the Secretary of State. Analysis of the GTC consultation responses conveyed the very strong impression that people were relishing the prospect of removing the TTA (as an unrepresentative, unaccountable, undemocratic body) and arguing that its activities and functions should be transferred to a more professionally accountable and reflective council.

How the Government will respond to such tensions once the GTC is firmly established is as yet unknowable. The terms of the Act leave enormous areas of the GTC activity and structure to be filled in through later regulation by the Secretary of State. This invests him and his successors with considerable scope for redefining all the 'ifs, mights and maybes' with which the legislation is currently littered.

Professional standards

This failure at a structural level to consider the relationship between the GTC and the TTA is not simply a minor point which can wait for piecemeal resolution, but strikes directly at the heart of the status of the teaching force. The concern is that there are some vital areas where issues that might be regarded as falling within the remit of the profession (Ingvarson 1998) are being undertaken by the TTA. At the centre of these are questions of Standards both for entry to the profession and for subsequent professional development. If there is to be any meaning to 'professional ownership', then there has to be influence on these matters by the appropriate professional body. We have already discussed in some detail the determinative role played by the TTA in the formulation of professional standards for teachers. This stands in marked contrast to the situation for most professional associations which tend to jealously guard their 'knowledge base' for the twin purposes of regulating entry to and progression within the profession, and for defining the professional field itself. Once again, the contrasts with doctors and nursing are quite stark.[2] The key point to note in this context is that if the nature of constitutive professional knowledge is to be radically redefined (as it has been under the auspices of the NPS framework), then this will carry important consequences for the definition of the profession concerned. This will be exacerbated if the reconstitution of that knowledge base is accomplished without the involvement of, or in the face of opposition from, the profession concerned. Hence the critical significance of the interface between the remits and powers of the TTA and the GTC. These issues remain unresolved but clearly will need to be worked out if, as Carol Adams says, the Council is to advise 'the Secretary of State on, for example, standards of teaching and professional development' and if there is to be an opportunity for teachers 'to shape change and influence policy'. Clarity on such issues becomes even more urgent in the light of the Green Paper and the establishment of a performance-management regime which is so tightly hinged to 'Standards', since patterns of progression, career enhancement, security, conditions of service and equitable reward structures and opportunities are all tied into this frame.

We would not want to argue that the GTC should represent or be answerable only to 'the profession', nor that it should possess autonomy over what are to count as professional standards for entry and progression, but if it is to operate as a professional body then it needs to occupy a central place in the deliberative process, not be given a merely advisory role on a par with a whole host of other bodies. Certainly, many would argue that the TTA possesses neither the status nor the experience to define and enforce such standards. Neither its practices of consultation nor its ministerially appointed board are substitutes for a properly established system of professional debate and decision-making, subject to appropriate mechanisms of transparency, accountability and political ratification.

The government's stated intention to enhance the status and standards of teaching cannot be accomplished without giving the GTC much more say in the whole 'standards' establishment and regulation process. At present there is a central ambivalence in the government's proposals which revolves around issues of power and control. As one of the consultation respondents put it, 'whose standards are these?' The government is not going to want to give up its power and the TTA acts as a very helpful lightning conductor in this respect. The government can maintain all of the control it wants and divert the attendant 'professional antagonism' around standards to the TTA. It is perhaps hardly surprising that it is leaving unresolved the problematic interface between the two bodies.

> I think if your ultimate model is a profession which is of very high status, and achieving very high standards by any kind of international comparisons, then the only appropriate model for that is a very high degree of self-government and self-regulation. But you know, that also requires a very high level of political trust and I don't see any politician around at the moment who is willing yet to hand that over. And while that's still the case then you know, I think the jury will remain out.
>
> (TTA Board member)

The issue of 'professional standards' is closely linked to questions of 'professional gatekeeping'. It is intended that the GTC should have a role as the *registration agency* for teachers, indeed after an interim period its activities will be financed through the registration funds it receives from teachers. However, important though such registration is, it is difficult to see it as other than an administrative function if the establishment and control over the criteria (standards) which form the basis for registration reside entirely elsewhere. As a very experienced campaigner for the GTC said to us in an interview,

> ... if you've got a system as we've now got as such, external regulation of teaching standards and all the rest ... the risk is of driving out any kind of inner motivation and sense of commitment and responsibility in the profession itself, and I see the Teaching Council as symbolic of all that and actually saying this is the visible and outward sign that the teaching profession is responsible for its own development, ... and the way you give it that is partly by internal regulation ...
>
> (Education Association Officer)

Professionality and power

In the light of our earlier comments on the politics of 'professionality', it is important to note that the language within which the introduction of the GTC is being couched is full of references to 'the profession' and 'professionalism'. For example, the most recent consultation document says

> The GTC ... will be a new professional body for teachers. Independent of government and with at least half a million members, it will be able to speak with authority on behalf of the teaching profession.
>
> (DfEE 1999g, p. 2)

However, on the basis of issues such as those we have outlined above, we are left reflecting on the extent to which the proposed GTC constitutes a 'professional council' in any meaningful respect. Even if we revert to the most mundane functionalist or trait theories of professionalism (which treat control over entry, establishment of a distinctive knowledge base, self-regulation, responsibility for training methods, control over assessment of competence and certification as defining characteristics of professions), there is little basis for viewing the GTC as comparable with professional bodies in other occupational sectors. An MP we interviewed put the issues very firmly in the context of what he called the concentration of 'the mechanics of the establishment' of the GTC.

> There has not been enough work done to define the nature of professionalism. If this body is to determine entry into the profession we surely have to have a very clear definition of what a professional teacher is. That must be to do with entry qualifications, of course, but it must also be to do with things like commitment to constant professional development, self-criticism and issues like that and it seems to me that that's the missing piece of the jigsaw at the moment when we actually look at the role of the GTC.

The pervasive nature of the official discourse of 'profession, professional, professionalism' leads us to question what work this language is being employed to accomplish. There is no doubt that the language of 'professionality' carries significant historical, cultural, symbolic and personal power in England. The terms have come to function as 'hurrah' words in denoting a committed and responsible approach to doing one's work well; alternatively, to be called 'unprofessional' is to stand accused. But they are also highly collusive terms and contain new forms of cultural incorporation and plausibility outside of which it is difficult to step. In terms of Third Way language it is the vocabulary to use if you are to remain 'on-message' rather than being sidelined as a 'whinger'. The question is raised as to whether in relation to the new GTC we are in the presence of a token gesture, a chimera which pretends to take the body of teachers seriously as 'professionals' whilst effectively 're-engineering' them as cohorts of workers under the auspices of a new work order. Or whether we are in the realm of a new form of state functionary, carrying with it the gloss of profession and an appearance of professional autonomy, whilst deeply embedded within *structures* of incorporation within which there are rewards for compliance but little room for manoeuvre.

Thus alongside the genuine welcome for the GTC we reported earlier there was also some scepticism about the extent of the powers which might be accorded to such a council. As one of our interviewees said,

> ... I've always been very sceptical about a GTC. I don't think the state is likely to give up its regulative functions to a professional body in the 1990s and it would probably like to take some of them away from existing professional bodies. So I think we would get a form of General Teaching Council which helped to mollify the profession, but not actually give it real powers. So I actually think it is an illusion. I'd rather it was much clearer who was pulling the strings.
>
> (Policy analyst)

A number of people whom we interviewed also expressed dissatisfaction with the idea of a GTC if that was 'designed to enhance professional autonomy'. One can detect a will to think beyond the rock of professional autonomy and the hard place of an unelected, unrepresentative agency of government, even though evidence from the consultations on the GTC indicates that awareness of issues of inclusivity are disappointingly low. Given all the goodwill it carries, it remains to be seen whether the English GTC can escape some of the problems McPherson and Raab (1988) saw as characterising the Scottish GTC. They described these problems as

> ... as much a battle for internecine squabbling, as it was a professional body enhancing the corporate status of teachers. (p. 279)

And they go on to say that

> ... because it was more a colony of its constituent interests than it was their aggregator, the Council could only double the parts, neither enriching the polyphony nor performing solo. (p. 281)

We have found these concerns echoed in the comments of interviewees with the additional anxiety that internal disputes and a highly directive hand from central government may make it difficult for the GTC to establish an independent agenda or an autonomous identity.

Most of the considerations we have addressed so far are 'insiders'' versions. It could be argued that they are dominated by professionally parochial concerns about remits, representation, membership and powers which, whilst of vital significance to educational practitioners, fail to connect with or even recognise wider democratic issues that could and should be raised in discussions of educational governance. Beyond this insiders' perspective and the protective fence of professionalism, there is a whole other debate with which we need to engage, which focuses on issues of accountability, public debate and inclusivity. Teacher education is not some obscure, esoteric matter. Teachers possess strategically significant access to young (and not-so-young) learners in society and have a sanctioned position as conduits of the knowable, the thinkable and the profane. They are literally paid to change consciousness, not always or everywhere in progressive directions. As an occupational cohort they may see themselves as in possession of a communal professional identity or define themselves as servants of the state, perhaps neither, perhaps both at the same time. Deliberations on such issues require contexts in which they can be responsibly and seriously debated and where it does not feel as though 'dissensus will be identified with adolescent behaviour' (as one of our interviewees put it). In such contexts we find new grounds for what is happening to teachers and teaching which are more general than particular, more public than professional, more transnational than localised. This takes us into broader considerations of the nature of emergent patterns of governance and their implications for power and control in the societies within which we live.

Governance, representation and accountability

Many political analysts and commentators argue that what we are witnessing, far from being a new form of democracy emerging, is a growing 'democratic deficit' (Benhabib 1996; Ranson and Stewart 1994 and 1998; Raulston Saul 1997; Weir and Beetham 1999). Anxieties over democratic governance are exposing shortcomings in the formulation, steering and implementation of policy. The questions of representation, accountability and transparency which we have been discussing are by no means limited to teacher education nor even the public sector. Concern spreads far beyond the UK, for if such a deficit is consequent upon increasingly dominant competitive-economic models then the future of democracy and the forms that it takes in our complex societies are dilemmas for all those undergoing current transformations. One particular expression of the dilemma of democratic legitimacy resides in the ever-present tensions of centralisation/decentralisation/regionalism, which is a major issue in many other European (and non-European) contexts (Henry *et al.* 1999; Lindblad 2000).

In our questionnaire survey we asked a number of questions which referred to centralisation, decentralisation and the significance of context.

Figure 6.1 shows that some three-quarters of our respondents felt that NPS *should* define general parameters which could be locally interpreted, whilst less than 30 per cent felt that such local flexibility was actually possible within the Standards. Similarly, whilst nearly 70 per cent agreed that the Standards paid too little attention to social contexts, almost the same number saw the NPS as constituting an attempt to exercise greater political control over education. Time and again our interview respondents, even those who were perhaps sympathetic to the ethos of NPS, emphasised the salience of context to teachers' orientations.

> ... a wonderfully endearing but problematic feature of the teaching profession is that there is an inherent insistence on local context. ... Now, I think there's terrific strength in that. That's part of the professionalism of teachers in that they want ownership. They know their clients, their children. They often know the parents. They believe in their community. They are rooted in their community and they get to know it and they love it and they see everything from that point of view and they ... put their kids first and put their class first and put their marking and preparation first. ... Teachers are there with the kids and that does make you contextualise ...

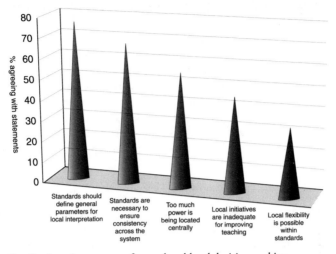

Figure 6.1 Implications for patterns of central and local decision-making.

You have to admire the individuality of every school. Every school is a different place to work in. It's a different combination of individuals, both the kids and the teachers. And that's highly problematic when it comes to standardisation and that's going to be a problem with the Green Paper threshold, I think.

(Chief Education Officer)

The attendant political and logistical implications were also given important emphasis.

I think we're in a very dangerous position indeed if we're seen to have a nationally and centrally driven education service and there is nothing between that and 25,000 schools. All of which are perfectly and indeed increasingly capable of managing their own affairs, bringing about their own kind of development and whatever but who actually need and ... are looking for some kind of local broker-age that can enable things to happen. Because if you wait for central brokerage you will wait forever because with 500,000 teachers and 25,000 schools there is not enough person power centrally to make all of that happen. And in any event, they can't take into account local needs, requirements, context, change and varia-tions and whatever.

(Professional Development Officer)

There was little sense or hint of 'regionality' within any of the official documentation preceding the proposed GTC framework. Insofar as 'regional offices' were referred to it was purely as

... part of the government's plan ... to get things out of London, and therefore obtain cheaper labour. It was cheaper to run and you'd get better quality staff for the same amount of money if you move out of London. So it was kind of purely economic reasons, got nothing to do with the value of the regionalisation.

(Education Association Officer)

More recently, however, Carol Adams, the newly appointed Chief Executive of the GTC, has made positive comments about the importance of 'regionality', which may stem from her previous work as a CEO in a major 'non-metropolitan' LEA. She is surely correct in recognising that it is a vital issue to engage with, not least because of what is known about how and where good practice flourishes; how energy and commitment are maintained; the importance of trust in supporting teachers' creativity and the danger of throttling or constraining local developments within centralised systems.

> They [teaching standards] won't make a difference as being something that's sort of imposed as some incredible detailed theological dictate from on high. They will only make a difference if people can engage on them, build some ownership and understanding of them and that has to mean to some extent some customising, flavouring into the local context. ... there are issues about teaching, the task of teaching in somewhere like ... which have a very different emphasis and flavour and terminology than in other parts of the country. So perhaps naively they thought that they were going to suddenly become instantly sort of applied everywhere. ... They can't have seriously believed that schools were going to actually take hold of them and seriously apply them.
>
> (LEA officer)

Ranson and Stewart (1998) express very much the same sentiments but in a more generalised form when they say

> Many tiers in organisational hierarchies separate ministers from action and impact. Central government cannot easily encompass diversity of circumstance or achieve diversity in response. Yet learning comes from a recognition of diversity of need, diversity of aspiration and diversity of response. ... A central government can achieve learning if it uses the diversity of local government as its base.
>
> (pp. 268–9)

Considerations such as these pose dilemmas about the new forms of representation and accountability which will best form the basis for democratic governance in the future. They also raise important questions about the nature and form of political accountability in this current historical, political context. There are three levels at which it is possible to consider accountability:

Accountability upwards – which is predominantly the model of accountability through which bodies like the TTA operate via its relationships with ministerial departments and parliamentary committees;

Accountability sideways or horizontally – on which basis most professional associations operate in acting upon, reporting to and being largely responsive to the wishes of their members; and

Accountability downwards – which is a much more tangled and neglected area which is presumed to be covered through conventional electoral processes.

But as Ranson and Stewart (1994) say,

> Our current form of public accountability is inadequate or, more precisely, incomplete. It offers members of the public a particularly exiguous form of participation (periodic voting) which has been used to distance them from the polity. It establishes the polity as something out there, not something *we* as citizens are members of or believe we have any responsibility for.
>
> (p. 235, emphasis in original)

If increased participation is being proposed as a better alternative to 'consumer democracy', then debates will have to take account of the ways in which our societies are increasingly diversified. Within most official documentation in our country it would be very surprising not to find lip-service being paid to the interests of parents, students, employers and the much-vaunted 'community interests'. However, the significance of this, when fleshed out, often tends to appear somewhat tokenistic. Clearly this is no easy issue even though – for some politicians, policy-makers, administrators and educationists – the resolution to the dilemmas seems straightforward. You form a defined policy (perhaps after officially sponsored exploration of alternatives and consultation) and then implement it with clarity and determination. Policies on 'standards', 'outcomes', 'quality' and 'effectiveness' would be good contemporary exemplars of such an approach. All too often, however, such policies are insufficiently grounded in the nature of the educational experiences which most people encounter. They are legitimated by consultations that have drawn on too narrow a base, have failed to access or hear the 'voices' of those who are most excluded from the communicative loop, fail to reflect upon or leave adequate space for the detailed specifics of circumstances, privilege certain interests over others, and operate with totalising orientations which fail to take account of structural, sectional, and regional differentiations. None of this may be intentionally malicious but it does not make for good democracy, although some would argue that it does make for strong government. Anna Coote (1999) has recently argued that

> Unless an organisation is prepared to cope with unwelcome or unpredictable results, the exercise will be counter-productive. The 'involved' public may feel that they are being manipulated or exploited, or believe that whatever they do or say will make no difference – whatever methods are used to involve them. More important still, those who are severely deprived and marginalised are usually much harder to involve than those who are more resourceful and assertive, and so unless special efforts are made to reach excluded groups, public involvement strategies

> may compound inequalities and deepen divisions between those with a voice and
> those without.   (p. 123)

There are different levels at which the representation of different 'voices' within the
policy process are clearly crucial:

- adequacy of representation on the policy-making bodies themselves;
- sensitivity of the criteria, values and purposes underpinning policy to the needs of
  different constituencies;
- quality of communicating policy outcomes and their rationales and the extent to
  which they both speak and listen to the responses of diverse, perhaps conflicting,
  bodies of interest.

At a technical level many people, academics, policy analysts and practitioners have
been exploring various ways of 'enhancing public participation'. These include inno-
vations in democratic practices such as citizens' juries, deliberative opinion polls, citizens' panels, consensus conferences, mediation groups, community forums,
stakeholder conferences, scrutiny panels and so on. Recently the DETR, in conjunction with LGA and LGMB, have sponsored a major research project on *Enhancing
Public Participation in Local Government* (Lowndes 1998). This attempted to provide a comprehensive review of the diversity of participation initiatives available to
local authorities, many of which have received little attention in relation to education
policy. In tandem with this, the international academic community in the course of
its struggles with new meanings and forms of 'democracy' is also recognising the crucial importance of establishing institutional procedures which will enable more
inclusive and responsive forms of deliberation to take place (Benhabib 1996).

Anne Phillips (1996) describes and analyses the tensions and collisions which are
involved in attempting to take account of the cacophony of 'voices' which make up
contemporary societies. In her discussion of what she calls the 'new pluralism' she says

> ... much of the contemporary work on democracy and difference operates with
> notions of a more active and vigorous democracy that depends crucially on public
> debate. Rejecting both the false harmony that stamps out difference and the
> equally false essentialism that defines people through some single, authentic
> identity, many look to a democracy that maximises citizen participation and re-
> quires us to engage and contest with one another.   (p. 143)

She fully recognises the dilemmas which arise when recognition of diversity may
exacerbate division and fragmentation and which apparently pull against the quest
for wider community and solidarity. In her own words, however, '[T]he ultimate
goal is a wider sense of belonging, which is why difference can be neither denied nor
simply left as it is' (1993, p. 157). Her arguments are grounded in the need for a
transformative politics which recognises power, domination and structural
oppressions. Although not specifically about education, her lengthy quote from Iris

Young (1990) brings us back to our own substantive focus by revealing what is currently missing from the routine debates on educational governance.

> Group representation unravels the false consensus that cultural imperialism may have produced, and reveals group bias in norms, standards, styles and perspectives that have been assumed as universal or of highest value. By giving voice to formerly silenced or devalued needs and experiences, group representation forces participants in discussion to take a reflective distance on their assumptions and think beyond their own interests. When confronted with interests, needs and opinions that derived from very different social positions and experience, persons sometimes come to understand the limitations of their own experience and perspective for coming to a conclusion about the best policy for everyone. Coupled with the knowledge that the perspectives expressed by oppressed groups also carry a specific vote, and thus that they cannot be ignored if the whole body is to come to a decision, such enhanced communication best promotes just outcomes.
>
> (Quoted in Phillips 1993, p. 158)

These general concerns connect with the more educationally specific conclusions of Whitty *et al.* (1998) where they have recently argued that contemporary social justice requires a politics of both *recognition* and *redistribution*. Their comparative analysis of the tensions which arise between centralisation, devolution, choice and entitlement ends with an injunction to explore the refashioning of educational politics and decision-making to take account of wider constituencies of representation. Like Phillips, they lay no claims to easy solutions, indeed, as they say,

> Future policies need both to recognise and redistribute, although pursuing both paths simultaneously is not straightforward. For instance, as Fraser (1997) argues, the politics of recognition tend to involve the highlighting and valuing of group differences, while the politics of redistribution look to erode the basis of social difference. (p. 138)

These debates take us well beyond the confines of education policy, let alone the even more specific terrain of teacher education, but addressing such issues is vital if there is to be a sustainable public debate about education and the role of teachers within it.

7 Addressing the future

Positives, negatives, obstacles and spaces

> [Hawksmoor] was not sure if all the movements and changes in the world were part of some coherent development, like the weaving of a quilt which remains one fabric despite its variegated pattern. Or was it a more delicate operation than this – like the enlarging surface of a balloon in the sense that, although each part increased at the same rate of growth as every other part, the entire object grew more fragile as it expanded? And if one element was suddenly to vanish, would the others disappear also – imploding upon each other helplessly as if time itself were unravelling amid a confusion of sights, calls, shrieks and phrases of music which grew smaller and smaller?
>
> (Ackroyd 1985, p. 126)

We have been privileged to have had the opportunity and resources to explore the dilemmas, tensions, joys and demands currently confronting teachers and teacher-educators. This privilege carries with it certain responsibilities to give something back which will prove to be of value. In this spirit our conclusion is offered as an agenda of concerns and as a contribution to a dialogue rather than as a policy intervention or claim in its own right. In our view too many people are already 'reaching for policy' prematurely without having adequately addressed the processes and structures through which policy deliberation may be firmly and equitably founded.

At the start of the book we referred to the idea of critical policy analysis, and in particular to the injunction that

> If ... policies are an amalgam of progressive and regressive elements ... then the task of critical policy analysis is to help to develop strategies to harness their progressive potential.
>
> (Taylor *et al.* 1997, p. 156)

We are conscious that the bulk of what we have reported is deeply depressing and disturbing, especially to those teachers and teacher-educators who have received such a 'hard pounding' from policy over the last two decades or so. We have a great deal of interview data spanning both the last years of John Major's Conservative administration and the early years of Tony Blair's 'new' Labour government which gives voice to teachers working in what has been well characterised as a climate of fear and uncertainty. Such a climate has also at times provoked high levels of anxiety in us which have been little alleviated by a change of government.

> Let no one, no sceptic, no energy sapper, erode the enthusiasm and the hope that currently exists ... if you are not with us, then step aside for there is no room in the education service for those who do not believe we can do better. This is a can-do government and you must lead a can-do service.
>
> (Blunkett 1997)

In the first flush of electoral success such an oratorical challenge is (perhaps) understandable. When such a style is maintained over time it becomes both threatening and confrontational. We have come across almost no-one who does not believe that 'we can do better', but we would urge the Secretary of State for Education to distinguish between complacency or indifference on the one hand and legitimate debate or disagreement on the other. As an expression of how far we have travelled along a road of what our Australian colleagues would call 'corporate managerialism', compare David Blunkett's comments above with those made in 1986 by a former Secretary of State for Education and leader of the Labour Party, Neil Kinnock.

> The objectives of *choice, standards* and *relevance* must be central themes of education. They have been debased by the present government in order to mobilise prejudice, feed propaganda and provide excuses for narrowing and reducing provision ... The expansion of choice, the raising of performance standards, the increase of relevance, together with other objectives of education like social and cultural enlightenment, good behaviour, responsibility, self confidence, the encouragement of the appetite for knowledge, the fulfilment of potential, the development of the individual regardless of sex, race, or economic circumstances, are desirable. But they are only significant if they are supported and reinforced by adequate resources and implemented in a partnership with the professionals that can foster success.
>
> (Quoted in Demaine 1999, pp. 9–10, emphasis in original)

As well as expressing a political transition, this quotation also highlights the way in which certain concepts have been appropriated, their boundaries mandated and interpretive debate constrained. 'Standards', 'effective' and 'accountability' are three which spring to mind. In each case there is a rich tradition of debate around these terms, the familiarity and grasp of which would both enhance the sophistication of policy-making and empower democratic understanding. Amongst many other things it is the ignoring or denial of such histories which leads to concerns that we are in the grip of 'control-freakery'. The dilution of such a tradition of debate and legitimate disagreement in favour of 'presentational' politics is, in our view, a powerful indictment of any supposedly democratic society.

During the course of our argument we have referred to a wide range of features of policy which are distorting practice and eroding the confidence and vitality of the public sector. Primary amongst these is the negativity which is expressed towards any-thing which lies within the public sphere and the elevation of that which is 'private'. Whilst resourcing levels for the public sector have not been cut, they have been restructured in the drive for economic competitiveness. This 'restructuring' has chan-nelled resources into the re-engineering of the 'service' along private-sector lines of financially driven, quantitative modes of performativity and effectiveness which take too little account of the forms and quality of non-calculative contributions to social life. These operational assumptions and their associated technologies are embedded within managerialised models of organisational structures and social relationships which privilege hierarchical and competitive work structures and hold these in place through strong and non-negotiable regulative controls.

At macro-levels there has been an intentional sifting and grading of educational institutions (schools and HEIs) through simplistic outcome and best-value indicator systems and the crudest productions of league-tabling, which serve as proxies for the profitability and Stock-Exchange indicators of the private sector. Such dynamics allow (or encourage) the production of fragmented, highly stratified, differentiated segmentations both within and between communities, with all the consequential short-term and longer-term impacts on life-chances and opportunity structures.

In our explorations of the policy-making process we have been dismayed by the limitations we have encountered. Politicians and policy-makers are oriented towards a 'short-termism' which possesses limited perspective on the past and scarcely stretches beyond the electoral cycle. We are faced with a politics of the 'solution' but without an adequate definition of the problem which it is deemed to solve. Little attention appears to have been paid to how problems might be defined and who should be involved in the process of defining them, or to what the parameters and impact of 'so-lutions' might prove to be in terms of the consequences (intended or otherwise). LeGrand has recently argued that the government 'is too swamped by the day-to-day preoccupations of office to engage in the necessary reflection' (quoted in Demaine 1999, p. 16). This links to what might count as 'evidence' and the deeply selective use made of it. For example the very thin version of pedagogy being proposed by current policy appears to have paid little attention to the much richer models of pedagogy and curriculum content being developed elsewhere (Lingard 1999b). Similarly there appears to be a resounding clash between policies of performance management as strategies for the attraction of 'talented young graduates' and the recent research by the team at the University of North London which has indicated that amongst teach-ers leaving teaching for other occupations

> The major advantages of the new jobs (in comparison with teaching) were oppor-tunities to use creativity and initiative. This finding seems particularly worrying; for many teachers these were the very aspects that attracted them to teaching in the first place.
>
> (Hutchings *et al.* 2000, pp. 19–20)

Nor does much consideration appear to have been given to historical evidence of what policies have been tried (successfully or unsuccessfully) in the past, or to the wealth of experiential evidence and insight which is available in ethnographic or oral research on teachers' lives and work. A number of consultants whom we interviewed reminded us that a great deal of what is now recognised as good practice within the mainstream school improvement movement was actually developed by teachers in classrooms, usually supported by local or national networks into which they volunteered. The limitations of voluntaristic models of professional learning are substantial, policy imposition, however, is not an answer to these conundrums, not even imposition which claims to have evidential backing. Evidence is not a weapon but an aid to reflection and decision-making. Evidence does not act as a substitute for thought, nor as a proxy for responsibility. On the contrary, it has to be used with responsibility and as an aid to thought, for evidence does not speak for itself. There are many sources of evidence; they do not by any means point in the same direction, they do not derive from given starting points, nor is there any agreement as to what counts as the data which should form the basis of evidence. To grant these things is not to dissolve into helpless relativism but to recognise that while we need a place to stand, we may have to shift our position if we are persuaded that it is untenable. Grasping this could generate a more grounded mode of policy-making, leading in the direction of richer and fuller versions of participation that are likely to be more productive and less alienating. At times it has almost appeared as if there is an unwillingness to develop and enhance inclusive procedures where these might contest 'control' and 'vision'. One of the elements which has caused us genuine distress as we have worked on this research has been the complexity of the forms of 'distortion' which we have encountered at every level. Sometimes this has been the consequence of intentional or unintended 'bad practice'. Sometimes it has taken the form of 'the noble lie' which is intended to result in better things. Sometimes it is because the 'resources' were not available to do an honest job where performances were expected, results demanded and sanctions waiting in the wings. Sometimes it has resulted from people not daring to reveal that the 'emperor has no clothes'. The list goes on. For many people we have interviewed, being involved in such distortion is both upsetting and genuinely threatening to their sense of self-respect, self-worth and 'professional' integrity.

Running through accounts of teaching, and other public-sector occupations, during the 1980s and 1990s has been a concern about the destruction of 'trust' relationships and their substitution by the 'discourse of derision' (Ball 1990). Taken together, these have had a devastating effect on the morale and sense of dignity of serving teachers and, externally, have disinclined people from wishing to become teachers (Coulthard and Kyriacou 2000). David Hartley locates this clearly within the managerialist turn in education.

> Particularly in Britain, the education policies of the post-1979 Conservative government have had the effect of undermining trust within the professions of the welfare state. The professions were not to be trusted; rather, they were to be subjected to contractual relationships. The high-trust, *professional* accountability of the 1960s and 1970s gave way in the 1980s to low-trust *public* accountability;

and this public accountability has been set subsequently within an almost Darwinian *market* accountability.

(Hartley 1997, p. 143, emphasis in original)

In an earlier account which has contemporary resonance Gerald Grace pointed to the implications of this process for patterns of teacher recruitment.

> Complementing any process of *technical restructuring* must also be a process of *relational restructuring*. The quality of teacher–state relations is greater than the sum of its technical parts. ... These may be summed up as *trust relationships* and as *consultation and partnership relationships*. ... The 1980s [and we would add, the 1990s] have been inimical to these relationships and in this sense have constituted an experience of deeper structural alienation. It will be necessary, if teaching is really to be 'an attractive career', to find new forms in which trust, consultation and partnership arrangements can be expressed in contemporary conditions.
>
> (Grace 1991, p. 13, emphasis in original)

As we have already seen in earlier chapters, these new forms of trust relationships will need to be set within boundaries that are respectful, respected and rigorous and that will require forms of accountability which move upwards, sideways and downwards but are not predefined within regulatory, centralised parameters.

Regrettably, such negative elements have become all too familiar features of the critical educational landscape over the last two decades – not just for teachers and teacher-educators but, as we keep insisting, for other workers and clients of the public sector. Nevertheless, within education there are possible grounds for bounded optimism. Some positive developments and understandings exist which would provide a basis for progressive growth if only there was a willingness to listen. These songs seldom feature on the song-sheet and are drowned out in the howls of 'naming and shaming', and by the relentless thumping of the drumbeats of 'standards', 'effectiveness', 'quality', 'performance', 'leadership' and 'modernisation'.

We know from our experience of working with and alongside teachers at all stages of their careers, the sophistication they and their schools can bring to understandings of learning, motivation and progression. If we compare the skills which teachers from the 1970s onwards have brought to their understandings of curriculum, pedagogy and assessment with those with which we and our generation entered teaching the contrast is humbling. This has remained true throughout the troubled years of the 1980s and 1990s. This is, of course, not to deny that there have always been dodgy, even downright damaging teachers. We still remember the history teacher who began the day smelling of whisky and finished it the same way and whose grasp of pedagogy was to have individuals read the textbook out loud all day, every day. We recall the primary teacher who at the end of each term collected the pupils' work books, carefully tore out the clean paper for later use, and, in front of the children threw away their work. There are incompetent, lazy, sad, sexist, racist, homophobic, cruel and blisteringly nasty individual teachers – and doctors, solicitors, journalists, educationalists and footballers. This we know, but they do not characterise the members of those occupations.

In our experience, backed up during this research process, the majority of teachers bring genuine engagement and commitment (albeit sometimes troubled) to the learners, schools and communities with whom and in which they work. As we have said in a number of places, 'context' is genuinely important to teachers and most do care both about the learning process and the circumstances within which that learning takes place. Teachers work within a number of vectors simultaneously and can grasp that these interact to constitute the learning situation. Personal relationships, security and encouragement, sensitivity to context are not alternatives to learning but the setting within which it grows and develops – and are as necessary for teachers as for young people.

A genuine gain in the educational landscape has come from the wide appreciation of the place of partnership and collaboration within the educational process. Well before the clumsy fiats of the mid-1980s, organic collaborations had been instigated between some schools, HEIs and LEAs. Inevitably they were sometimes hesitant and exploratory and usually under-resourced. Nonetheless, they began to negotiate a common vocabulary within teaching, higher education and professional development. Through the encountering of shared questions, divergent judgments and material problems, the parameters for what might count as the development of competence and capability began to be established. These practices were both spreading and deepening and with a little goodwill and resourcing could have been fostered and enhanced. Instead, an administration with a deep distrust of teacher education and LEAs attempted to mandate 'partnerships' which were mechanistic, ungrounded in practice and proved overly bureaucratic for all concerned. It is to their mutual credit that reciprocities have continued to develop between schools, LEAs, HEIs and other knowledge, training and development providers, often in conditions of resource strain and ritualistic regulation. These have brought much greater managerial, financial and logistical sophistication in their train, but the principles which underpin such developments and the politics which could inform their enhancement and bring benefit for the constituent communities are too often marginalised through the pressures of resourcing and bureaucracy.

As with 'joining-up' across a variety of other areas of service provision, support and welfare agencies, if this is to be more than either tokenism or a cloak for ever more punitive social policies, the form and basis of such partnerships need to be carefully analysed and effectively grounded in resourcing, commitments, values and experiences. Within these 'learning partnerships' there is a general acceptance of the extensive need for articulation across phases of teachers' and other educational workers' careers and a growing recognition that teachers will move in and out of teaching at various stages, both because of the so-called 'portfolio' career and because of their domestic circumstances. This needs to be built in to allow for appropriate training and induction, but also to make use of the other experiences entrants have acquired and which would repay sharing. There is also recognition (and celebration) of diversities both within and between our communities. The slow, grudging, nervous moves away from equiphobia may perhaps signal an understanding that, for example, minority ethnic teachers are not just a potential resource to 'solve' a recruitment crisis, nor are the careers of minority ethnic teachers exempt from broader questions of progression and enhancement.

There are welcome movements and transitions across knowledge areas, made possible both by interactions between paradigms and by the porosity of conceptual categories and facilitated by 'intelligence systems'. Of course all of this has to be grounded in certain basic capabilities. However, there are huge questions to be asked about the 'basic' understandings of literacy, numeracy and ICT which need to be unpacked and explored within communities of practice. In his important analysis of reflexive modernisation and teacher education Michael Young (1998) has this to say about the notion of 'core technologies of teaching and learning' found in some strands of the school-effectiveness movement:

> ... the idea of core technologies implies that teaching and learning are like other technologies, relatively well understood and agreed. Nothing, of course, could be further from the truth.   (p. 172)

We cannot fully understand the nature of what teaching should be like without an adequate grasp of what it is that we want children to learn and how we want them to engage with the learning process. For example, whilst there may be some people who would claim that the acquisition of basic skills of literacy and numeracy are unimportant or irrelevant, this is certainly not a position we would support. However, saying this is not, in our view, to say very much. It is certainly not to support the imposition of a particular approach to literacy, let alone a highly directive, not to say autocratic mode of pedagogy and classroom management. Miriam Henry and her colleagues (1999) provide an extended debate on these issues and effectively relate them to the intersections between national and global impulses.

> Preoccupation with so-called literacy standards as a political response to unemployment is hardly new, but in the globalized economy has taken on an extra edge. Additionally in Australia, literacy has become a kind of equity surrogate, ... However, despite the rhetoric of providing 'literacy for all' and assertions of the need for multi-skilled, adaptive and problem-solving workers in the new work order, current approaches to literacy tend to reflect a narrow outcomes-focus and an obsession with reductionist forms of standardized testing ...   (p. 93)

But, and this is a critical 'but', we are not claiming infallibility in such views. There are legitimately and honestly held divergent views on these issues which tap directly into questions of entitlement and the social distribution of knowledge resources. It is the 'how' of both recognising such diversity and the 'how' of reaching deliberative decisions which remains crucial.

The new National Curriculum offers the possibility of some progressive inflections to the framework currently in place.

Equality of opportunity is one of a broad set of common values and purposes which underpin the school curriculum and the work of schools.

(DfEE/QCA 1999)

If rhetoric becomes reality, here is a real chance that the work schools do in contributing to the values of the future will be recognised.

There are also a number of reports that represent important landmarks for reopening debates about teaching and learning – the Citizenship Report (QCA 1998) for example, argues that

> For teachers to confine their endeavours to the inculcation of knowledge and the transmission of skills, no matter how useful they may be, is to restrict the enterprise of schooling to just a scheme of training.
>
> (QCA 1998, p. 57, para. 10.5)

And the Robinson Committee on Creativity, Culture and Education not only comments on the role of assessment and inspection, but also questions whether teachers are being adequately prepared for their role.

> Assessment and inspection have vital roles in raising standards of achievement in schools. But they must support and not inhibit creative and cultural education. ... Raising standards should not mean standardisation, or the objectives of creative and cultural education will be frustrated. ... The new provisions in initial teacher education present serious difficulties to the future of creative and cultural education.
>
> (NACCCE, p. 11)

The GTC has also come into being expressing fresh commitment and respect for teachers as well as an initial commitment to recognising the importance of regionality and the significance of where teachers work in their interpretations and judgments about their work. On his appointment as Chair of the GTC, David Puttnam was interviewed in the 28 December 1999 edition of the *Guardian* newspaper. He had this to say about the teaching profession:

> It is kinder, more committed and more hard-working than anything that gets presented ... People must come to understand the degree to which all of us rely on the quality of the teaching profession. (p. 17)

Echoing the sentiments of some points we have made above, the report went on to say that

> He thinks that there are few dreadful teachers these days. Chris Woodhead's decision to identify 12,000 incompetents was a 'miscommunication'. If the figure was right, the chief inspector should have said the proportion was as little as 3%. If only the same could be said for journalists and ministers.

From the point of view of their students, we would argue that this is 12,000 too many. However, the current climate of damning by association will not address the problem, any more than punishing a whole class for the misdemeanours of a few is generally regarded as either fair or productive.

Carol Adams as Chief Executive of the GTC has also come into her new position with a reputation for respecting and valuing teachers.

> ' ... teachers have gone into the classroom day after day and carried out this emotionally and intellectually demanding job, which requires enormous skills and expertise – and that needs much greater recognition,' she argues.
> ... she's well known for the high regard in which she holds teachers as professionals, and the tough defences she's mounted of their work.
>
> (Moriarty 1999, p. 15)

The membership and composition of the GTC also represents a distinct advance, which we should like to see broadened further and provided with an even stronger and more responsive regional and local deliberative framework. Such movements would provide a basis for a form of 'extended or democratic professionalism' which could seek, in Geoff Whitty's terms,

> to demystify professional work and build alliances between teachers and excluded constituencies of students, parents and members of the community on whose behalf decisions have traditionally been made either by professions or by the state
>
> (Whitty 1999, p. 9)

It is difficult to believe that, however its agenda develops, the GTC will not wish to play a fuller part in the definition and negotiation around teaching standards for entry, induction and professional development. Such a process will mesh with the redefinition and delimitation of the powers of the TTA, which itself has recently been appearing to make genuine attempts to break free from the combative and negative orientation with which it was established. If the Agency is to have any form of continued existence, such moves will need to be matched by a genuine and well-considered change in its attitudes towards the commitments and expertise which teachers and other educators bring to their work.

A further development which would go some way to creating a more positive ambience within which teaching can be conducted is the 'softening' of the performance-management machinery proposed in the Green Paper. There are signs that the government has already begun to move away from a crude performance-related pay model, that the proposals for the appraisal procedures are becoming more developmental and less stridently individualistic, and that in recent consultation documents, the discourse of the NPS framework is beginning to play a more subdued part. Although many features have still to be fully engineered and struggled over, perhaps the hard edges are becoming more softly focused with the growing awareness of criticism and resistance, the dawning realisation of the scale of transaction costs and risks of adverse litigation, and the belated revelation that its potential for attracting new recruits into teaching may have been deeply misconceived, driven by belief and dogma rather than informed by evidence.

This is not to say that the dangers of the pedagogical fix are past. As David Hartley puts it,

> Educational discourse is currently suffused by managerial jargon. Information technology is waiting in the wings, ready to translate and to transmit standardized curricula in time-compressed, easily consumable, totally portable packages called modules. The insight of re-engineering is that performativity lies in the direction of redesigned curricular content and structure which can be electronically accessed and monitored. Once the curricular fix is taken, then the technical fix is practically possible. Education may be disembodied and replaced by charismatic software. ... Choice will be a chimera, confined to the selection available in the multi-provider educational boutiques, franchised out by the state which may adopt near-total regulatory powers. (p. 137)

In all societies there are widespread interests in how teachers are themselves educated, in discussions about the content and purpose of their education, and in the values which their training and education entail and promote. The international transformations in education and teacher education have not only occurred in 'prosperous' countries but also, most demandingly, in developing countries. In a detailed report on the impact of the 'structural adjustment' policies of bodies such as the World Bank, IMF and OECD on teacher education, the ILO (1996) said

> For developing countries ... this has been an especially painful process, made even more difficult by developed country financial policies and falling commodity prices in the 1980s. (p. 103)

Within these changes we have argued throughout that questions of the most enormous democratic significance are being raised on an international scale by the increasingly smudged nature of the relationships between what we used to call the public and private sectors (Niemi 1999). In an English context this was recently dramatically highlighted in the *Times Educational Supplement* under the headline 'Assessors reap rewards'. The article went on to say

> Teachers' bids to cross the new performance threshold will be vetted by assessors [hired by Cambridge Education Associates, a private firm] who could earn more in six days than the successful applicants will receive.

And later,

> Hay McBer, the management consultants who have been helping ministers to develop a performance-related pay scheme, are believed to have been given a

£3 million contract. The project leader is said to have been charging £2,500 a day but Hay McBer would not confirm the figure.

(Barnard 2000, pp. 1–2)

In the literature on public policy which has been developing over the past decade there has been an extremely vigorous discussion about the consequences of the transformations occurring throughout the public sector for issues of social inclusion and exclusion. This literature has its confusions and complexities not least because: there is no consensus in the social policy field itself about the nature of the transformations (or 'reinventions') which are occurring; there is debate about the general explanatory power of the various models/paradigms which have been proposed; there are problems about the extent to which different explanatory models succeed in explaining changes in disparate substantive fields, for example education, health, social security, the prison service; and there is disagreement about the scope of the transformations and the extent to which we are operating within national political specifics or within global parameters set by such bodies as the OECD. Nonetheless, despite these vigorous and healthy debates, wherever one turns in contemporary social policy, the issue of 'governance' occupies a critical space in the analysis. How and through what procedures are decisions to be made and resources allocated? What forms of representation and voice can best provide a common foundation of entitlement whilst accommodating diversity? Can reconciliations be drawn between the tensions of national, regional and local priorities? In the education field this quest for the development of robust and representative governance structures for teaching is significant not only for present and future cohorts of teachers, but for children or students with whom they work and also for the communities in which they are embedded. Complex issues of access and equity, entitlement and diversity, representation and accountability pose dilemmas which lie at the heart of sociality and require democratic arenas for their contestation and resolution. We currently find some evidence to suggest that, in our own context at least, such arenas are beginning to be tentatively considered in some quarters.

In our focus on recent developments in England in relation to governance (which has become particularly pertinent at a time of a major restructuring of teaching), we have attempted to raise a number of general issues which bear consideration if we are even to grasp the parameters of what it will mean to move forwards equitably, collectively, progressively and democratically. In our view we could not begin to construct an agenda for change in teacher education without first addressing questions such as the following.

- Who ought to have a say in the education and professional development of teachers?
- On what basis should these constituencies be determined and by whom?
- What are the structural and sectional characteristics of such constituencies and how they might be built into deliberative procedures in ways that make them genuinely inclusive?

- What are the mechanisms which currently privilege and amplify some voices whilst silencing others, and how can these be reconstructed?
- How can conflict, contestation and disagreement be recognised, respected and resolved?
- How can existing deliberative and decision/policy-making processes be made more adequately accountable to diverse constituencies?
- What are the public and communicable grounds on the basis of which it can be argued that genuine inclusion would make education 'better'?

Behind such an agenda lie the beliefs that the resulting debates will establish procedures which will enhance the whole range of individual and collective learning and development capabilities that young people will need for the future, and both connect to, and generate a perception of teaching that will prove appealing enough to attract enough new teachers of high quality. If these are not the issues to be engaged with and understood by present and future citizens, then it is genuinely difficult to know what would count as debates that should be informing the future. Referring to the impact of emerging cultures of Europeanisation, the European White Paper on Education and Training (1997) makes the claim that

> The future of European culture depends on its capacity to question constantly and seek new answers without prejudicing human values. This is the very foundation of citizenship and is essential if European society is to be open, multicultural and democratic. (p. 12)

Directly comparable sentiments are expressed by the NACCCE Report.

> The foundations of the present education system were laid at the end of the nineteenth century. They were designed to meet the needs of a world that was being transformed by industrialisation. We are publishing this report at the dawn of a new century. The challenges we face now are of the same magnitude, but they are of a different character. The task is not to do better now what we set out to do then: it is to rethink the purposes, methods and scale of education in our new circumstances. This report argues that no education system can be world-class without valuing and integrating creativity in teaching and learning, in the curriculum, in management and leadership and without linking this to promoting knowledge and understanding of cultural change and diversity.
> (NACCCE 1999, p. 15)

A grasp, collectively shared, of the uncertainties of the future – global, national, local and interpersonal – and of its diversities and pluralisms is no longer an option which can be tacked on to traditional cultures of knowledge and power. It is time to move on from the politics of ruthlessness and to redesign a mode of education policymaking that will form a constructive element for the social architecture of the future.

Notes

1 The reconstruction of teaching in context

1 Docking (2000) points out that some shift of emphasis may be taking place in that the recent statement of values in the revised National Curriculum (QCA 1999) puts 'the well-being and development of the individual' at the top of the list and 'a productive economy' lower down. Ozga and Lawn (2000) also point out that historically 'policy-makers have been ambivalent about the economising of education, and where the influence of elite provision and tradition has diluted the impact of vocationalism, at least in some types of schooling' (p. 221).

2 Although we much prefer to use the term ITE (Initial Teacher Education) rather than ITT (Initial Teacher Training) we have used the latter because this is now the label which is used in Government documents.

3 The campaign papers are held in the UCET archive, situated at the Institute of Education, Bedford Way, London.

4 Technically the TTA is an NDPB, although Weir and Hall stress that these should be included in the general QUANGO count.

5 At the time of writing it is not possible to say to what extent these questions will be influenced by the Freedom of Information Bill currently receiving Parliamentary attention.

6 This is a reference to the work undertaken by Lord Dearing in 'slimming-down' the complexities and detail of the National Curriculum.

7 We have not dealt directly with the issue of teacher recruitment partly because it is a complex (mine)field in its own right and partly because it is being carefully researched elsewhere, for example, by the team at the University of North London (Hutchings *et al.* 2000) and by John Howson, whose regular contributions in the educational press provide regional as well as national data and predictions. However, while we fully recognise the centrality of the issues involved, we would also argue that it is not a 'technical' issue which can be separated from questions to do with teachers' education, professional development, career structures or patterns of working life (Welton *et al.* 1995). In this respect it is an issue to which we shall make reference at various points in our argument.

2 Standards in teaching

1 We have decided to use the term National Professional Standards (NPS) in order to distinguish the standards for teachers from the standards for school students. We shall follow this convention throughout, only varying it when quoting other formulations, e.g. in official texts or other commentaries.

2 In addition to the 'traditional' routes into teaching there now exists a range of alternatives including SCITT provision, modular courses, part-time programmes and the Graduate and Registered Teacher

Programme (GRTP), which is an employment-based route. All of these are designed to lead to QTS and hence be subject to the requirements of the QTS Standards.

3 A more detailed account of this element of our research can be found in Hextall and Mahony (2000).
4 For an account of the New Right and their influence on the politics of policy-making during the Conservative administration, see Ball (1990). Two prominent members of the TTA Board were publicly associated with the New Right.
5 The EOC is not alone in this respect, at that time the CRE was also not routinely circulated. The TUC is also not included on the TTA's routine circulation list whilst employer organisations, such as the CBI, are. This makes an interesting point in the light of Michael Apple's reference in Cultural Politics and Education (1996) to the Ontario Federation of Labour's nine key positions on training pp. 100–101.
6 TTA figures claim one hundred and seven but one was misidentified.
7 Paradoxically the National Curriculum itself, at least for young people up to the age of fourteen, is not particularly vocationalist in orientation though there are clear dangers inherent in the current 'back to basics' movement.

3 Managing and modernising teaching

1 See Yeatman (1994) and Ball (1998) for accounts of the emergence of the 'performative state' and its implications for policy formation and implementation
2 The citations for the DfEE 'advice' and some of the other submissions can be found in the references at the end of the book.
3 The interaction between the 'self' and transformations in contemporary forms of work and occupational relationships are explored in Clarke and Newman (1997), Casey (1995) and Gee *et al.* (1996), and we shall return to them later.
4 See ATL; LGA; NEOST; NAHT; NASUWT; NUT; PAT; SEO; SHA; UCET – all 1999.

6 Governance and accountability

1 For the remainder of this section we shall only be applying our arguments to the arguments surrounding the English GTC. It is worth noting that there has been a GTC in Scotland for over three decades and that currently the Irish government is in the process of establishing a Teaching Council. See Department of Education and Science (1998) Report of the Steering Group on the Establishment of a Teaching Council, Dublin, Stationery Office.
2 It is interesting to note that the TTA make regular references to the medical profession in their justifications for restructuring the teaching profession. As Walby and Greenwell (1994) have pointed out, issues of certification and control as well as definitions as to what counts as 'professionality' carry quite different resonances for doctors and nurses. These raise complex questions about the restructuring of public services under the auspices of 'new managerialism' and raise important issues of power, hierarchy and their intersection with gender relations.

Further reading

Acker, S. (1995) 'Gender and Teachers' Work', *Review of Research in Education, No. 21, 1995–96*, Washington: American Educational Research Association, pp. 99–162.

Ackroyd, P. (1985) *Hawksmoor*, London: Abacus.

Ainsworth, S. and Johnson, A. (2000) 'The TTA Consultation Documents on ITT: What no Values?', in D. Lawton, J. Cairn and R. Gardener (eds) *Education for Values: Morals, Ethics and Citizenship in Contemporary Teaching*, London: Kogan Page (forthcoming).

Angus, L. (1993) 'The Sociology of School Effectiveness', *British Journal of Sociology of Education*, 14, 3, pp. 333–45.

Angus, L. (1994) 'Sociological Analysis and Education Management: the social context of the self-managing school', *British Journal of Sociology of Education*, 15, 1, pp. 79–91.

Apple, M. (1996) *Cultural Politics and Education*, Buckingham: Open University Press.

Armstrong, M. and Baron, A. (1998) *Performance Management: The new realities*, London: Institute of Personnel and Development.

ARTEN (1998) *Response to the Green Paper: Teachers – Meeting the Challenge of Change*, Birmingham: Anti-Racist Teacher Education Network.

Ashton, D. and Green, F. (1996) *Education, Training and the Global Economy*, Cheltenham: Edward Elgar Publishing Ltd.

ATL (1996) 'Evidence to the Parliamentary Education and Employment Committee', *Inquiry into the Professional Status Recruitment and Training of Teachers*, London: Association of Teachers and Lecturers.

ATL (1999a) *Meeting the Challenge of Change, Comment*, London: Association of Teachers and Lecturers.

ATL (1999b) *Response to the DfEE's consultation on The Performance Management Framework and on the proposed regulations for headteacher and teacher performance review*, London: Association of Teachers and Lecturers.

Ball, S. (1990) *Politics and Policy -making in Education*, London: Routledge.

Ball, S. (1998) 'Performativity and fragmentation in "postmodern schooling"', in J. Carter (ed) *Postmodernity and the Fragmentation of Welfare*, London: Routledge, pp. 182–203.

Barnard, N. (2000) 'Assessors Reap Rewards', *Times Educational Supplement*, 21 January.

Bartlett, L., Knight, J. and Lingard, B. (1992) 'Restructuring Teacher Education in Australia', *British Journal of Sociology of Education*, 13, 1, pp. 19–36.

Benhabib, S. (ed) (1996) *Democracy and Difference: Contesting the Boundaries of the Political*, Princeton: Princeton University Press.

Bennett, C. and Ferlie, E. (1996) 'Contracting in Theory and Practice: some evidence from the NHS', *Public Administration*, 74, Spring, pp. 49–66.

Blackmore, J. (1999) *Troubling Women: Feminism, Leadership and Educational Change*, Buckingham: Open University Press.

Blunkett, D. (1997) Speech to the 1997 conference of the National Association of Headteachers, *Times Educational Supplement*, 6 June, pp. 7–8.

Bottery, M. (1998) *Professionals and Policy: management strategy in a competitive world*, London: Cassell.

Bottomley, V. (1993) 'Foreword', in *Ethnic Minority Staff in the NHS: A Programme of Action*, London: National Health Service Management Executive.

Broadfoot, P. (1999) 'Assessment and Lifelong Learning'. Paper presented to British Educational Research Association Annual Conference, University of Sussex, 2–5 September.

Budge, D. (1997) 'In Search of Foreign Correspondences', *Times Educational Supplement*, 5 December.

Brush, L.D. (1999) 'Gender, Work, Who Cares? Production, Reproduction, Deindustrialization and Business as Usual', in M.M. Ferree, J. Lorber and B.B. Bush (eds) *Revisioning Gender*, Thousand Oaks: Sage, pp. 161–89.

Cabinet Office (1999a) *Modernising Government*, London: Cabinet Office.

Cabinet Office (1999b) *Professional Policy Making for the Twenty-First Century*, London: Cabinet Office.

Carr, W. and Hartnett, A. (1996) *Education and the Struggle for Democracy*, Buckingham: Open University Press.

Carrington, B. Nayak, A., Tomlin, R., Bonnett, A., Demaine, J., Short, G. and Skelton, C. (1999) *Ethnic Diversity and Teaching: Policy and practice in Sixteen English Initial Teacher Training Institutions*. Interim Report 2 to the TTA, London: Teacher Training Agency.

Casey, C. (1995) *Work, Self and Society after Industrialism*, London: Routledge.

Cerny, P. (1990) *The Changing Architecture of Politics: Structure, Agency and the Future of the State*, London: Sage Publications.

Clark, D. (1996) 'Open Government in Britain: Discourse and Practice', *Public Money and Management*, January–March, pp. 23–30.

Clarke, J. and Newman, J. (1997) *The Managerial State*, London: Sage Publications.

Clarke, J., Cochrane, A. and McLaughlin, E. (eds) (1994) *Managing Social Policy*, London: Sage Publications.

Clay, J. and George, R. (1993) 'Moving Beyond Permeation', in I. Siraj-Blatchford (ed) *'Race', Gender and the Education of Teachers*, Buckingham: Open University, pp. 125–36.

Collinson, D. and Hearn, J. (1996) 'Breaking the Silence: On Men, Masculinities and Managements', in D. Collinson and J. Hearn (eds) *Men as Managers, Managers as Men*, London: Sage Publications, pp. 1–24.

Connell, R. (1993) *Schools and Social Justice*, Sydney: Pluto Press.

Connell, R.W. (1995) *Masculinities*, Sydney: Allen and Unwin.

Coote, A. (1999) 'The Helmsman and the Cattle Prod', in A. Gamble and T. Wright *The New Social Democracy*, Oxford: Blackwell, pp. 117–30.

Coulthard, M. and Kyriacou, C. (2000) 'Does Teaching as a Career Offer What Students Are Looking For?' Paper to Regional Dimensions of Teacher Supply and Retention Conference, University of North London, 19 January.

CRE (1997) *The Leadership Challenge*, London: Commission for Racial Equality.

CRE (1999) *The Leadership Challenge: Progress Report 1999*, London: Commission for Racial Equality.

Dale, R. (1982) 'Education and the capitalist state: Contributions and contradictions', in M. Apple (ed) *Cultural and Economic Reproduction in Education*, London: Routledge and Kegan Paul, pp. 127–61.

Daley, D. (1999) 'Unbowed and Professional', Paper to British Educational Research Association Annual Conference, Brighton, University of Sussex, 2–5 September.

Deakin, N. and Walsh, K. (1996) 'The Enabling State: The Role of Markets and Contracts', *Public Administration*, 74, Spring, pp. 32–46.

Deem, R. and Ozga, J. (2000) 'Transforming post-compulsory education? Femocrats at work in the academy', *Women's Studies International Forum*, (forthcoming).

Demaine, J. (1999) 'Education Policy and Contemporary Politics', in J. Demaine (ed) (1999) *Education Policy and Contemporary Politics*, London: Macmillan, pp. 5–29.

Department of Education and Science (1998) *Report of the Steering Group on the Establishment of a Teaching Council*, Dublin: The Stationery Office.

Deshpande, P. and Rashid, N. (1993) 'Developing Equality through Local Education Authority INSET', in I. Siraj-Blatchford (ed) *'Race', Gender and the Education of Teachers*, Buckingham: Open University, pp. 154–68.

Devereux, C. (1996) *Cross-Cultural Standards of Competence in Customer Service*, Cheam: W.A. Consultants.

Devereux, C. (1997) *Rigour without Rigidity*, Cheam: W. A. Consultants.

DfE (1994) The Remit Letter for the TTA, 5 October 1994, London: Department of Education.

DfE and Welsh Office (1993) *The Government's Proposals for the Reform of Initial Teacher Training*, London: Department for Education.

DfEE (1995) *Benchmarking School Budgets*, London: Her Majesty's Stationery Office.

DfEE (1996) National Curriculum for ITT, Letter to Geoffrey Parker, Chair of Board of TTA, London: Department for Education.

DfEE (1997a) *Excellence in Schools*, London: The Stationery Office.

DfEE (1997b) *Teaching: High Status, High Standards. General Teaching Council; a Consultation Document*, London: Department for Education and Employment.

DfEE (1998a) Green Paper *Teachers: Meeting the challenge of change*, London: The Stationery Office.

DfEE (1998b) *Teaching: High Status, High Standards, Circ. no. 4/98*, London: Department for Education and Employment.

DfEE (1998c) *Teaching: High Status, High Standards. The Composition of the General Teaching Council; a Consultation Document*, London: Department for Education and Employment.

DfEE (1999a) *Quinquennial Review of the Teacher Training Agency: Prior Options Report*, London: Department for Education and Employment.

DfEE (1999b) *Teachers meeting the challenge of change: technical consultation document on pay and performance management*, London: Department for Education and Employment.

DfEE (1999c) *Teachers: Taking forward the challenge of change – detailed summary of responses to the Green Paper consultation exercise*, London: Department for Education and Employment.

DfEE (1999d) *Teachers: Taking forward the challenge of change – response to the consultation exercise*, London: Department for Education and Employment.

DfEE (1999e) *Performance Management Framework for Teachers: Consultation Document*, London: Department for Education and Employment.

DfEE (1999f) *Explanatory note on how we expect the performance threshold to operate in 2000–2001* (submission to the STRB), London: Department for Education and Employment.

DfEE (1999g) *The General Teaching Council for England: The Register of Teachers – a Consultation Paper*, London: Department for Education and Employment.

DfEE/QCA (1999) *The National Curriculum: Handbook for primary teachers in England*, London: Department for Education and Employment and Qualifications and Curriculum Authority.

Docking, J. (ed) (2000) *Raising the Standard: New Labour's Policies for Schools*, London: David Fulton.

Dominelli, L. (1996) 'Deprofessionalizing Social Work: Anti-Oppressive Practice, Competencies and Postmodernism', *British Journal of Social Work*, 26, pp. 153–75.

Down, B., Hogan, C. and Chadbourne, R. (1997) 'Making Sense of Performance Management in Schools: Official Rhetoric and Teachers' Reality', Paper presented to the Australian Association for Research in Education Conference, Brisbane, 30 November–4 December.

Dunleavy, P. and Hood, C. (1994) 'From Old Public Administration to New Public Management', *Public Money and Management*, July–September, pp. 9–16.

Eliassen, K.A. and Kooiman, J. (eds) (1994) *Managing Public Organisations: Lessons from Contemporary European Experience*, London: Sage Publications.

Elliott, J. (1999) 'Introduction: global and local dimensions of reforms in teacher education', *Teaching and Teacher Education*, 15, pp. 133–41.

Elwood, J., Epstein, D., Hey, V. and Maw, J. (eds) (1998) *Failing Boys? Issues in Gender and Achievement*, Buckingham: Open University Press.

Epstein, D. (1995) (ed) *Challenging Lesbian and Gay Inequalities in Education*, Buckingham: Open University Press.

Eraut, M. (1994) *Developing Professional Knowledge and Competence*, London: Falmer Press.

European White Paper on Education and Training (1997) *Teaching and Learning: Towards the Learning Society*, Brussels: Commission of the European Communities.

Exworthy, M. and Halford, S. (eds.) (1999) *Professionals and New Managerialism in the Public Sector*, Buckingham: Open University.

FENTO (1999) *Standards for Teaching and Supporting Learning in Further Education in England and Wales*, London: Further Education National Training Organisation.

Fergusson, R. (1994) 'Managerialism in Education', in J. Clarke, A. Cochrane and E. McLaughlin (eds) *Managing Social Policy*, London: Sage Publications, pp. 93–114.

Ferlie, E., Pettigrew, A., Ashburner, L. and Fitzgerald, L. (1996) *The New Public Management in Action*, Oxford: Oxford University Press.

Flett, K. (1999) Letter, *Times Educational Supplement*, 23 July.

Foreman, J., Bedingfield, R. and Coussey, M. (1997) *Decentralisation and Devolution: the impact on equal opportunities at work*, Ware: Wainwright Trust.

Fraser, N. (1997) *Justice Interruptus: Critical Reflections on the 'Postsocialist' Condition*, New York: Routledge.

Frith, R. and Mahony, P. (1995) *Factors Influencing Girls' and Boys' Option Choices in Year 9. Report to Essex Careers and Business Partnership*, London: Roehampton Institute London.

Fullan, M. and Hargreaves, A. (1992) *What's Worth Fighting for in your School?* Buckingham: Open University Press.

Gee, J.P., Hull, G. and Lankshear, C. (1996) *The New Work Order: behind the language of the new capitalism*, Sydney: Allen and Unwin.

Gewirtz, S. (1998) 'Conceptualizing social justice in education: mapping the territory', *Journal of Education Policy*, 13, 4, pp. 469–84.

Ghouri, N. (1998) 'Race Chief attacks training negligence', *Times Educational Supplement*, 3 July.

Gilbert, R. and Gilbert, P. (1998) *Masculinity goes to School*, Sydney: Allen and Unwin.

Gill, B. (1998) 'Excluding Racism from Schools – Policies and Practice', *Arena: Newsletter of the National Anti-Racist Movement in Education*, 47, Birmingham: National Anti-Racist Movement in Education, pp. 3–4.

Gillborn, D. (1999) 'Race, Nation and Education: New Labour and the New Racism', in J. Demaine (ed) *Education Policy and Contemporary Politics*, London: Macmillan, pp. 82–102.

Glatter, R. (1996) 'Context and capability in educational management', Paper presented at BEMAS Annual Conference, Coventry, 22 September 1996.

Grace, G. (1991) 'The State and the Teachers: Problems in Teacher Supply, Retention and Morale', in G. Grace and M. Lawn (eds) *Teacher Supply and Teacher Quality: Issues for the 1990s*, Clevedon: Multilingual Matters.

Grace, G. (1995) *School Leadership*, London: Falmer.

Graham, J., Gough, B., and Beardsworth, R. (1999) *Partnerships in Continuing Professional Development*, London: University of East London and Standing Council for the Education of Teachers and Trainers.

Griffiths, Morwenna (1998) *Educational Research for Social Justice: getting off the fence*, Buckingham: Open University.

Hall, V. (1996) *Dancing on the Ceiling: a study of Women Managers in Education*, London: Paul Chapman.

Halsey, A.H., Lauder, H., Brown, P. and Wells, S.A. (eds) (1997) *Education Culture Economy Society*, Oxford: Oxford University Press.

Hartley, D. (1997) *Re-schooling Society*, London: Falmer.

Hatcher R. (1997) 'Labour's Education Policy: implications for social justice', paper to British Education Research Association Annual Conference, York, 11–14 September.

Henry, M., Lingard, B., Rizvi, F. and Taylor, T. (eds) (1999) *Journal of Education Policy Special Issue*, 14, 1, pp. 85–97.

Hextall, I. and Mahony, P. (1998) 'Towards a General Teaching Council: Issues of Professionalism and Democracy', Paper to European Educational Research Association Annual Conference, Ljubljana, 16–20 September.

Hextall, I. and Mahony, P. (1999) 'Representation and Accountability in the Formation of Policy on Teacher Education: the GTC (England)', *Larutbildning och Forskning i Umeå*, 6, 1, pp. 7–25.

Hextall, I. and Mahony, P. (2000) 'Consultation and the management of consent: Standards for Qualified Teacher Status', *British Education Research Journal*, 26, 3, pp. 323–42.

Hextall, I., Lawn, M., Menter, I., Sidgwick, S. and Walker, S. (1991) 'Imaginative Projects: Arguments for a New Teacher Education', in G. Grace and M. Lawn (eds) *Teacher Supply and Teacher Quality: Issues for the 1990s*, Clevedon: Multilingual Matters.

Hextall, I., Mahony, P. and Sidgwick, S. (1999) 'Access denied: redefining a social justice agenda for teacher education', Paper to British Education Research Association Annual Conference, Brighton, 2–5 September.

Hill, D. (1999) 'New Labour and Education: New Ideology? New Politics?', Paper to British Educational Research Association Annual Conference, University of Sussex, 2–5 September.

Hodkinson, P. and Issitt, M. (1995) *The Challenge of Competence: Professionalism through Vocational Education and Training*, London: Cassell.

Hoggett, P. (1996) 'New Modes of Control in the Public Service', *Public Administration*, 74, Spring, pp. 9–32.

Hood, C. (1991) 'A Public Management For All Seasons', *Public Administration*, 69, pp. 3–19.

House of Commons, Education and Employment Select Committee (1999) *The Work of OFSTED, vol. I*, London: The Stationery Office.

Hoyle, E. and John, P. (1995) *Professional Knowledge and Professional Practice*, London: Cassell.

Hughes, O. (1994) *Public Management and Administration: An Introduction*, London: Macmillan.

Hustler, D. and McIntyre, D. (eds) (1996) *Developing Competent Teachers*, London: David Fulton Publishers.

Hutchings, M., Menter, I., Ross, A. and Thomson, D. (2000) 'Teacher Supply and retention in London – Key findings and implications from a study carried out in six boroughs in 1998/9', Paper to Regional Dimensions of Teacher Supply and Retention Conference, University of North London, 19 January.

Hyland, T. (1994) *Competence, Education and NVQs: Dissenting Perspectives*, London: Cassell.

ILO (1996) *Impact of structural adjustment on the employment and training of teachers*, Geneva: International Labour Organization.

Ingvarson, L. (1998) 'Professional Development as the Pursuit of Professional Standards: The Standards-Based Professional Development System', *Teaching and Teacher Education*, 14, 1, pp. 127–40.

Ironside, M. and Seifert, R. (1995) *Industrial Relations in Schools*, London: Routledge.

Itzin, C. and Newman, J. (eds) (1995) *Gender, Culture and Organizational Change*, Routledge: London.

Jenkins, R. (1986) *Racism and Recruitment: managers, organisations, and equal opportunity in the labour market*, London: Cambridge University Press.

Jones, C. and Mahony, P. (eds) (1989) *Learning our Lines: Sexuality and Social Control in Education*, London: The Women's Press.

Jones, C., Maguire, M. and Watson, B. (1997) 'The School Experience of Some Minority Ethnic Students in London Schools During Initial Teacher Training', *Journal of Education for Teaching*, 23, 2, pp. 131–44.

Kane, I. (1996) 'A training agency fit for the scrap heap', *Times Higher Educational Supplement*, 15 November.

Kanter, R.M. (1993) *Men and Women of the Corporation*, New York: Basic Books. 2nd edn.

Kelly, L., Regan, L. and Burton, S. (1991) *An Exploratory Study of the Prevalence of Sexual Abuse in a Sample of 16–21 Year Olds*, Child Abuse Studies Unit: University of North London.

Kirkpatrick, I. and Lucio, M.M. (1996) 'The contract state and the future of public management', *Public Administration*, 74, Spring, pp. 1–8.

Kohli, J. (1996) (Untitled) *Kaleidoscope*. Summer edition.

Labour Party (1995) *Excellence for everyone: Labour's crusade to raise standards*, London: Labour Party Office.

Lawn, M. (1994) 'The End of the Modern in Teaching? Implications for Professionalism and Work', in D. Kallos and S. Lindblad (eds) *New Policy Contexts for Education: Sweden and the United Kingdom,* Umea, Sweden: Umea University, pp. 169–90.

Lawn, M. (1995) 'Restructuring teaching in the USA and England: moving towards the differentiated, flexible teacher', *Journal of Education Policy*, 10, 4, pp. 347–60.

Lawn, M. (1996) *Modern Times? Work, Professionalism and Citizenship in Teaching*, London: Falmer.

Leithwood, K., Jantzi, D. and Steinbach, R.(1999) *Changing Leadership for Changing Times*, Buckingham: Open University Press.

Levitas, R. (1998) *The Inclusive Society? Social Exclusion and New Labour*, London: Macmillan.

LGA (1999) *Response to the Green Paper and the Technical Consultation Document*, London: Local Government Association.

Limerick, B. and Lingard, B. (eds) (1995) *Gender and Changing Educational Management*, Rydalmere: Hodder Education.

Lindblad, S. (2000) *Report on Educational Governance and Social Integration and Exclusion in Europe*, Uppsala, Sweden: University of Uppsala.

Lingard, B. (1995) 'Re-articulating Relevant Voices in Reconstructing Teacher Education', The Annual Harry Penny Lecture, University of South Australia.

Lingard, B. (1999a) 'It is and it isn't: Vernacular Globalisation, Educational Policy and Restructuring', in N. Burbules and C. Torres (eds) *Globalisation and Educational Policy*. New York: Routledge, pp. 79–108.

Lingard, B. (1999b) 'Utilising School Reform for Improving Student Outcomes?', Keynote address to Powerful Partnerships for the New Millennium Conference, Adelaide, 27 August.

Lingard, B. and Douglas, P. (1999) *Men Engaging Feminisms*, Buckingham: Open University Press.

Lingard, B. and Rizvi, F. (1997) 'Globalization, the OECD and Australian Higher Education', in J. Currie and J. Newson (eds) *Globalization and Universities: Critical Perspectives*, California: Sage, pp. 257–73.

Lloyd, C. (2000) 'Excellence for all children: False promises! The failure of current policy for inclusive education and its implications for the 21st Century', *International Journal of Inclusive Education*, 14, 2, pp. 133–51.

Louden, W. (ed.) (2000) *Standards of practice. Professional standards in education*, Melbourne: Australian Council for Educational Research.

Lowndes, V. *et al.* (1998) *Enhancing Public Participation in Local Government*, London: Department of Environment, Transport and the Regions in conjunction with Local Government Association and Local Government Management Board.

Macpherson, W. (1999) *The Inquiry into the Matters Arising from the Death of Stephen Lawrence*, London: The Stationery Office.

McPherson, A. and Raab, C. (1988) *Governing Education: A Sociology of Policy since 1945*, Edinburgh: Edinburgh University Press.

Maguire, M. (1999) '"A touch of class": inclusion and exclusion in initial teacher education', *International Journal of Inclusive Education*, 3, 1, pp. 13–26.

Mahony, P. (1989) 'Sexual Violence and Mixed Schools', in C. Jones and P. Mahony (eds) *Learning our Lines: Sexuality and Social Control in Education*, London: The Women's Press, pp. 157–90.

Mahony, P. (1997) 'Talking Heads: Feminist Perspectives on Public Sector Reform in Teacher Education', *Discourse*, 18, 1, pp. 87–102.

Mahony, P. (1998) 'The Rise And Fall Of Standards in Teaching', Paper to Professional Standards and the Status of Teaching Conference, Edith Cowan University, Perth, 24–26 February.

Mahony, P. (1998) 'Girls will be Girls and Boys will be First', in J. Elwood, D. Epstein, V. Hey and J. Maw (eds), *Failing Boys? Issues in Gender and Achievement*, Buckingham: Open University Press, pp. 37–55.

Mahony, P. (1999) 'Teacher Education Policy and Gender', in J. Salisbury and S. Riddell (eds) *Gender Policy and Educational Change*, London: Routledge, pp. 229–41.

Mahony, P. and Harris, V. (1996) 'Profiling in Practice: the Goldsmiths Experience', in D. Hustler and D. McIntyre (eds) *Developing Competent Teachers*, London: David Fulton Publishers, pp. 9–28.

Mahony, P. and Hextall, I. (1997a) 'Problems of Accountability in Reinvented Government: a case study of the Teacher Training Agency', *Journal of Education Policy*, 12, 4, pp. 267–78.

Mahony, P. and Hextall, I. (1997b) 'Sounds of Silence: the social justice agenda of the Teacher Training Agency', *International Studies in Sociology of Education*, 7, 2, pp. 137–56.

Mahony, P. and Hextall, I. (1997c) 'Effective Teachers for Effective Schools', in G. Weiner, R. Slee and S. Tomlinson (eds) *School Effectiveness for Whom?*, London: Falmer, pp. 128–43.

Mahony, P and Hextall, I. (1998) 'Social Justice and the reconstruction of teaching', *Journal of Education Policy,* **13,** 4, pp. 545–58.

Mahony, P. and Smedley, S. (1998) 'New Times Old Panics: the Underachievement of Boys', *Change: Transformation in Education,* **1,** 2, pp. 41–50.

Mansfield, B. and Mitchell, L. (1996) *Towards a Competent Workforce,* Aldershot: Gower.

Marsden, D. and French, S. (1998) *What a Performance: Performance-related pay in the Public Services,* London: Centre For Economic Performance, London School of Economics.

Mason, A. and Palmer, A. (1996) *Queer Bashing: A National Survey of Hate Crimes Against Lesbians and Gay Men,* London: Stonewall.

Menter, I. (1999) 'The Green Paper – Colour Blind or Visionary?', in J. Graham (ed) *Teacher Professionalism and the Challenge of Change,* Stoke on Trent: Trentham Books.

Millett, A. (1996a) *Chief Executive's Annual Lecture,* London: Teacher Training Agency, 29 October.

Millett, A. (1996b) 'Pedagogy – Last Corner of the Secret Garden', Invitation lecture, King's College, 15 July.

Millett, A. (1997) *The Chief Executive's Annual Lecture 1997,* London: Teacher Training Agency, 3 December.

Millett, A. (1998a) 'Professionalism, Pedagogy and Leadership', *TES/KEELE Lectures on Educational Leadership in the Millennium,* University of Keele, 3 June.

Millett, A. (1998b) *Corporate Plan Conference: Address by Anthea Millett,* London: Teacher Training Agency, 19 May.

Millett, A. (1999) *Valedictory Speech, Teacher Training Agency: Annual Review 1999,* London: Teacher Training Agency, 8 December.

Moghadam, V. (1999) 'Gender and the Global Economy', in M.M. Ferree, J. Lorber and B.B. Bush (eds) *Revisioning Gender,* Thousand Oaks: Sage, pp. 128–60.

Moos, L. (1996) 'Insights into School Culture', *Managing Schools Today,* **5,** 8, pp. 22–4.

Moos, L., Mahony, P. and Reeves, J. (1998) 'What Teachers, Parents, Governors and Students Want from their Heads', in J. Macbeath (ed) *Effective School Leadership: Responding to Change,* London: Paul Chapman pp. 60–79.

Moriarty, M. (1999) 'Speaking up for the classroom teacher', *Teachers,* December, London: Department for Education and Employment.

Murlis, H. (1992) 'PRP in the context of Performance Management', in H. Tomlinson (ed), *Performance-Related Pay in Education,* London: Routledge pp. 55–72.

Myers, K. (2000) (ed) *Whatever happened to Equal Opportunities in schools: Gender equality initiatives in education,* Buckingham: Open University.

NACCCE (1999) *All Our Futures: Creativity, Culture and Education,* London: National Advisory Committee on Culture, Creativity and Education.

NAHT (1999) *Response to the Green Paper 'Teachers: Meeting the Challenge of Change' and Technical Consultation Paper on Pay and Performance Management,* Haywards Heath: National Association of Head Teachers.

NAME (1998) *Response to "Excellence in Schools",* Birmingham: National Anti-Racist Movement in Education.

NASUWT (1999) *Response to the Green Paper … working hard to make it work,* Birmingham: National Association of Schoolteachers and Union of Women Teachers.

NEOST (1999) *Employers' Evidence to the School Teachers' Review Body Concerning the 1 April 2000 Review of Pay and Conditions,* London: National Employers' Organisation for School Teachers.

Newman, J. (1995) 'Gender and cultural change', in C. Itzin and J. Newman (eds) *Gender, Culture and Organizational Change*, Routledge: London, pp. 11–29.

Newsam, P. (1993) 'Pestered with a Popinjay', *Times Educational Supplement*, 17 September.

Niemi, H. (ed) (1999) *Moving Horizons in Education: international transformations and the challenges of democracy*, Helsinki: University of Helsinki.

Nolan (Lord) (1995) *First Report of the Committee on Standards in Public Life*, London: Her Majesty's Stationery Office.

NUT (1999) *Teaching at the Threshold*, London: National Union of Teachers.

OECD (1994) *Quality in Education*, Paris: OECD.

OFSTED (1997a) *Framework for the Assessment of Quality and Standards in Initial Teacher Training 1997/98*, London: Office for Standards in Education.

OFSTED (1997b) *Secondary ITT Subject Inspections 1997–98: subject guidance for the quality of training and assessment*, London: Office for Standards in Education.

OFSTED (1997c) *Secondary ITT Subject Guidance*, London: Office for Standards in Education.

Osborne, A. and Gaebler, T. (1992) *Reinventing Government: How the Entrepreneurial Spirit is Transforming the Public Sector*, Reading MA: Addison Wesley.

Osler, A. (1997) *The Education and Careers of Black Teachers*, Buckingham: Open University.

Ozga, J. (1995) 'Deskilling a profession: professionalism, deprofessionalism and the new managerialism', in H. Busher, and R. Saran (eds) *Managing Teachers as Professionals in Schools*. London: Kogan Page, pp. 21–37.

Ozga, J. and Lawn, M. (2000) 'Modernizing the [Dis] United Kingdom: deregulation, devolution and difference', in S. Lindblad and T. Popkewitz (eds) *Public Discourses on Educational Governance and Social Integration and Exclusion: analysis of policy texts in European contexts*, Uppsala, Sweden: University of Uppsala, pp. 205–61.

PAT (1999) *Teachers: Meeting the Challenge of Change*, Derby: Professional Association of Teachers.

Pepperell, S. and Smedley, S. (1998) 'Calls for more men in Primary Teaching: Problematizing the Issues', *International Journal of Inclusive Education*, 2, 4, pp. 341–57.

Phillips, A. (1993) *Democracy and Difference*, Cambridge: Polity Press.

Phillips, A. (1996) ' Dealing with Difference: a Politics of Ideas, or a Politics of Presence?', in S. Benhabib (ed) *Democracy and Difference: Contesting the Boundaries of the Political*, Princeton: Princeton University Press, pp. 139–52.

Pollitt, C. (1993) *Managerialism and the Public Services*, Oxford: Blackwell. 2nd edn.

Power, S. and Whitty, G. (1999) 'New Labour's education policy: first, second or third way?', *Journal of Education Policy*, 14, 5, pp. 535–46.

Pring, R. (1992) 'Standards and quality in education', *British Journal of Educational Studies*, 41, 1, pp. 4–22.

QCA (1998) *Education for Citizenship and the teaching of democracy in schools*, London: Qualifications and Curriculum Authority.

Raab, C.D. (1994) 'Where are we now: Reflections on the sociology of education policy', in D. Halpin and B. Troyna (eds) *Researching Education Policy: Ethical and Methodological Issues*, London: Falmer Press, pp. 17–30.

Ranson, S. (ed) (1998) *Inside the Learning Society*, London: Cassell.

Ranson, S. and Stewart, J. (1994) *Management for the Public Domain*, Basingstoke: Macmillan.

Ranson, S. and Stewart, J. (1998) 'The Learning Democracy in S. Ranson (ed.) *Inside the Learning Society*, London: Cassell.

Reeves, J. and Casteel, V. (2000) 'Not as easy as it looks: Designing the implementation of the Scottish Qualification for Headship', *Journal of Teacher Development* (forthcoming).

Richardson, J.J. and Jordan, A.G. (1979) *Governing Under Pressure: the Policy Process in Post-Parliamentary Democracy*, Oxford: Martin Robertson.

Richardson, R. (1999) *Performance-Related Pay in Schools. An Evaluation of the Government's Evidence to the School Teachers' Review Body*, London: London School of Economics.

Robertson, S. (1996) 'Teachers' Work, Restructuring and Postfordism: Constructing the New "Professionalism"', in I. Goodson and A. Hargreaves (eds) *Teachers' Professional Lives*, London: Falmer, pp. 28–55.

Rogers, S. (1999) *Performance Management in Local Government*, London: Pitman/Financial Times.

Salisbury, J. and Jackson, D. (1996) *Challenging Macho Values: Practical ways of working with adolescent boys*, London: Falmer Press.

Saul, J.R. (1997) *The Unconscious Civilization*, Victoria, Australia: Penguin.

Sayer, J. (1999) *The General Teaching Council*, London: Ward Lock.

Seddon, T. (1994) *Context and Beyond*, London: Falmer.

Seddon, T. (1997) 'Education: Deprofessionalised? Or reregulated, reorganised and reauthorised?', *Australian Journal of Education*, 41, 3, pp. 228–46.

Sennett, R. (1998) *The Corrosion of Character*, London: W.W. Norton.

SEO (1999) *Response to 'Teachers: Meeting the Challenge of Change'*, Manchester: Society of Education Officers.

SHA (1999) *Response to the Government's Green Paper 'Teachers: Meeting the Challenge of Change'*, Leicester: Secondary Heads Association.

Shakeshaft, C. (1995) 'Gendered Leadership Styles in Educational Organisations', in B. Limerick and B. Lingard (eds) *Gender and Changing Educational Management*, Rydalmere: Hodder Education, pp. 12–33.

Shand, D. (1996) 'The New Public Management: an International Perspective', Paper to Public Services Management 2000 Conference, University of Glamorgan, 11 October.

Showunmi, V. and Constantine-Simms, D. (eds) (1996) *Teachers for the Future*, Stoke-on-Trent: Trentham Books.

Sidgwick, S., Mahony, P. and Hextall, I. (1994) 'A Gap in the Market?', *British Journal of Sociology of Education*, 15, 4, pp. 467–79.

Sidgwick, S., Allebone, B., Griffiths, J. and Kendall, S. (2000) 'The Involvement of Schools in ITE and the Induction of Newly Qualified Teachers in Greater London', Paper to Regional Dimensions of Teacher Supply and Retention Conference, University of North London, 19 January.

Simey, M. (1985) *Government by Consent: The Principles and Practice of Accountability in Local Government*, London: Bedford Square Press.

Sinclair, A. (1995) 'The Seduction of the Self-Managed Team and the Reinvention of the Team-as-Group', *Leading and Managing*, 1, 1, pp. 45–62.

Siraj-Blatchford, I. (ed) *'Race', Gender and the Education of Teachers*, Buckingham: Open University.

Smyth, J. and Dow, A. (1998) 'What's wrong with Outcomes', *British Journal of Sociology of Education*, 19, 1, pp. 291–303.

Smyth, J. and Shacklock, G. (1998) *Remaking Teaching: ideology, policy and practice*, London: Routledge.

Smyth, J., Shacklock, G. and Hattam, R. (1997) 'Teacher Development in Difficult Times: lessons from a policy initiative in Australia', *Teacher Development*, 1, 1, pp. 11–19.

Spring, J. (1998) *Education and the Rise of the Global Economy*, Mahwah NJ: Lawrence Erlbaum.

Stewart, M. and Bapat, G. (1996) *The Cement Roof: Afro-Caribbean People in Management*, Ware: Wainwright Trust.

Taylor, S., Rizvi, F., Lingard, B. and Henry, M. (1997) *Educational Policy and the Politics of Change*, London: Routledge.

Taylor-Gooby, P. and Lawson, R. (eds) (1993) *Markets and Managers: New Issues in the Delivery of Welfare*, Buckingham: Open University Press.

TEA (1994) *TEA Members' Briefing*, London: Teacher Education Alliance.

TES (1999a) 'Teacher trainers "cannot deliver"', *Times Educational Supplement*, 5 November.

TES (1999b) 'Trainers slate standards as impossible', *Times Educational Supplement*, 19 November.

Thorne, B. (1993) *Gender Play: Girls and Boys at School*, Buckingham: Open University Press.

Thornton, K. (1999) 'Disabled access to cost millions', *Times Educational Supplement*, 17 December.

Tomlinson, J. (1995) 'Professional Development and Control: the Role of General Teaching Councils', *Journal of Education for Teaching*, 24, 1, pp. 59–68.

TTA (1995) *Annual Report 1994/1995*, London: Teacher Training Agency.

TTA (1996a) *Corporate Plan*, London: Teacher Training Agency.

TTA (1996b) *TTA 11/96 Press notice: National Standards for Teachers*, London: Teacher Training Agency.

TTA (1996c) *A Strategic Plan for Teacher Supply and Recruitment: a discussion document*, London: Teacher Training Agency.

TTA (1997a) *Standards for the Award of Qualified Teacher Status*, London: Teacher Training Agency.

TTA (1997b) *Proposed Training Curriculum and Standards for New Teachers Consultation*, London: Teacher Training Agency.

TTA (1997c) *Report on the Outcomes of Consultation on the Proposed Training Curriculum and Standards for New Teachers*, London: Teacher Training Agency.

TTA (1997d) *Training Curriculum and Standards for New Teachers: Consultation Summary June 1997: Chief Executive's Foreword*, London: Teacher Training Agency.

TTA (1998a) 'Foreword', in *1998 National Standards for SENCOs, Subject Leaders and Headteachers*, London: Teacher Training Agency.

TTA (1998b) *Corporate Plan 1998–2000*, London: Teacher Training Agency.

TTA (1998c) *National Standards for Headteachers*, London: Teacher Training Agency.

TTA (1999a) *Corporate Plan 1999–2001*, London: Teacher Training Agency.

TTA (1999b) *CRE Review of Government Policy: Race Equality. Report on the Work of the TTA*, London: Teacher Training Agency.

TTA/CRE (1998) *Teaching in Multi-Ethnic Britain*, London: Teacher Training Agency.

UCET (1999) *Teachers: Meeting the Challenge of Change*, London: University Council for the Education of Teachers.

Walby, S. and Greenwell, J. (1994) *Medicine and Nursing: Professions in a Changing Health Service*, London: Sage Publications.

Waldegrave, W. (1993) Speech to the Public Finance Foundation. OPSS, Cabinet Office, 5 July.

Waller, W. (1961) *The Sociology of Teaching*, New York: Wiley.

Weiner, G. (1995) 'Contrasting Perceptions of Women as Educational Leaders', in B. Limerick and B. Lingard (eds) *Gender and Changing Educational Management*, Rydalmere: Hodder Education, pp. 23–33.

Weir, S. and Beetham, D. (1999) *Political Power and Democratic Control in Britain*, London: Routledge.

Weir, S. and Hall, W. (1994) *EGO TRIP: Extra-governmental organisations in the United Kingdom and their accountability*, London: Charter 88 Trust.

Welton, J., Howson, J. and Bines, H. (1995) 'Managing partnership: future directions', in H. Bines and J. Welton (eds) *Managing Partnership in Teacher Training and Development*, pp. 207–24.

Whiting, C., Whitty, G., Furlong, J., Miles, S. and Barton, L. (1996) *Partnership in Initial Teacher Education: A topography*, London: Institute of Education, University of London.

Whitty, G. (1996) 'Professional Competences and Professional Characteristics: The Northern Ireland Approach to the Reform of Teacher Education', in D. Hustler and D. Mclntyre (eds) *Developing Competent Teachers*, London: David Fulton, pp. 86–97.

Whitty, G. (1998) 'New Labour, Education and Disadvantage', *Education and Social Justice*, 1, 1, pp. 2–8.

Whitty, G. (1999) 'Teacher Professionalism in New Times', Paper to Annual Conference of Standing Committee for the Education and Training of Teachers, Dunchurch, 26–28 November.

Whitty, G., Power, S. and Halpin, D. (1998) *Devolution and Choice in Education: the School, the State and the Market*, Buckingham: Open University Press.

Wolf, A. (1995) *Competence-based Assessment*, Buckingham: Open University Press.

Woods, P., Jeffrey, B., Troman, G. and Boyle, M. (1997) *Restructuring Schools, Reconstructing Teachers: Responding to Change in the Primary School*, Buckingham: Open University Press.

Yeatman, A. (1994) *Postmodern Revisionings of the Political*, London: Routledge.

Yeatman, A. (1996) 'Interpreting Contemporary Contractualism', *Australian Journal of Social Issues*, 31, 1, pp. 39–54.

Young, I.M. (1990) *Justice and the Politics of Difference*, Princeton NJ: Princeton University Press.

Young, I.M. (1993) 'Justice and Communicative Democracy', in R. Gottlieb (ed) *Tradition, Counter Tradition, Politics: Dimensions of Radical Philosophy*, Philadelphia PA: Temple University Press, pp. 23–42.

Young, M.F.D. (1998) *The Curriculum of the Future: from the 'new sociology of education' to a critical theory of learning*, London: Falmer.

Zmroczek, C. and Mahony, P. (1999) *Women and Social Class – International Perspectives*, London: UCL Press.

Index